Glasgow Media Group Reader, Volume 2

The work of the Glasgow University Media Group has become a core part of many media and journalism study courses and has made a great contribution to our understanding of the relationship between the mass media and society. In recent years, the Group's assertion of the role the media plays in shaping audience understandings of current events has provided a crucial counter argument to theorists of postmodernity such as Jean Baudrillard.

These two Readers bring together key articles and new writings by members of the Group from the early 1970s to the present, making newly available for students material from the Group's classic books, *Bad News*, *More Bad News*, *Really Bad News* and *War and Peace News*.

This volume of the collected writings of the Glasgow University Media Group reprints classic articles on the reporting and audience reception of industrial and economic news, including coverage of the 1984–5 Miners' Strike. The Reader also includes more recent material on media coverage of conflicts in Northern Ireland, the Falklands and the Persian Gulf. In a new essay, Greg Philo examines the media strategies of political parties in the 1980s and considers the effects of recent changes in the legal and commercial structure of broadcasting.

Overall, the Reader illustrates how the struggle by various groups to 'manage the media' has interrelated with a transformation of political life, as traditional values of consensus have been challenged by those of the free market.

Greg Philo is Reader in Sociology and Research Director of the Media Unit, University of Glasgow and a founder member of the Glasgow University Media Group.

D1040567

Communication and Society
General Editor: James Curran

Glasgow Media Group Reader, Volume 2

Industry, economy, war and politics

Edited by Greg Philo

Bad News and *More Bad News* by Peter Beharrell, Howard Davis, John Eldridge, John Hewitt, Jean Oddie, Greg Philo, Paul Walton and Brian Winston

Really Bad News by Greg Philo, John Hewitt, Peter Beharrell and Howard Davis

War and Peace News by Lucinda Broadbent, John Eldridge, Gordon Kimmett, Greg Philo, Malcolm Spaven and Kevin Williams

London and New York

First published 1995
by Routledge
11 New Fetter Lane, London EC4P 4EE

Simultaneously published in the USA and Canada
by Routledge
29 West 35th Street, New York, NY 10001

Typeset in Times by Solidus (Bristol) Limited
Printed and bound in Great Britain by
TJ Press (Padstow) Ltd, Padstow, Cornwall

British Library Cataloguing in Publication Data
A catalogue record for this book is available from the British Library

Library of Congress Cataloguing in Publication Data
A catalogue record for this book has been requested

ISBN 0–415–13036–0 (hbk)
ISBN 0–415–13037–9 (pbk)

Contents

Part III Politics and media

Illustrations

Chapter 6

Chapter 8

Acknowledgements

We must thank all the people who have helped us over the last twenty years. There are many who have contributed in an extraordinary number of ways – so thanks for all that encouragement, support and goodwill. We must thank everyone who has helped us assemble data and produce our publications. Thanks for technical assistance to Trevor Graham, Parlane McFarlane, Cathy Irvine and to Kathleen Davidson and Joanne Yuill for their tireless help in preparing manuscripts. Great thanks are also due to Frank Mosson for all the help and time which he gave and to Jacquie Reilly and Lesley Henderson for their work. Thanks to all those inside the media who have given us so many insights and so much of their time. Thanks especially to Alex Graham and Alan Horrox (who can now put this on their own personal files). There is another special thanks to all the people who have helped in the production of this volume – so thanks to Greg Lanning, John Underwood, Sue Inglish, Sue Elliott, John Pilger, Sylvia Harvey, Tom O'Malley, John Corner and thanks to James Curran for his constant good humour and encouragement to our work. We also owe our thanks to Michael Cockerell, Andrew Gamble, Bill Miller, Will Hutton, Chris Pond, Paul Convery, Roger Simon, Liz Curtis, Jane Winter, Michael Ritchie, Mark Stephens and to Len Masterman.

On a personal note, thank you to our families for supporting us and putting up with grumpy academics around the house. Thanks to Mary, Johnny and Sarah Philo, Rene and Dick Philo and to Emma Waddell and Caitlin Miller and Margery McMahon.

There are so many people who have helped us over these years that it would take another book to express our gratitude adequately. But please accept our grateful thanks – without you it would not have happened.

Introduction

The two volumes of *Media Group Readers* bring together in an accessible form key pieces of work written by the Group over the last twenty years. The first volume focused largely on our early work on news content including our studies of language and visual imagery. This volume includes material from our case studies of industrial, economic and political news as well as war reporting. The work spans an extensive time period and this enables comparisons to be made, for example, between political news in the 1970s and 1990s or between media coverage of the Falklands and Gulf Wars. The collection also illustrates the development of theory and methods within the group. There have been two key themes in this. First we have always insisted on the crucial importance of empirical research. Of course, all such work is informed by theoretical assumptions and our approach is neither empiricist nor a-theoretical, but it has been our view that attempts at grand theorizing without empirical reference often drift into mere speculation. We have had little time for the increasingly abstract and contemplative drift of some recent cultural studies. Second, in our own substantive work we have attempted as far as possible to develop an approach which analyses the communications process as a totality. We began our work in the mid-1970s with a study of media content and subsequently developed new methods for the analysis of production processes and the reception of messages by audiences. In our more recent research we have developed an approach which attempts to analyse all these processes simultaneously. This volume gives a clear indication of these developments in our work.

The first two chapters deal with industrial and economic news in the 1970s. They summarize the case studies which we produced in this period, notably on the coverage of strikes in the car industry, the decline of the economy and how problems such as inflation were alleged to relate to trade-union activity. Chapter 3 extends the argument to looking at how different audience groups related to media coverage of a specific dispute – in this case the 1984/5 miners' strike.

The analysis of war reporting has also been a major focus for our case studies. One of the key themes in these has been the relationship between the state and the media and the limits on journalism in time of war. In chapter 4, David Miller discusses government information policy in relation to the Northern Ireland conflict and analyses the effects of the broadcasting ban which had been imposed on some groups of interviewees. One of our major studies in the 1980s was of the Falklands War and in chapter 5, we discuss the limits on news coverage during the conflict. Lucinda Broadbent then contributes a chapter on images of women during that war and the manner in which public opinion was reported. We also include here, as chapter 7, a report on media coverage of the Gulf War. This makes possible some very interesting comparisons between these conflicts. John McArthur (1992) has recently suggested that the Falklands War was an important moment in the growth of information policy and provided inspiration to the American military in the development of the approach eventually used in Operation Desert Storm. He quotes a US navy 'public affairs specialist' writing for his military colleagues: '"In spite of a perception of choice in a democratic society, the Falklands War shows us how to make certain that Government policy is not undermined by the way a war is reported"' (quoted in MacArthur 1992: 138). The lessons learned according to the public-affairs specialist were to: '"Control access to the fighting, invoke censorship, and rally aid in the form of patriotism at home and in the battle zone. Both Argentina and Great Britain showed us how to make that wisdom work . . . [also] to effect or help assure 'favourable objectivity', you must be able to exclude certain correspondents from the battle zone"' (ibid.: 130–40).

American journalists at the time of the Falklands War in 1982 expressed dismay at the limits which had been imposed on their British colleagues. But by the time of the Gulf War in 1991, it was clear that the development of the 'pool system' and the policy of favouring some journalists, while excluding others, paralleled much of the earlier British experience.

In the third section of this volume we look at the coverage of politics in the media and the extraordinary changes which have taken place in political life and its representation over a twenty-year period. When the Media Group began its research in 1975, the postwar consensus was at a peak with the development of the 'social contract' by the Labour government of Harold Wilson. We showed in our work at the time how this was received very favourably within the prevailing social-democratic and consensual ethos of television. By contrast, the Left of the Labour Party and the politics of grassroots movements were seen as something of a 'threat'. In chapter 8, we illustrate the differences in treatment which were accorded to various political views at that time. Chapter 9 then looks at the historical rise of consensual politics and explores some of the other key factors which have shaped the content of contemporary media.

The last two chapters analyse more recent politics and media accounts of them. Chapter 10 focuses on the growth of political advertising in the 1980s and examines why the Labour Party was unable to contest the dominance of the Conservatives, especially in representations of key areas such as the economy. Chapter 11 offers a broad analysis of the contemporary transformation of consensual politics with the rise of the New Right and the election of a succession of Conservative governments from 1979. It illustrates the effect of these political changes on both the legal and commercial basis of broadcasting and on the manner in which television reproduced the political and social debates of this time. The chapter traces all these changes from the initial attacks on broadcasting by the Conservatives in the early 1980s to the impact of the new Broadcasting Act in the 1990s. It shows how these developments had important effects on the relationship between broadcasting and the state and asks what the prospects are for a critical and independent journalism.

One of the most interesting dimensions of this collection as a whole is that the illustrations and analysis cover an extended time period. It can thus show, for example, how the struggle between contending political forces to 'manage the media' interrelates with changing material circumstances. In the mid-1980s, the Conservatives were thought of as the masters of information management. But the increasingly evident decline of the British economy created very specific problems for the development by them of an effective information policy. Taken as a whole we hope that the collection will provide some insight into such processes. It should also help teachers and researchers who are interested in the methods and analytic approaches which we have developed over these years. We commend it to all those who along with us have seen the media as a key dimension of the struggle to legitimize the social relationships of our world and to those who have sought to challenge propaganda and crude ideology with a critical understanding.

Greg Philo

REFERENCE

MacArthur, J. (1992) *Second Front: Censorship and Propaganda in the Gulf War*, Berkeley: University of California Press.

Part I

Industrial and economic reporting

Chapter 1

'And now they're out again'
Industrial news*

Greg Philo, John Hewitt and Peter Beharrell

> Most meetings are at 7.30 as we start work. Being on strike, the unions
> fixed them all for two hours later, which gave us more time to read the
> papers and listen to the radio and in the end the morale went.
>
> (BL worker on the defeat of the 1981 Leyland strike,
> *Guardian*, 4 November 1981)

When we began our research we were interested in the picture given of the
industrial world: of what were presented as its problems and potential
solutions. Our method was to look first at the *possible* explanations for the
economic crisis, for what was causing problems in industry; then to see which
of these occurred in news coverage and which were excluded. Second, we
examined how some explanations were featured prominently and how others
were downgraded.

One of our first detailed studies was of coverage of the car industry. We
found ourselves looking mainly at strikes and wage claims. These are not of
course the only things that happen in industry, but they are what is called the
news. In January 1975 a dispute occurred at British Leyland. This received
extensive coverage over a period of five weeks. The association of British
Leyland with strikes has now entered the folklore of our society: no football
match is complete without a barrier proclaiming that 'KENNY [or whoever]
STRIKES FASTER THAN LEYLAND'. In January 1979 the *Daily Telegraph*
reported: 'The public in every opinion poll shows that it believes the trade
union situation to be more responsible than any other factor for the nation's
problems.' We wanted to see how much this view underpinned television
news coverage and how it was related to other possible causes of the car
industry's problems.

---

*This chapter was originally published in 1982 in *Really Bad News* (London: Writers & Readers
Co-operative). We would like to acknowledge the help of Lilian Weir in preparing the 'Leyland
again – déjà vu' section of this chapter.

Editor's note: Every effort has been made to locate the original illustrations but in some cases
these had to be filmed from earlier publications so quality is consequently not high, especially
in cases where the original was filmed from a television screen.

WHAT'S WRONG WITH LEYLAND?

At the time of our study much 'alternative' information on the car industry was available. This fell into two main areas: low investment and bad management. British industry as a whole has suffered from underinvestment for at least thirty years. In the case of the car industry, the *Daily Express* reported in February 1975 that a Toyota worker in Japan was working with machinery worth the equivalent of £11,780 while a British Leyland worker had only £1,000 worth. There are a number of reasons for this lack of investment. One is that capital is being exported from Britain to countries such as South Africa where profits are higher. Another is that within the British economy, people with money choose to invest it where they will receive the highest return. This is often not the manufacturing industry. For speculative reasons, literally thousands of millions of pounds have, over the years, been directed away from production into areas such as the buying up of property and land. In the period 1974–5 each of the top three property companies in London had assets greater than the total value of British Leyland. A third factor is the distribution of profits as dividends to shareholders.

The Ryder Report on Leyland commissioned by the government, showed that between 1968 and 1972 the company had distributed 95 per cent of its profits as dividends. In these years Leyland had made £74 million in profits; of this only £4 million was retained for reinvestment, while £70 million was distributed as dividends. Leyland had more obsolete and worn-out machinery than its competitors. The most important effects of this were that cars cost more per unit to produce and also that the machinery was likely to break down. In 1975, the management's own figures showed that they were losing more through ineffective machinery, and factors such as management errors, than they were losing through strikes at Leyland. At this time Leyland was a hotchpotch of all the different parts which had been absorbed into it and different sections produced models which were in competition with each other. Management and organizational structure were obviously chaotic.

Such explanations conflict with the more common accounts that the problems of industry are caused by strike-prone workers.

'AND THERE WAS MORE TROUBLE TODAY'

On 3 January 1975 Harold Wilson, then Prime Minister, made a speech at his Huyton constituency. In it he dealt with the future of government investment in industry and criticized the past record of car production using the words 'manifestly avoidable stoppages of production'. The precise origin of these stoppages and who was to blame were left ambiguous. Here is the way it was presented on the first BBC bulletin of that night:

The Prime Minister, in a major speech tonight on the economy, appealed

'The Prime Minister, in a major speech tonight on the economy, appealed to management and unions.'

to *management and unions* in the car industry to cut down on what he called 'manifestly avoidable stoppages'. He said this was especially important now that government money was involved. The decision to help British Leyland was part of the government's fight against unemployment, but the help couldn't be justified if it led to continuing losses. Mr Wilson singled out for particular blame British Leyland's Austin–Morris division, which he said were responsible last year for a fifth of the stoppages in man days of the whole car industry.

(BBC 1, Early Evening News, 3 January 1975)[1]

The bulletin continued with filmed extracts of Wilson speaking:

This is an industry which itself makes a disproportionate contribution to the loss of output through disputes, because with just over 2 per cent of the total employees, 2 per cent of all those working in the whole of Britain, it accounted for one-eighth of all the man days lost in 1974 through disputes and that was a year, of course, which was inflated by the coal-mining dispute, which we rapidly brought to an end, and it accounted for getting on for one-third of the total national loss through disputes in 1973. *Whether this loss of production was acceptable or not with private capital involved, or whether it was simply that private capital was unable to deal with such problems, is a matter now for historical argument.* What is not a matter for argument for the future, is this: with public capital and an appropriate degree of public ownership and control involved the government could not justify to parliament or to the taxpayer the subsidizing of large factories involving thousands of jobs, factories which could pay their way but are failing to do so because of manifestly avoidable stoppages of production.

(BBC 1, *Early Evening News*, 3 January 1975)

There are three points in Wilson's speech which are of interest here. First, the introduction, where Wilson is reported as having criticized 'management and unions'. Second, in all the sections of the speech we are shown, Wilson does not use the word 'strike' but uses the less emotive term 'dispute'. He even rewords well-known phrases such as 'the coal-miners' strike' into 'the coal-mining dispute'. Third, he singles out the problems of what he calls 'private capital' and notes that 'whether this loss of production was acceptable or not with private capital involved, or whether it was simply that private capital was unable to deal with such problems, is a matter now for historical argument'.

On the same channel an hour and forty-five minutes later, these three things have changed. The speech is now introduced as an appeal to workers alone. It is referred to from now on as a speech about strikes and the sections on the problems of private capital are no longer shown.

The Prime Minister has appealed to *workers* in the car industry to cut down on avoidable stoppages. He said the industry had a record of strikes out of proportion to its size, and he singled out for particular blame, British Leyland's Austin–Morris division, which he said was responsible last year for a fifth of the industry's lost production through strikes. Mr Wilson said

'The Prime Minister has appealed to workers in the car industry.'

that unless labour relations improved, government help for British Leyland would be put in doubt.

The bulletin continued with these extracts from the speech:

Parts of the British Leyland undertaking are profitable, others are not, but public investment and participation cannot be justified on the basis of continued avoidable loss-making. Our intervention cannot be based on a policy of turning a private liability into a public liability.

[*BBC cut here*] What is not a matter for argument for the future is this. With public capital and an appropriate degree of public ownership and control involved, the government could not justify to parliament, or to the taxpayer, the subsidizing of large factories which could pay their way, but are failing to do so because of manifestly avoidable stoppages of production.

(BBC 1, *Late News*, 3 January 1975)

The BBC 2 coverage that evening was still working with the definition of the speech as being about both sides. It was introduced as a 'blunt warning to the car industry' and later in the bulletin there was a discussion between an industrial correspondent and the newscaster in which they made it quite clear that the speech was not simply a criticism of the work force.

NEWSCASTER: Many of the phrases in the Prime Minister's speech are pointed directly at the unions and the labour force, some are pointed at management, like the need for more efficient working methods. Do the management accept that they have got to do some pretty radical rethinking about production methods and that sort of thing?

(BBC 2, 23:16, 3 January 1975)

This is important as the speech was referred to on a very large number of occasions (forty-four in all) in conjunction with the coverage of the dispute at Leyland. This was the last time it was referred to as being critical of management.

The ITN coverage at no point acknowledged these criticisms. In the introduction Mr Wilson was said to have given 'workers a blunt warning'. In addition to showing excerpts from the speech ITN also had a reporter on the spot who summarized to a camera what he believed it to be about. These summaries again emphasized the speech as an appeal to the workforce:

This was a stern message to come from a Labour Prime Minister, but it was received politely enough by the audience here in a Labour club in his constituency; but the speech was clearly prompted by the growing number of companies going to the government for help and the large sums of public money involved. Mr Wilson clearly expects a greater degree of restraint from the *workforce* in firms where the government has stepped in to help and he has appealed directly to *working people* not to rock an already very leaky boat.

(ITN, 22:00, 3 January 1975)

This bulletin continued with reports of attitudes to the speech and to the source of Leyland's difficulties. Elsewhere the alternative history of these difficulties was well documented. The problems of investment and distribution of dividends were in fact highlighted as early as 1972, as for example in this excerpt from the journal *Management Today*:

> Capital expenditure had been very low for many years, and depreciation was correspondingly small. The high profits about which so many boasts were made, were thus derived from a declining asset base and too high a proportion was paid out to shareholders.
>
> (*Management Today*, August 1972)

But such alternative accounts were reduced on the news to mere tokens. In the above ITN bulletin, the story on Leyland lasted over 5 minutes, and the first 4 minutes and 50 seconds were taken up with the speech, summaries of it and the definition of it as being about the workforce. The bulletin continued immediately with a *15-second* reference to the alternative view. Leslie Huckfield MP, was quoted as saying that the main problem in Leyland was the management failure to invest. This account was immediately 'sandwiched' by following it with two other views that refuted it, those of the Leyland management and of Mr Prior, the Conservative spokesman.

> Mr Wilson's comments on British Leyland got a cool reception from one Labour MP, Mr Leslie Huckfield of Nuneaton. *He said* the Prime Minister clearly knew very little about the car industry, the real cause of the trouble was the chronic failure of management to invest, *he said*. But the opposition's employment spokesman Mr James Prior, and the British Leyland spokesman, both supported Mr Wilson's remarks. Mr Prior said Mr Wilson was at least stating some home truths which others have been expressing for a long while.
>
> (ITN, 22:00, 3 January 1975)

Huckfield's view is effectively discounted, all the more since it was heavily parenthesized with a double 'he said'. ITN left us in no doubt as to which side they wished to emphasize. They literally 'underlined' one interpretation of the speech and used this to introduce their coverage of the dispute. The above bulletin continued:

> *As if to underline Mr Wilson's remarks*, British Leyland's Austin–Morris plant in Cowley announced that 12,000 men are being laid off because of a strike by 250 workers. The striking workers are engine tuners, who want to be graded as skilled workers. They rejected a plea to call off the strike which could cut production by a thousand cars a day.
>
> (ITN, *Late News*, 3 January 1975)

The BBC used the same form of 'sandwich' and also linked the speech and the dispute. We know here that the BBC is about to talk of strikes since it uses the words 'and there was more trouble today':

> Mr Wilson's speech has been welcomed by the opposition spokesman on employment, Mr James Prior. He said the Prime Minister had told car workers some home truths, although it was a pity he hadn't done so before, but Mr Leslie Huckfield, a Labour MP with a lot of car workers in his constituency of Nuneaton, said the speech was disgraceful. The real culprits were the management, not the workers. British Leyland said tonight they shared Mr Wilson's exasperation at the series of futile disputes in the corporation *and there was more trouble today*. Twelve thousand workers at the Cowley plant near Oxford were laid off because of a strike by 250 in the tuning department.
>
> (BBC 1, *Late News*, 8 January 1975)

This sets the pattern for the subsequent use of the speech in relation to the dispute. It is constantly recalled as the events at Cowley are reported. The apparently routine coverage of a dispute is now underpinned by a series of insertions which point to one interpretation of Leyland's problems.

The last of these references occurred seventeen days after the speech was actually made. As the coverage of the dispute moves further away from the actual event of the speech, so the original definition is reworked, always in the direction of blaming the workforce. Wilson's original reference to 'manifestly avoidable stoppages' is recalled variously as being about 'senseless strikes', 'unnecessary strikes' and a warning to 'workers in general, but car workers in particular'.

The typical pattern is as follows:

> and now they're out again, *within a week in fact of the Prime Minister's warning that what he called unnecessary strikes were putting jobs in the car industry at risk*. And indeed, as a result of this action this morning, 12,000 other British Leyland car workers may well have to be laid off immediately.
>
> (ITN, 13:00, 9 January 1975)

> Cowley in Oxford, *specially picked out by Mr Wilson in his warning last night about strikes*, is at a standstill for a second day because of industrial trouble. Twelve thousand workers at the plant are being laid off because 250 engine tuners who want to be higher graded are stopping work on Monday. In his speech last night, Mr Wilson warned workers in general, but car workers in particular, that the government could not justify subsidizing large factories which were losing money because of manifestly avoidable strikes. The speech has been welcomed by some Conservative MPs, but condemned by some left-wing Labour members.
>
> (ITN, 13:00, 4 January 1975)

First the fresh strike at British Leyland's. The management at Cowley said this evening that despite the renewed stoppage by the 250 tuners there, they have managed to achieve 80 per cent of a normal day's output. The 12,000 other people who work at Cowley, *the plant which was specifically mentioned by the Prime Minister last week when he talked about senseless strikes in the motor industry* – they were angry this morning when they learned that the tuners had voted to walk out again and that they faced the threat of layoffs for the second time in four days.

(BBC 2, *Late News*, 9 January 1975)

Alternative explanations of Leyland's problems are not used to organize coverage in the same way. For example, two days after the Wilson speech Jack Jones made a statement criticizing Leyland's management. This was referred to three times on BBC 1, three times on ITN and not at all on BBC 2. The Jones statement disappeared very rapidly from the news and significantly was not used as an organizing principle for coverage. It simply occurs as a fragment which is quickly passed over. By comparison, the Wilson speech with its new definition was referred to 13 times on BBC 1, 8 times on BBC 2 and 21 times on ITN.

The definition of Wilson's remarks is used to give authority for a limited explanation around which the flow of coverage is being organized. But the view that strikes are the problem has become so firmly implanted in the normal account of journalists that at times they feel quite able to embrace it as their own. For example on 4 January an ITN journalist gave a report from Cowley and concluded:

The Austin–Morris plant at Cowley is now totally shut down. Twelve thousand men have been laid off because 250 engine tuners want their jobs regraded. It's the kind of strike that has contributed significantly to the dire economic problems of British Leyland.

(ITN, 22:00, 4 January 1975)

While the theme that strikes are the problem is embraced in this way, at no point in this five-week period of coverage are any of the other explanations of Leyland's problems treated in a similar manner. Journalists never concluded: 'it's the kind of chronic investment failure that has done so much to contribute to the problems of Leyland'.

Information which contradicts the dominant view, if it appears at all, exists as fragments and is never explored by news personnel as a rational alternative explanation. It is not used by them as a way of organizing what they cover, of selecting what they film or of structuring their interviews. Where alternatives do occasionally surface, as for example when shop stewards are interviewed, then these accounts are simply fitted into the dominant flow. This may occur even when the content of such an interview seriously contradicts the assumption that the journalist is pursuing when asking the questions. At

".. and tell the viewers, Mr X, when did you stop sleeping on the night shift?"

Leyland the shop stewards' convenor was interviewed. The reporter set up the interview once again in relation to Wilson's speech, and asked how the men at Cowley were reacting to it. The shop stewards' convenor argued that this approach did not help, and gave two critical pieces of information that severely contradicted the media view of Leyland. He said that since April of the previous year the men had been working consistently to avoid disputes. The level of disputes in Leyland had in fact fallen in the period to which he was referring. Second, he argued that most of the production had been lost through breakdowns or shortages of materials, a point born out by the management's own figures on production losses. Reports confirming the shop steward's view later appeared in four national newspapers, but were never given on the television news.

In this interview the news journalist simply ignores the evidence given to him.

SHOP STEWARD'S CONVENOR: ... Since April of last year, we have worked consistently, all of us, to try and avoid any disputes whatsoever. In fact most of the production that has been lost, has been lost through either breakdowns or shortage of materials and we do recognize that British Leyland has got a problem, a cash-flow problem, and we have worked very, very hard, both union and members, to try and eradicate this position.

BBC REPORTER: How does the prospect of no government cash for British Leyland strike you if the strike record doesn't improve?

(BBC 1, 21:00, 6 January 1975)

In the face of the evidence that the level of disputes at Leyland has gone down and that anyway most production is not lost through this, the journalist persists with the view that the critical issue is what will happen if the strike record does not improve! It is so much on the tip of his tongue that the journalist (presumably accidentally) actually uses the word 'strike' twice in the same sentence.

HAIR-RAISING STORIES

This treatment of people on the shop floor may be compared with that of the *Financial Times*. Its journalists were sent to Leyland and interviewed shop stewards. On 6 January 1975 the *Financial Times* reported: 'Cowley shop stewards tell hair-raising stories about managerial failings, and point at the moment to constant assembly-track hold-ups caused by non-availability of supplier component parts.'

Journalists claim in their defence that they play 'devil's advocate' in interviews; that it is their role to present the opposition case and that this provides lively television. Our study showed that they simply did not do this. They do not typically attack the management using the arguments of shop stewards. We can compare the above interview with one in which an ITN journalist interviewed a British Leyland manager. One question does take up briefly the theme of Mr Jones's criticism of management, the other six speak for themselves:

1 Would workers at Leyland approve of a one-year strike truce?
2 Jones yesterday said management was largely to blame for stoppages – how do you take this?
3 What are stoppages caused by?
4 Isn't this a criticism of the unions as they apparently have so little control over their men?
5 Do you think there are people at work at Leyland who simply want to disrupt the thing?
6 What danger is there to jobs in Leyland if these sort of strikes go on?
7 With government coming to the aid of British Leyland, aren't the workers going to think their jobs are safe anyway?

(ITN, 13.00, 6 January 1975)

We may also note that the shop steward was interviewed with his back to a wall outside the factory gates while the Leyland manager was brought into the comfort and style of the ITN studios for a lengthy face-to-face discussion with the newscaster. What is at stake in all this coverage is the routine processing of information, reports and interviews around one view of industrial crisis. Information that contradicts this is either discounted or ignored and at times is actually used as if it supports the dominant view. In one instance, government figures were released showing that overall car sales were down. The main cause of this was the oil crisis, and the increasing cost

ITN, 13:00, 6 January 1975.

BBC 1, 21:00, 6 January 1975.

of fuel. Television programmes showed fields full of cars that could not be sold. These were cars that had been completed and had left the factory. They were unlikely, therefore, to be affected by strikes. Logically if there were less strikes there would be even more cars which would not be sold. Yet ITN actually ran the story of the unsold cars directly in conjunction with the alleged strike problem at Leyland.

> On the day that it has been announced by the government that new car sales last year were down by 25 per cent on 1973, *the director of British Leyland's Cowley plant has warned of a calamity if the strike situation there gets-worse. Figures out today show that private car and van registrations dropped* from 1,688,000 in 1973 to 1,273,000 last year and all vehicle registrations were down nearly as much, by 20 per cent. The warning came in a letter from the plant director, Mr John Symons, to Leyland employees as the company and the Engineering Union agreed to talks tomorrow at the Conciliation and Arbitration Service to try to solve the strike of engine tuners at Cowley. Mr Symons said that the strike had meant that Cowley was failing to meet what he called its survival budget. He also gave a warning that a further deterioration would be calamitous with the strongest likelihood of a major reduction in manufacturing and employment at Cowley.
>
> (ITN, 22.00, 22 January 1975)

The news is one-dimensional in that it pursues one explanation at the expense of others. A count of the causes of Leyland's problems which were referred to in the Cowley coverage gives some indication of this. *Excluding* all of the references to Wilson's speech they were as follows. On BBC 1 there were 22 references to the strike problem at Leyland, 5 references to the problem of management and only 1 to investment. On BBC 2 there were 8 references to the strike theme, 3 to management and 2 to investment. On ITN there were 33 to the strike theme, 8 to management and none to investment. Such a count actually overestimates the presence of alternative explanations since these occur only as fragments and are never pursued. By contrast the strike theme runs through the coverage of the car industry. The news is organized around the logic of this explanation. When strikes are presented as a source of industry's problems we know and are informed exactly of what strikes do. The resources of the media are organized to give us this information. A kind of chain of information is set up by which we know what a strike is, what it does, who it affects, the damage it causes and who is to blame. We are routinely told who is on strike, who is responsible, who is left-wing, if there are splits in the unions and how many exports are lost. When themes such as left-wing influence and deliberate wrecking are inserted they create the links in how we are to understand what is happening. Such insertions may occur quite gratuitously, even when there is no immediate story. In this sense, to be on the news you do not have to do anything 'newsworthy' at all. For a left-wing shop steward, complete non-action will still cause a personal history of months before to be once more regurgitated. In this piece of ITN news, also 'unavailable for comment' was Mr Alan Thornett:

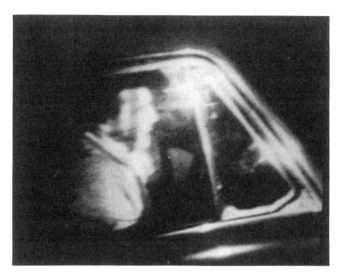

'Other officials refused to comment at all. These included . . . the man at the centre of last summer's strike.'

Other officials refused to comment at all. These included district secretary Mr Malcolm Young and shop steward Mr Alan Thornett. He was the man at the centre of last summer's strike when Leyland sought to have him removed from union office, because they claimed he was seeking deliberately to disrupt production.

(ITN, 22:00, 6 January 1975)

Similarly the view that strikes are the problem is put forward so routinely that it may occur even when the immediate subject does not call for it, as for example in the description of a new Leyland car which is about to be launched:

Onlookers outside the Cowley factory gates have been getting an unplanned preview of a new British Leyland car. It's the successor to the Austin 1800 range, code-named 8071 and due to be launched in spring, *strikes permitting*. British Leyland hope it will revive interest in their cars in a sagging home market.

(BBC 1, 21:00, 9 January 1975)

The news is underpinned by a key ideological assumption. It is that production in our society is normal and satisfactory unless there are problems with the workforce. All the other problems which may be generated by a productive system based on private interest – such as the export of capital and the flow of investment funds away from manufacturing, the running down of some sections of the economy and the rapid expansion of others, the need to keep shareholders happy and to distribute dividends – are closed off in the flow of coverage. Although these factors are clearly responsible for major disruptions in the economy they remain unexamined by journalists as sources of trouble. For them production is normal until there is a dispute. As for example in this coverage from ITN:

> For a week now the company has been keeping production up to 80 per cent of normal and stockpiling cars for the tuners to attend to when the dispute is settled.
>
> (ITN, 13:00, 20 January 1975)

What is crucial is that normal production and full production are treated as synonymous and are equated with being strike-free. In the coverage of the above dispute ITN informed us that:

> With the engine tuners back at work at least for the time being, the Austin–Morris plant, singled out by the Prime Minister for particular criticism, *was also back in full production*.
>
> (ITN, 13:00, 7 January 1975)

A production stoppage or a problem in industry becomes equated in general usage with a strike. This occurs across industrial reporting. Here, for example, in coverage of Chrysler, a reporter notes that stocks must be good because there have been no strikes:

> With a touch of irony, Chrysler point out that they'd had a run *without production stoppages, without strikes*, so stocks must be good, but for all their optimism their workforce is going on a three-day week for the rest of January.
>
> (BBC 1, 21:00, 9 January 1975)

The journalist's view of the 'normal' covers up the nature of a system which through its own logic can produce chaos and decline, independent of the wishes or actions of the workforce – but it is at their door that the blame is laid.

LEYLAND AGAIN – DÉJÀ VU

In February 1979 we took an additional sample of coverage of a Leyland dispute to compare with earlier results. For two weeks, we recorded the main evening bulletin on BBC 1 and ITN and the Sunday evening *News Review* on BBC 2. On 7 February the workers at the Longbridge plant in Birmingham came out on unofficial strike. They said they were protesting at management's refusal to make back-dated parity payments which had been agreed by both sides in return for higher levels of productivity. In the context of the agreement the unions had conceded that redundancies could take place. The shop stewards pointed out that 7,000 redundancies had occurred and claimed that management were attempting to conceal the true levels of production at both Austin–Morris and Jaguar. Management claimed that productivity had not been high enough to justify the payments, that the men had misunderstood the terms of the agreement and that the shop stewards were breaking procedure.

Given that management and unions had competing explanations to offer for the dispute, in principle each of these might have been explored in an even-handed way. In the main, however, coherence and rationality are granted to management and not to the workforce. The different ways in which each group is interviewed reflect this. It is not enough to analyse formal balance in terms of the time allocated to the two groups (in this case the workers and their representatives had more than management). The style of the interview also matters. Questions put to management tend either to be an open invitation to give their views or to lead directly to these. As a result such interviews are fairly harmonious: the 'devil's advocate' role and the 'difficult' questions are reserved largely for shop stewards.

Interviews with Pat Lowry (personnel director of BL cars) and Ray Horrocks (managing director of Austin–Morris) began with an open invitation to them to elaborate upon their views. These were allowed to stand without interruption or challenge. On the rare occasions when a second question was put to them, it was encouraging rather than challenging. Thus on BBC 1, a journalist interviews Horrocks:

JOURNALIST: ... when I spoke to the boss of Austin–Morris, of which Longbridge is the biggest part, I asked him if the workers had been deliberately misled by the stewards.
HORROCKS: I am saying they were given wrong information without any shadow of a doubt at all and that is now very evident. Because against the background of the same information, 66,000 workers in 27 plants right across the country have voted to stay at work.
JOURNALIST: So what's the message in that for Longbridge?
(BBC 1, 21:00, 9 February 1979)

And on ITN:

JOURNALIST: If Longbridge doesn't go back, Leyland say other plants are going to be hit. And there is a long-term threat too.
HORROCKS: In what I think is the unlikely event that Longbridge stay out – there's no doubt at all in my mind, I shall have to ask the chief executive of BL Ltd. that I should reappraise the Austin–Morris plant, and that will have long-term implications for the company.
JOURNALIST: What sort of implications?
(ITN, 22:00, 7 February 1979)

The aggressive questions put to shop stewards and pickets stand out in marked contrast. Here, for example, a BBC journalist interviews the Longbridge convenor of shop stewards:

> JOURNALIST: The vote was in favour of an instant walk-out. There have been dire warnings that another stoppage could spell the end of British Leyland. After this one would there be a plant or a job to come back to?
>
> SHOP STEWARD: I'm confident we shall have a plant and a job to go back to. I note that Mr Edwards might not have a job. Indeed, he's already seeking tax exile. I wish that some of our members on the wages that we get could seek tax exile, at the same rate as himself.
>
> JOURNALIST: *Leyland workers over recent years have got a reputation* with the public *for perhaps doing things very quickly and doing sometimes stupid things* – is this one of them?
>
> SHOP STEWARD: I wouldn't have thought so. But you know, you were here last year when we persuaded our members not to. If anyone's adopted a responsible attitude it's the workers at Longbridge.
>
> JOURNALIST: *Was it responsible to go ahead with this strike?*
>
> (BBC 1, 21:00, 7 February 1979)

And on ITN:

> JOURNALIST: There were clashes this morning between pickets and drivers trying to get building materials through to a plant that will build the new Mini – the car that is the key to the company's future. *Aren't the men cutting their own throats?*
>
> SHOP STEWARD: We're on strike. It's been forced upon us. We've got no alternative. And we intend to use the full force of our membership in picketing this plant to ensure that nothing moves in and nothing moves out. We regret that we have to do these things. But until such time as the management come down to earth, that's how it will continue.
>
> JOURNALIST: *Even if it destroys the company?*
>
> (ITN, 22:00, 8 February 1979)

Management or official views tend to form the basis of such news accounts. At times, they are embellished to give them maximum emphasis, as in this report by a BBC correspondent: 'BL management wasn't slow to *blast back* at the Longbridge stewards for acting unconstitutionally, breaking procedure, overturning the secret ballot vote and spreading inaccurate information.' He refers to output and productivity figures and tells us: 'Now the extra productivity is measured against output in 1977 – *goodness knows, a bad year for disputes*.' The report ends with the declaration:

> An all-out strike could mean BL revising the corporate plan it has submitted to the NEB, cutting back investment, cutting back jobs. The

failure of British car companies to produce cars means a boost for imports which, we learn, accounted for 54 per cent of all sales last month, when *incidentally*, BL cars were market leader for the fourth consecutive month.

Management are not typically challenged and they emerge as victims – having to revise the corporate plan, cut jobs and investment because of the strike. There is no longer any room for a logical alternative view. The last phrase – 'BL cars were market leader for the fourth consecutive month' – is literally treated as incidental information. It could within an alternative frame have been used to contradict or at least challenge the conventional view that BL is failing to produce cars because of frequent strikes.

The effect of all this is to produce a critical distinction between responsible citizens and those few individuals or unions that are rocking the boat. The solid consensus of right-thinking, decent, law-abiding, hard-working taxpayers is compared with the wild, irresponsible minority. At its crudest, this is presented as the unions on one side and the taxpayers on the other. On 8 February 1979 ITN opened its main news with the headline: 'LEYLAND UNIONS SAY: LET THE TAXPAYERS PAY.'

This was a factually incorrect report of the unions' views. At the time Leyland was desperately short of capital. The chief negotiator of the unions recalls to us that he told a reporter that Leyland would be a good investment for the National Enterprise Board. The state already owned most of the assets of Leyland and had lent it money. But on such loans up to $15\frac{1}{2}$ per cent was being charged in interest – the taxpayer was not *giving* anything. More importantly, such a statement misses the issues of *who* the taxpayers are, and what their real interests are. At this time over half a million people were employed directly or indirectly by Leyland. They paid about £750 million in tax a year, which is very much more than the state lends to Leyland. It is absurd to imply that Leyland workers are different from other taxpayers and even more absurd to suggest that taxpayers as a whole would be better off if Leyland collapsed. The effect on the economy would be, at the least, to put an enormous number of people out of work, given all the industries that depend upon car production. Unemployment pay would then have to be met by those that still were paying tax.

Such headlines are no more than crude ideology. The blaming of the unions on the one side and the championing of the 'taxpayer' on the other lay the foundations for the most conservative economic policies. This plays right into the hands of monetarists – who believe that market forces should be unleashed for a competition in which only the strong survive. In this bleak vision the state should no longer intervene to hold back unemployment and recession. Instead, these should be allowed to develop so that wages will be forced down to the benefit of those who employ labour. Television has done much to make this scenario possible. Working people are presented as having brought unemployment upon themselves. The taxpayers, those that are left, can rest easy.

NOTE

1   All italics in quotes from television news programmes throughout this volume represent our own emphases unless otherwise stated.

Chapter 2

'Reasonable men and responsible citizens'

Economic news*

Greg Philo, Peter Beharrell and John Hewitt

Just as the coverage of industry is organized around limited and conservative explanations, so is news on the economy as a whole. In this case we show how television news was organized around an account which blamed inflation mainly on wages and then linked this explanation to the political policy of wage restraint. Here again what underpins media coverage is scrutiny of working people rather than an analysis of 'normal' operations of the economy and its ability to generate crisis.

SKY-HIGH PRICES

The key problem underlying Britain's economic decline is the failure of industrial investment. On rare occasions this has been acknowledged on the television news. In January 1975 the industrial editor of ITN made the following reference: 'Since the war, Britain's overriding problem, almost universally agreed, has been a failure to invest adequately' (ITN, 22:00, 21 January 1975). We have already shown how this affected particular industries such as cars. In fact the decline of investment was widespread across the whole of the manufacturing sector. Between 1960 and 1972 Britain reinvested 16–18 per cent of its gross product each year. By comparison Japan was investing 30–35 per cent, almost twice the rate (Yaffe 1973: 16).

In some areas the difference was staggering. While in 1978 Mr Callaghan was announcing a government grant at around £100 million for the computer industry, the Japanese government and industrial interests were going ahead with the injection of £35,000 million into theirs (Evans 1979: 93). The main reason for the long-term decline of manufacturing investment in Britain has been simply that profit returns from it have been low. Consequently those with capital have invested in other areas. This had the effect of lowering productivity relative to Britain's competitors and also fuelled inflation as the

---

*This chapter was originally published in 1982 in *Really Bad News* (London: Writers & Readers Co-operative).

money found other purposes. For example, the *Investor's Chronicle* here describes the effect on prices when the property boom began to take off:

In the summer of 1973, the government was allowing the amount of money for use in the country to expand rapidly in the hope that industry would use it to invest in new plant to produce more goods and earn more foreign exchange by exporting.

It did not work out that way, because industry was not confident that it could sell enough goods profitably enough to cover the money for new plant. So the extra money being pumped into the economy found other uses.

At first some of it found its way into buying shares where it helped to force prices up. More important, vast amounts of money were being lent by the banking system to buy property. Since property is in limited supply, the main effect was to force prices sky high.

(*Investor's Chronicle*, 11 September 1974)

The relative fall in investment had another disastrous consequence: it raised the serious prospect of major unemployment. Since World War II all western governments had been committed to maintaining high levels of employment and to intervening in the economy to ensure that there was no return to the slump of the 1930s. Capitalism was not to be abolished by either Labour or Conservative policies, but it could be modified in the name of producing social harmony. In effect what happened was that successive governments were forced to step in either to buy up the bankrupt sections of manufacturing industry or to prop up the weak sections with grants and loans. This, together with regional aid grants and indirect subsidies to industry, such as expenditure on motorways, had a major effect on government spending. In May 1975 the *Observer* reported that public borrowing by the government had quadrupled in just over one year to £10,000 million. In effect the government was making up for the failures of private investment. The problem was that in doing this, it was spending more on this and in other areas such as welfare than it was raising through taxation. This was a major factor in the development of inflation, since the government was effectively printing the extra money. A critical problem by the mid-1970s was how to claw this money back out of the economy. The three chosen solutions were to increase taxation, cut 'unnecessary' spending in areas such as hospitals and schools, and hold down wages. At the time of our study in 1975, wage restraint was very much in the air and political figures such as Denis Healey were arguing that wages had caused inflation as a way of justifying these policies. This view was espoused by most of the Right and Centre of the Labour Party. The unions did not in general agree that they had caused inflation and the TUC was divided over whether or not wage restraint was an acceptable way to reduce it.

The argument that wages had caused price increases was a dubious one. It hinged on the view that wages were shooting ahead and somehow dragging prices along behind them. In fact in the whole period 1970–5 real wages had remained about the same and for the first six months of 1975 had actually fallen. In any case prices do not have to rise simply because wages do. If sufficient investment is undertaken, then productivity can increase and manufacturers can afford to increase wages and in some cases may even lower the cost of the product. Workers in countries such as Germany and France, where there are higher levels of investment, receive higher wages, yet the rate of inflation there is lower than in Britain.

The view that wages were responsible for the crisis was rejected by large sections of the trade unions, and was also criticized from the Right. Monetarists in the Conservative Party blamed inflation on excessive state spending. Obviously they did not relate this spending to a general theory of capitalist crisis. They saw the decline as coming from 'subsidized incompetence', 'lazy workers' and 'lack of initiative'. They were against subsidizing weak sections of industry and saw the solution as allowing the economy to move into a slump. In this situation unemployment would force wages down and the new conditions would hopefully be taken advantage of by the owners of capital who survived the crisis. Although these policies were clearly not designed to help working people, it is the case that the theory behind them definitely implied that wages were not the initial cause of inflation. This was stated quite openly by monetarists at the Conservative Party conference of October 1976. The policies of wage restraint were denounced as a 'con trick' on these grounds. As early as January 1974 Nicholas Ridley (Under-Secretary for Trade and Industry in Edward Heath's Conservative government) wrote:

> Contrary to the popular view, the cause of inflation is not high wage settlements but the way in which they are financed. In the public sector, wages must be paid for out of the earnings of the firm. If this is done, no inflation results. It is only when the Government pays for high public sector wage settlements or receives bankrupt companies with money that it prints, that inflation results.
>
> (*Sunday Times*, 20 January 1974, emphasis added)

There were other arguments about what had contributed to inflation, such as the effects of oil-price increases. Most economists are agreed that this had some effect, but it cannot really explain Britain's economic problems since the oil crisis affected all western countries in much the same way. Yet Britain's inflation rate was much higher than most.

RAMPANT WAGES?

There were three main positions on what had caused the economic crisis and inflation, but only one of these directly blamed wages. Yet the news consistently pursued the theme that wages were the cause of inflation. Our study of the first four months of 1975 showed that on the news statements that wages were the main cause outnumbered by 8 to 1 those reports which rejected this view. The argument that wages were the problem was linked by news journalists to political policies such as the need for wage restraint. For example, the industrial correspondent of the BBC commented in January 1975: 'With wages now as the main boost in inflation, just getting inflation down to a reasonable level seems to imply tougher pay restraint' (BBC 1, 21:00, 20 January 1975).

In this period there were seventeen occasions when views were given on the news that the policies of wage restraint and lower wages were *not* the best way to solve the economic crisis. There were 287 occasions when the view was featured that these were exactly what *was* needed.

As we showed in the case of the car industry, the importance of these references is not so much how many times they appear, but that they are used to organize coverage around limited explanations. Here again, the alternatives, where they appear, are mere fragments, while the dominant theme of wage inflation and the need for restraint is at the core of news gathering and reporting. The link between wages and prices was simply assumed in a series of discussions and reports. Month after month on the news we were shown graphs and charts to illustrate how much wages and prices had gone up. The link is a dubious one since, of course, many factors apart from wages can cause price increases. The conclusion of all these reports was that wages were ahead of prices. For example, BBC 1 informed us in one bulletin in January 1975 that 'wage inflation is still accelerating sharply with earnings keeping well ahead of prices' – that 'average earnings also soared' and that they were 'far outstripping the retail price increases'. Such coverage was typical over the first four months of 1975. Its conclusions are even more dubious since it is not clear that wages were in fact ahead of prices at this time. In a study of real income published in 1976, Frances Cairncross concluded that 'the purchasing power of the average male worker's earnings has been virtually unchanged for four years' (*Guardian*, 8 October 1976).

UNRELIABLE GUIDES

One reason why wage rises constantly appeared on the news as if they were ahead of prices was that the official figures on these were often reported without important qualifications. These included at the very minimum the need to allow for tax and other deductions to indicate the real value of wage increases. Without these qualifications wages could be made to look as if they were 'outstripping' prices. In the case of ITN, on 11 occasions when they gave the figures, 6 made no reference to what *real* wages were. For the BBC the gross figures were given without reference to real wages on 17 occasions out of a total of 20 in their reports on wages and prices figures. The difference is clear if we compare a report which includes the qualifications and one from which they have been dropped. In its early evening news report on 20 January the BBC reported:

Meanwhile the nation's wage bill is going up faster than ever before. Official figures today show that average earnings last November were 25 per cent higher than in the same month in 1973, a record increase. Our economics correspondent says that *after taxation, the actual rise in spending power is just over 20 per cent.* That is still ahead of the increase in retail prices of 18.3 per cent.

(BBC 1, 17:45, 20 January 1975)

On the same channel three hours later, the qualifications have been dropped:

NEWSCASTER: The figures published today by the Department of Employment show that wage inflation is still accelerating sharply, with earnings keeping well ahead of prices. During 1974 basic weekly wage rates rose by a record $28\frac{1}{2}$ pence in the pound. While in the year up to last November, *average earnings,* which include overtime and bonus pay, *also soared by a record 25.3 per cent, far outstripping the retail price increases* of 18 per cent during the same period.

(BBC 1, 21:00, 20 January 1975)

Indeed the BBC became so wedded to the view that wages were far ahead of prices that at one point it actually altered the normal way in which these figures are reported, to draw the conclusion more firmly. The usual way of measuring increases in pay is the index of average earnings. Both channels have acknowledged that this is the most reliable guide; for example, a BBC correspondent noted that 'it is the best guide that there is to the relationship

'This is the comparison which really counts, the average earnings.'

between pay and prices' (BBC 1, 17:45, 19 February 1975). Similarly ITN in comparing wages and prices figures had concluded: 'This is the comparison which really counts, the *average earnings* of 7 million workers' (ITN, 22:00, 20 January 1975).

There is another index of wages called the index of basic weekly wage rates. This can be unreliable since it measures only what the basic rate is supposed to be. If, for example, people are on short time because of recession, then the figures will overestimate what people are receiving. This is exactly what was happening by April of 1975. Yet the BBC main news introduced the wages and prices figures for that month as follows:

> Well, these figures rub in Mr Healey's warnings about wage-led inflation, and pay rises well in excess of the cost of living. And they reveal a widening disparity between pay and prices. The percentage increase in *basic weekly wage rates* for the year to March is 32.5 per cent against an increase of 19.9 per cent in the latest retail price index in the twelve months to February.

(BBC 1, 21:00, 16 April 1975)

Of the six BBC bulletins which discussed these figures (on 16, 18 and 20 April) only two mentioned even briefly the index of average earnings. The average-earnings index showed that falling industrial output was holding back the rise in real income. *The Times* in fact commented on the day after the above BBC bulletin:

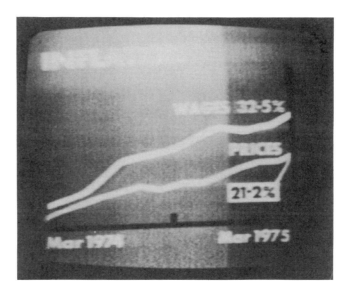

'These figures rub in Mr Healey's warnings. . . . The percentage increase in basic weekly wage rates.'

There is accumulating evidence that falling industrial output and the increase in short-time working is beginning to hold back the rise in actual earnings, which include payments for overtime and bonuses.

(The Times, 17 April 1975)

Figures and information on the economy were thus organized to lay the blame for inflation on wages. The above example shows how this account was then used to 'rub in' the views of Healey.

RUBBING IN MR HEALEY'S WARNINGS

We are obviously not complaining here about the presence of Mr Healey on the screen. It would be naive to suggest that a national television service could or should avoid reporting the views of the Chancellor. Our criticism is that the resources of the media were used to underline, develop and give legitimacy to these views. They provide the logic around which coverage is organized – they are embraced by the journalists and are constantly reiterated and given credence by being linked with apparently incontrovertible information. For example in the BBC coverage of March 1975 a speech by Healey on the 'lunacy of wage increases' is linked to *unqualified* figures on wages and prices.

NEWSCASTER: From the Chancellor of the Exchequer, Mr Denis Healey, *a stern warning* on the effect of wage inflation. The Chancellor told a meeting of the parliamentary Labour Party this morning that *to ignore*

BBC 2, 17:45, 19 March 1975.

current wage rises was irresponsible lunacy. At the same time official figures were published showing that wages are now about 29 per cent higher than a year ago while prices have risen by 10 per cent less. Here's our economics correspondent. . . .

ECONOMICS CORRESPONDENT: The gap between wages and prices is one of Mr Healey's big problems as he plans his budget. He said this morning wage settlements were just not close enough to the social-contract guidelines and were responsible for the worst rise in prices.

(BBC 1, 17:45, 19 March 1975)

The report is consistently from the point of view of Mr Healey. Journalists feel quite able to underline what he knows and doesn't know. Later in the same report we are told:

Last year wages did keep ahead of prices and current wages are also doing so, for thousands of workers in many trades, getting rises of 35 and 40 per cent above a year ago. *Mr Healey knows this can't go on.*

It might be noted that thousands of workers were not receiving such increases. *The Times* reported in August of that year that average earnings in the first six months of 1975 had *fallen* in real terms by 10 per cent. In the above bulletins the correspondent's claims on the effects of wages were followed by further references to what Mr Healey wanted. After these is what amounts to a throwaway line referring to alternative views on the economy:

He [Mr Healey] wants more modest wage deals and better output per man. Without it he forecasts prices will be rising twice as fast in Britain as in those countries competing with us. The message from the Chancellor called for belt-tightening *and the party meeting rejected a call from the left-wing Tribune group for an opposite give-away budget.* This afternoon MPs were gloomily forecasting higher income tax.

(BBC 1, 17:45, 19 April 1975)

A whole tradition of Keynesian economics is here reduced to a call for an 'opposite give-away budget'. There are no reports or information included to make sense of, or to underline, the *Tribune* view. What there is here is an illusion of balance, whereby statements are included from what appear as different sides. But the reported views have a totally different status, legitimacy and meaning in the text. Only one set 'makes sense' in that we are systematically given the information necessary to understand the explanations and policies to which they relate. When the budget did appear a month later, it was presented on the news as if it were a necessary response to the inflation that had allegedly been caused by trade-union activity. On ITN, for example, it was introduced as follows:

Good evening. In the toughest of budgets *the Chancellor, Mr Healey, has fired a broadside at all those who have taken high pay rises.* These, he said, were the main cause of the present rate of inflation.

(ITN, 22:00, 15 April 1975)

We may ask who were 'all those who had taken high pay rises'. ITN had reported in the previous month that according to the government, 75 per cent of all pay rises were being settled within the social contract. Most of these workers had in effect taken wage cuts.

The effects of the budget of that year were in fact heavily deflationary. It increased taxation and was designed to claw back money out of the economy. This was a bitterly controversial move: the unions predicted that it would massively increase unemployment. A justification and rationale for the budget were thus essential for the government. A series of reports was released from official sources, such as the Bank of England and the Price Commission, and these were used in the media to underline the necessity of the government's position. The report from the Price Commission appeared shortly after the April budget at a critical moment in the arguments. This was covered intensively on both channels. The message on wages and inflation was clear:

NEWSCASTER: And now the economy. Prices in Britain rose at their fastest rate ever between December and February, *mainly due to high wage settlements*, according to the Price Commission report published today. In three months up to last December, the Commission approved an average of £350 million in price increases each month, particularly in nationalized industries, but as subsidies started to be phased out and *the big pay increases started to push labour costs higher*, the Commission were forced to allow an average of £1,105 million in increases each month between December and February. This quarterly figure is about as large as the previous nine months combined. Well, here with a report is our industrial correspondent, Giles Smith:

GILES SMITH: Today's message from the Price Commission is grim and it's no less grim because it's not a new one. Inflation is now rampant and, according to the Commission, *wage inflation is almost entirely to blame*. Ominously, they say the pace of the prices explosion has so far been understated. In the three months covered, the retail prices index went up 5.8 per cent, wholesale prices 6.5 per cent, but the Commission's own index, which should be more up to date, rose 7.5 per cent. For this *the Commission firmly blame wage-cost increases*.

(ITN, 22:00, 29 April 1975)

ITN reported the Commission as saying that wages were 'almost entirely' to blame for inflation. The BBC that night actually put a figure on the precise effect of wages. They reported that 'between 60 and 75 pence in the pound' of all price increases came from wages. Such a heavy and unqualified repetition of the theme of wage inflation seemed extraordinary, given the alternative evidence that real wages (for most workers) were probably falling.

When we examined the actual document that the Price Commission published it was apparent that it blamed inflation on a range of factors, including, for example, the increase in oil prices. It had estimated the precise effect of each factor on price increases. The Commission had calculated that the direct contribution of labour costs to price increases was only 20 per cent. Yet both ITN and the BBC reported the effect of wages as massively above this. We were curious to see how this disparity had occurred. The reason was that the Price Commission had estimated upwards its own figures for the effect of wage costs on prices. According to the report in the *Financial Times* the following day, it had done this in two ways. First, in its revised figures, the Commission had *removed* the effects of oil from the calculation and this had put the contribution of wages up from 20 to 30 per cent. Second, they introduced the concept of 'indirect wages', on the grounds that everything, even raw materials, involved a wage element.

Of course such a very general conception makes the precise calculation of exactly what is happening to wages very difficult if not impossible. None the less the Price Commission concluded that the effect of 'indirect wages' could be calculated by multiplying the figure for the direct effect of wages by 'probably two to two and a half times'. The BBC had presumably arrived at its own figures by multiplying the figure of 30 per cent (which was wages after removing oil) by two to two and a half. Whatever the logic of all these calculations, mathematically they become simply absurd at this point. Percentages cannot be multiplied by fixed amounts in this way. Both BBC and ITN were in grave danger of having more percentages than would fit into a hundred. They had given such high figures for the effect of wages that all the other factors could no longer be accommodated. The logic of the report was that well over 100 per cent of all price increases now came from wages, oil and all the other factors.

These figures were indeed attacked the next day in the press – from both Right and Left. The *Daily Telegraph* argued from a monetarist position that wage increases 'are not themselves the cause of inflation' and blamed the problem on the government printing money. The *Morning Star* attacked the calculations in detail and argued that the Price Commission had used 'highly dubious arithmetic and reasoning'.

Given the history and established traditions of the television news it would be naive to think that journalists would be allowed to attack such an 'authoritative' source as a government commission. It would be inconceivable to imagine the news beginning with: 'Good evening, with highly dubious arithmetic and reasoning the Price Commission has claimed tonight that wages are almost entirely to blame for inflation.' Yet by the standards of impartiality and neutrality which broadcasters lay claim to, the reporting of such documents is totally inadequate. In the case of the Price Commission report at no point in any of the bulletins was there a comment on how the high figures for the effect of wages had been arrived at, and at no point is the information given that the proven figure for the effect of wages was only 20 per cent. This figure in fact represented a *decline* in the effect of wages on the previous quarter, which was again not reported on the news. On both BBC and ITN the highest possible estimate of the effect of wages on inflation was taken. The media here are not merely reporting the views of important people, but are actually developing them. The journalists feel able to step into the minds of senior civil servants and tell us what they are thinking or who is to blame. The above report on the Price Commission was followed on ITN by a list of the culprits:

> As the Commission chairman, Sir Arthur Cockfield, states, 'taking industry as a whole, the primary factor causing wages to rise is and can only be rising labour costs'. *Well, the sort of wage rises the Commission is thinking about are* those in the 30 per cent plus bracket and today there came another: the 11,000 London dockers who were on strike for five weeks just a while ago were today offered and accepted a pay deal which averages out at well over 30 per cent – on the face of it well outside the Social Contract guidelines. Tonight, too, a new threat from the electricity power engineers to strike in support of a 33 per cent pay claim.
>
> (ITN, 22:00, 29 April 1975)

There are shots of dockers at a mass meeting which function simply as 'wallpaper' over which the commentary about their pay award is read. No docker is asked to comment on the views of the Price Commission. The 'authoritative' source takes precedence and the shots of the meeting stand in sharp contrast to the picture of the Commission chairman and the high status which is given to his words.

The content of the news is organized in such a way that coherence is given to only one set of explanations and policies. What we are indicating here is not isolated pieces of 'bias'. The problem is much more profound than this. The logic of one group of explanations is built into the text. This logic dictates the flow of information, the range of accounts and the legitimacy that is given to these. In the case of economic news, the premise that wage increases have caused inflation and the economic crisis is followed through to the conclusion that wage restraint and higher taxation are necessary. This item from BBC 2 *News Review* summarizes this position:

> Now home, and as you know this week there's been a lot of heavy news on the country's economic front. Two figures from the week give the real story. Everything else in one way or another is reaction to those figures. One: prices rose in the last twelve months by the biggest ever increase, 21 per cent. Two: wages rose in the last twelve months by a far greater figure, 32 per cent. The Chancellor for one regards that extra 11 per cent on wages as the main cause of inflation. His answer, as we saw in the budget on Tuesday, is to take the extra money away in taxes.
>
> (BBC 2, 18:15, 20 April 1975)

A synthesis is thus made between a restricted and narrow economic explanation and the political policies that apparently flow from it. When this economic view is pursued the logic of who is to blame is inescapable. It seems perfectly natural to monitor wage claims, rather than the actions of those who own capital. This becomes so routine that journalists could dispense with apparently emotive terms such as 'excessive'. They have only to say, 'and tonight another wage claim', for everyone to know what they mean and at whom the finger is being pointed.

In fact journalists do sometimes use emotive terms and make their attitudes to trade unions quite clear. In the following interview, an ITN newscaster asks a trade unionist from the National Union of Bank Employees about their wage claims:

> INTERVIEWEE: Our job as a trade union is to maintain the purchasing power of our members' salaries and that's all we're trying to do with the pay claim that we've now formulated.
>
> ITN PRESENTER: But as *reasonable men and responsible citizens* can you say that's all you are trying to do and all you are interested in when you hear warnings from the Chancellor to the effect that increases of this sort are going to wreck the national economy?
>
> (ITN, 13:00, 24 February 1975)

Two months later the same newscaster is pursuing the same theme – this time with the general secretary of the train drivers' union:

> Can we look at your claim you've already got in; you see, I mean, you said to one of my colleagues not long ago on this programme that this claim was likely then – this was in February – to be in the range of 25 per cent to 30 per cent; now, you see, that is already between 5 per cent and 10 per cent more than the rise in prices *and it's just this excessive demand above the price rise that Mr Healey was saying was endangering our whole national economy.*
>
> (ITN, 13:00, 16 April 1975)

Wage claims in the period we studied were carefully monitored and examined on the news to see whether they were acceptable on the terms that were being set by the government – whether they were inside or outside the social contract. The most dire warnings interpenetrate such reports of wage claims. In this example we are unable to hear what the miners are doing without being told what Mr Healey would think about it:

> The Chancellor of the Exchequer, *Mr Healey, has warned again of excessive wage increases as the miners start negotiating on* their claim for up to 43 per cent. Mr Healey said in London tonight that Britain could be bankrupt if the national wage bill were too high this year – but it needn't happen if the workers stuck strictly to the social contract. During the day

the Coal Board twice increased their offer to the miners, mainly to the benefit of those working underground.

(BBC 1, 21:00, 11 February 1975)

The monitoring of pay claims and their 'acceptability' was consistently from the Healey point of view. At the time of our study the social contract was supposed to mean that wages should go up by about as much as the cost of living. In other words wages should not rise in real terms, but neither should they fall. But on the television news the social contract was deemed to have been broken *only* in the sense that workers were thought to have received 'too much'. There were cases in this period in which working people took wage settlements which could not possibly have kept up with the cost of living – which were in fact wage cuts. These were reported merely as being 'inside' the social contract. There were no fears expressed by television journalists on these occasions and no Chancellors were questioned on the breaking of acts of faith.

In subsequent years it became impossible to sustain this impression of wages soaring above prices. Living standards began to fall quite dramatically in many employment sectors. An analysis of the four years after 1975 demonstrates this, even if wages are taken in gross terms. In real terms, living standards fell between January 1975 and January 1977 by approximately 10 per cent. A study by us in 1979 showed that by then, wages and prices figures were being reported quite differently. They were still reported, but *separately* – without comparison. For example, the BBC reported on 14 February that the

BBC 1, 21:00, 16 February 1979 (prices without wages).

latest figures from the Department of Employment meant that most settlements were 'around 10 per cent'. Two days later, the same programme (BBC 1's *Nine O'Clock News*) carried a report on prices which said that 'inflation could be back in double figures by early summer'. The BBC did *not* report that for the low-paid the inflation rate would be even higher than the official figure suggested, since the cost of basic essentials such as food tends to rise faster than the general level of prices. Nor did the BBC point out that by the time tax was paid on the new wage settlements, living standards would continue to remain low and would probably fall for some groups. Direct comparisons of wage and price levels were now significantly absent.

If such comparisons *had* been broadcast, they would have shown that wage increases at the time were, on average, barely ahead of prices. Far from there being any 'wage explosion', these settlements had no hope of recovering even the real income levels of 1975. There were no headlines to announce that fact, nor any which linked 'official' figures, showing the fall in real income, to the industrial unrest of 1979. The television news used official information to criticize the trade unions for their alleged effects on the economy and on government policy. But the same figures were not used to draw conclusions which might be damaging to government policy, or which might question its economic logic or validity.

Though the precise content of the news changed between 1975 and 1979, the organizing principle remained the same. The news was still presented from the point of view of the government's pay policy: 'good news' was measured in terms of how well this was doing. So instead of comparing wages with prices, the BBC on 14 February 1979 compared them with earnings in the preceding phase of the pay policy.

In a similar vein, ITN reported the new earnings figures as follows:

> *The authorities were happy to announce* two bits of economic news today. First, Britain made a profit of a million pounds last month; they'd thought the balance of payments might be much worse because of the lorry drivers' strike – but it wasn't. And second, the official figure for earnings is that in the five months until the end of December – that's the first five months of Stage Four – they rose by just 3.4 per cent. That included the Ford settlement, but *the total of workers settling was only a million.*
>
> (ITN, 22:00, 14 February 1979)

Only a million? With such a small number, apparently, ITN could not find any of them to see if they were as 'happy' with the figures as the authorities were. Two days later ITN juxtaposed their report on retail price increases with a NUPE pay claim:

> the government will be able to say that the increases in basic rates which the unions are resigned to, have been kept to a strict 9 per cent – and that amounts to a significant morale booster in the battle against inflation.

This assumes not only a direct link between wages and prices as the source of inflation, but also that the battle to be fought is against wages, rather than, for example, against unemployment. And for whom are these figures supposed to be a 'morale booster'? Many economists believe that allowing wages to fall in real terms must produce high rates of unemployment. There is no single analysis which everyone accepts. The *Financial Times* noted (8 February 1979) that while some experts suggested higher wages would produce real growth, others argued almost exactly the reverse.

It is only because the BBC and ITN argue consistently from *one* point of view that they are able to use concepts such as 'wage inflation' and its 'dangers' quite uncritically, and to express 'hopes' and 'fears' from within such partial and limited assumptions. What is 'reasonable' and what is 'excessive' is determined from within the same limits. An interview with the Prime Minister on BBC 1's *Nine O'Clock News* (8 March 1979) was introduced with these words: 'Mr Callaghan has been concentrating a lot this week on the government's stand against excessive pay claims.' It would be difficult to imagine such an uncritical reference to trade-union policies – for instance that they had been 'concentrating a lot on getting a living wage for their members'.

On *News at Ten* the same day, Mr Callaghan was reported in the headlines as saying: 'There's no more money.' In the interview itself, which was shown on both channels, he commented: 'You can't get more money out of the bank than there is in it.' The interview was reported in conjunction with the government's decision to restrict credit by putting up interest rates. An ITN reporter underlined the whole message by declaring that the decision 'reinforces the government's determination to stand firm in the face of mounting pay claims. Mr Callaghan won't print what he calls "confetti money" to finance these claims.'

At no point in this coverage were any of the government's economic assumptions challenged. In the interview, there are no interruptions; nor do we see any questions put to Mr Callaghan on the news programmes of either channel. He gives his message unchallenged, direct to camera. Yet within the current political and economic spectrum, a wide range of critiques was available. On the same day as this interview, the *Financial Times* argued that the government's pay policy was a series of '*ad hoc* stop gaps', with each year's limit having no special coherence. Just three days earlier, on 5 February 1979, the *Financial Times* had attacked the very calculations which were being used to relate wage increases to inflation and unemployment.

While there is no sustained critique on the television news of the 'official' figures, or of the views of the 'authorities', there *are* severely critical analyses of calculations and claims made by other groups such as trade unions. Perhaps there is a fear – felt by the BBC and the IBA alike – of offending the powerful. 'A million workers' can be dismissed without worrying about the consequences, but the Cabinet, the Bank of England and the Treasury are altogether more immediate and potent forces. But such coverage leads inexorably to the view that working people are responsible for the crisis and that it is acceptable that they should pay for it. Alternative ways of understanding the crisis and other possible ways of resolving it are excluded.

REFERENCES

Evans, C. (1979) *The Mighty Micro*, London: Victor Gollancz.
Yaffe, D. (1973) 'The crisis of profitability', *New Left Review*, 80: 10.

Chapter 3

Audience beliefs and the 1984/5 miners' strike*

Greg Philo

We know that television affects us. TV news is our main source of information for national and international events. But what do *we* bring to our understanding of television? New research from the Glasgow University Media Group shows that what we understand and believe about the television message is influenced by our own personal history, political culture and class experience. In a new study (Philo 1990) groups of people from different parts of the country were given news photographs from the 1984/5 miners' strike. They were then asked to imagine that they were journalists and were invited to write their own news stories. They were also questioned about their memories of the strike and about what they believed about specific issues – for example, was the picketing that had taken place mostly peaceful or mostly violent?

One surprising result was the closeness of the 'news programmes' produced by the groups to original items which had appeared on the BBC news and ITN. One year after the strike had ended a group from Shenfield in Essex wrote the following 'news item': 'As the drift back to work in the mines began to gather momentum, violence erupted.' A group from Glasgow pursued a similar theme: 'On a day that saw an increased drift back to work ... further violence was taking place.' While on the original news from ITN we had heard: 'Worst picket violence yet but miners continue their drift back' (ITN, 17:45, 12 November 1984).

It is very interesting that a phrase such as 'drift back' should have stuck so clearly in people's minds. At the time of the strike, some journalists commented on how such phrases became a routine part of news coverage. Michael Crick from ITN's *Channel 4 News* published his own diary of the strike:

The national coal board's skilful propaganda claims that men are returning daily in hundreds, even thousands, and detailed figures are supplied first

---

*This chapter was originally published in *Social Studies Review*, May 1991, pp. 174–7.

thing to news desks every day. Some journalists don't bother to attribute the figures to the board ... and most have generally adopted the board's phrase 'the drift back' despite its suggestions of a continuous and inevitable process.

(Crick 1985: 17)

WHAT DOES TV TELL US?

The study shows that pictures and language can stick in our minds but it does not follow that we all believe what we have seen. For example, virtually all the people who were interviewed thought that most picketing shown on television news had been violent, but whether they believed that most picketing was *really* like this was another matter. The extent to which they believed in the television version of the world depended on several factors, particularly on whether they had access to alternative accounts. No one who had actually been to a picket line thought that picketing was mostly violent. The police described it as being rather like a rugby scrum. 'A lot of it was good-natured banter' and "Come on, lads, it's time for a good heave,"' said one officer. Mostly, people who had been there described it as being very boring, nothing happening at all for hours on end, as they just sat around. But for those without such direct experience, television was more likely to be an important source of information. A woman interviewed in Scotland described how initially she had believed in the television account and then came to change her mind:

> When I first saw the TV pictures I thought it was terrible because I thought it was really violent. Every time it came on I would just walk away and not watch it. Then most of my friends at work, their husbands are miners at Polkemmit pit – they stood at the picket lines and there was never any violence, never any. The camera men must have deliberately filmed a violent bit for television.

Other people also found that their beliefs were affected by their work experience and personal history. A woman working in a solicitor's office in Croydon, south London, wrote a very interesting news story, using the pictures provided. One of these pictures was of a shotgun lying on a table. Most people in the groups associated the gun with the striking miners or pickets but in her story it is the police who use 'arms' and 'threatening behaviour':

> Serious disruption and fear was caused by the police today at the coal mines, as a result of them using arms and threatening behaviour towards the pickets and the coal miners.

At first sight, we might understand this as a simple critique of police behaviour, but in fact the writer gave a very complex explanation of how she had arrived at her 'news story'. From her professional experience in seeing court cases reported, she thought that the media concentrated on the sensational. The reporting of a strike would therefore focus on violence but she did not herself believe that most picketing had been like this. She had also written in her replies to questions that her attitude to the police was, on the whole, positive and that she actually believed that the gun belonged to a striking miner. I asked her how she could reconcile these beliefs with what she had written in her news story. She replied:

I understand that the police do things which are not 'by the book'. It wouldn't surprise me if an officer had picked up the gun and used it. Things which I have been told by police officers which they have done to people taken in for questioning might surprise some people, but in certain circumstances it would be understandable. I can see why they do it.

I asked her, if she saw the police in this way, why she described them as causing 'serious disruption' in her news story? She replied:

In the miners' strike, I did see the police as a disruptive force. I didn't feel that all those police officers should be sent in. The miners and pickets may have sorted it out between themselves. When I see the police I associate them with criminals and the miners are not criminals. I do have very mixed feelings, I do sympathize with the miners but I tend to see things from both sides. All my life I have had dealings with the police in my work and socially. My father was a police constable and my boyfriend was a CID officer.

The final comment about being a policeman's daughter comes almost like a punchline at the end to explain the complexity of her attitudes. Because she was so close to the police, she could both sympathize with them and know they might sometimes break the rules. At the same time, she had a clear and professionally defined view of what police responsibilities are. Through this extraordinary set of filters she was able to envisage a situation in which the police might fire unlawfully at pickets, while retaining sympathy both for them and the miners. At the same time she used her professional background both to assess how the police should act and to reject the media account of what occurred in the events.

USING PERSONAL HISTORIES

In another case, a Salvation Army officer from Beckenham, Kent, used her personal history as well as religious material that she had read to inform her critique of news. As a child she had grown up in Durham and she believed that those in mining communities were decent people who would not be involved in violence. She stated:

With a TV camera you can take one shot and make it look like a hundred shots. You can take it from one angle and make it look like there are hundreds fighting – in short, cheat shots and manipulation.

She had read of this in a religious book, which had used the analogy of the manipulation of film images to comment on personal morality. As she said: if you didn't live your life correctly, you were doing 'cheat shots'. The example which the book had used was of stunt photography in Hollywood. But the woman had applied the analysis to television coverage of picketing and had decided that it was a 'cheat shot'.

Some people used simple processes of logic to criticize what they had seen on television. They commented on the scale of the strike and the numbers involved, saying that people could not have been fighting most of the time. This deduction could apparently be made irrespective of sympathies with the strike. One woman from Penge in south London was very critical of the striking miners and said that she would have shot them if she had been a working miner. But she also argued: 'Because of the amount who were actually on strike ... it can't all have been violent.' A print worker who was interviewed also commented: 'If they had been really violent, the police couldn't have coped. It would have been the army.'

Another reason for doubting television news was the comparison of it with other sources of information, such as the 'quality' and local press or 'alternative' current affairs programmes and radio. About 16 per cent of the sample of people in this study made such comparisons. Some people also made comments on the tendency of television to exaggerate and focus on violence to the exclusion of other events. About 14 per cent of the people made this criticism and gave it as a reason for rejecting what they had seen on the news. This is a relatively low proportion, given that the population is thought to believe, in general, that the media tend to exaggerate. But what is significant about this result is that even where such beliefs existed they were not always used to discount what was seen in the news.

MEMORIES OF THE STRIKE

The study also analysed how memories of the strike were affected by personal history, by cultural and class experiences. All the people interviewed for the study were asked what were their key memories of the strike. This revealed sharp differences between the various groups. For example, women from working-class areas of Glasgow and London remembered queues for food and the loss of jobs in the dispute. But, in a group of women from the very middle-class area of Bromley in Kent, no one gave these as their memories of the strike. The effect of experience on memory could apparently last for many years. A middle-class woman living in Essex, married to an accountant, gave as her key memory of the strike the hopelessness of families and 'shortage of money'. She explained this by speaking of her own personal history as a child in the steel works of Wales and the harsh consequences of unemployment for her own family.

It is clear that we can bring a great deal of our own history, culture and class experience to our reception of media messages. But we should not under-estimate their power and especially that of television to influence public belief. Most of the people in this study did not have direct experience of the events of the strike and did not use alternative sources of information to negotiate the dominant message on issues such as the nature of picketing. Over half the people interviewed for our main sample believed that picketing was mostly violent. Both television and the press were given as key sources of information, but people spoke of the special power of television, saying that its images were 'more immediate' and 'stuck more'. As one resident of Glasgow put it, 'Seeing is believing.'

This was apparently so for a large number of people, at least in relation to their beliefs about picketing. In all, 54 per cent of the main sample had believed that most picketing was violent. The source of this belief seems very clearly to have been the media. It is something of an indictment of news journalism that after coverage virtually every day for a year, such a large proportion of people had apparently no idea what a typical picket line was like. In the course of the interviews for this research, I sometimes read out the eye witness accounts which had been given by the police and others of experience on the picket lines. These were greeted with genuine surprise by many in the groups, who were convinced that what they had seen on the news was typical. Sometimes there was a sense of shock that they had been misled. As one woman from a group of workers in London, commented: 'People always say don't believe what you hear in the media, but this really gives you something to think about.'

CONCLUSION

Where does this leave research into the 'effects' of mass media? The earliest mass-communication researchers believed that the media had tremendous power to promote ideas and beliefs. They saw media power as akin to a hypodermic needle injecting society with ideologies and propaganda. Later it became apparent that *audiences* bring much of their own culture and history to their understanding of media messages.

However, our current research shows that some key elements of the information which is used when these audiences think about the world is itself provided by television and the press. It is also clear that it can be very difficult to criticize a dominant media account if there is little access to alternative sources of information. In these circumstances we should not underestimate the power of the media.

REFERENCES

Crick, Michael (1985) *Reporting the Strike*, Cambridge: Granta.
Philo, G. (1990) *Seeing and Believing*, London: Routledge.

Part II

War reporting: Northern Ireland, the Falklands and the Gulf War

Chapter 4

The media and Northern Ireland
Censorship, information management and the broadcasting ban

David Miller

Information and representation are not simply epiphenomena in modern societies. Communication is central to the conduct of politics and the lived experience of culture. Direct censorship is one of the key weapons of the information manager. It excludes information from the public sphere and helps to structure the information which is available. Censorship is centrally related to the exercise of power and the management of experience. It is not surprising, therefore, that the use of direct censorship increases in times of acute social, political or military conflict. But the use of direct censorship in societies legitimated by a commitment to liberal democracy presents the state with problems as well as opportunities. The legitimation of censorship is itself one of the major tasks of information management in liberal democratic societies.

LEGITIMATING INFORMATION CONTROL

The legitimation of information control varies with the outcome of struggles over the definition of the type and intensity of conflict. These relate both to the actualities of conflict and to the strength of internal opposition to the government. Such opposition will vary partly in relation to the success of official or alternative information-management attempts.

In a situation of total war such as between 1939 and 1945, the rights and liberties of peacetime are suspended in a battle for national survival. In partial engagements such as Suez, the Falklands or the Gulf, different rules apply. Comprehensive censorship is less easy to legitimate and dissent less easy to marginalize. A counter-insurgency conflict like that in Northern Ireland is a further step down in terms of the threat to the central state. Whereas, in the Gulf War of 1991, systematic disinformation was regarded as legitimate it has not been so regarded in Northern Ireland since the mid-1970s. A step down from counter-insurgency in intensity are serious internal disturbances, including inner-city riots/uprisings and large-scale industrial disputes. In Northern Ireland, it has been possible for the state to use the full range of information-management tactics. By contrast, the use of censorship and disinformation was not nearly so well developed in relation to the inner-city disturbances of the 1980s or the 1984/5 coal dispute. Instead, sophisticated public relations and the intimidation of the media were relied upon.

However, not all counter-insurgency campaigns are the same. The conflict in Northern Ireland is different from the fifty-three other counter-insurgency campaigns conducted by the British army between 1945 and 1969 (Ministry of Defence 1969). Northern Ireland is close to Britain and is, supposedly, an integral part of the UK state in which democratic conditions are held to obtain. Media access to and interest in Northern Ireland have also been greater than in previous colonial counter-insurgency campaigns. Such differences have made the practice of extrajudicial killing and systematic disinformation much more difficult and have, therefore, often hampered military strategists.

This point has been acknowledged by some counter-insurgency writers. In the late 1970s, David Charters was a colleague of Maurice Tugwell, the head of disinformation at British army headquarters in Northern Ireland in the early 1970s. Charters has written:

> The Army's counter-insurgency doctrine, evolved over 25 years of fighting insurgency in the Empire, was difficult to apply in Ulster because the doctrine was not designed for domestic use.... The restrictions and harsh measures which had made a successful campaign possible in Malaya could not be applied readily in Britain, with its long tradition of individual liberty and freedom of the press. In Malaya, thousands of miles away from home, operations beyond the jungle fringe could be conducted in almost complete secrecy; in Ulster, the daily movements of a patrol may be seen on TV that evening in Belfast and in London. Moreover, because Northern Ireland is constitutionally part of the United Kingdom, the problem is a domestic one, and politicians in London are more inclined to intervene directly in the actual conduct of security policy and operations
>
> (Charters 1977: 25–6)

Here we find one of the key military objections to the presence of the media in a counter-insurgency conflict like Northern Ireland. The army wanted to treat Northern Ireland as if it were simply another colony. We might ponder how the British army would have conducted itself had 'harsh measures' been possible. The legitimation of British rule in Northern Ireland, however, rested on the official propaganda view that Northern Ireland was an intimate part of the British state, and therefore the appearance of liberal democracy and the freedom of the press had to be preserved.

METHODS OF CONTROL

We can divide methods of information control into four: public relations, intimidation and the use of the law, self-censorship, direct censorship. This chapter briefly summarizes the impact of the first three limits and then goes on to examine the ban on broadcasting interviews with members of Sinn Féin and ten other Irish organizations.

Public relations

In the absence of serious political conflict or armed violence, the most important weapon of information control is routine public relations. In Northern Ireland routine official PR has been dedicated to promoting the view that the conflict is caused either by deep and irreconcilable divisions between Irish nationalists and Ulster Unionists, or simply by 'terrorism'. In either case it is nothing to do with the relationship between Britain and Ireland, and Britain is held to be a neutral arbiter. The routine PR operation includes a wide range of PR tactics. In areas of more controversy, such as the conduct of the 'security forces', disinformation becomes a more important PR tactic. This is to say that official sources, especially the army and the police, routinely release information which is known to be false when security personnel are involved in shooting incidents (Miller 1994).

Use of the law and intimidation

To support the PR effort there have been official attempts to impose tight controls on media practice. This is done, both by the use of the law and by the routine use of government intimidation of the media. In the former case, the number and severity of powers available to circumscribe the media have steadily increased since the 1970s. They include the Prevention of Terrorism Act, the Emergency Provisions Act, the Official Secrets Act and the Police and Criminal Evidence Act, which have all been passed and/or tightened since the 1970s (Ó Maoláin 1989). In particular the 1989 revision of the PTA allows the police to demand access to any journalistic material should they believe that it is likely to have 'substantial value' in a terrorist investigation. The 1989 Official Secrets Act further narrowed the sphere of debate by making it illegal for anyone associated with intelligence or security matters to speak or be reported in the media. No public-interest defence is permissible.

Intimidation is often used in tandem with the law or threats of the law. After a series of controversies in the 1970s, successive governments were able to stop broadcasters interviewing active members of the IRA and INLA. The INLA interview on BBC's *Tonight* was the last occasion on which such an interview was heard on British television. The controversy, in July 1979, was also Prime Minister Thatcher's first serious conflict with the broadcasters. Other major rows followed throughout the 1980s. In 1980 *Panorama* filmed the IRA on patrol in Carrickmore. The outcry in parliament and in the press allowed the police to seize the unbroadcast film. These two controversies represent a turning point in relations between broadcasters and the state.

The use of the Prevention of Terrorism Act against the media was considered for the first time with the INLA interview and Section 11 of the Act was actually used for the first time to seize the Carrickmore footage. The next major row was in 1985 and concerned the representation of Sinn Féin in an edition of the BBC series *Real Lives*. The government went further than ever before in trying to pressure the BBC not to broadcast the programme. The BBC buckled and pulled the programme. The government were less successful with Thames TV's *Death on the Rock* in 1988, which raised the possibility that the SAS killings in Gibraltar had been extrajudicial executions. The new powers available under the 1989 revision of the Prevention of Terrorism Act to seize material were supposed to be used to combat paramilitary racketeering. Yet in 1991 they were used against Channel 4 and an independent production company who alleged, in a *Dispatches* report, that there was a secret committee of Protestant paramilitaries, business people and security-forces personnel directing the assassination of Republican suspects. The broadcasters were found guilty, but pragmatically the court decided not to shut the channel down. Instead, in a landmark judgement, Lord Justice Woolf ruled that in the future, there would be no doubt about the scope of the law, thus warning programme-makers not to use unofficial confidential sources when reporting on Northern Ireland.

Self-censorship

The effect of the use of the law and intimidation has been that broadcasters have continually tightened the internal procedures used in making programmes about Northern Ireland (Miller 1994). All programme ideas on Northern Ireland had to be 'referred up' to senior management in the BBC and independent companies. The reference-upwards system was inaugurated in 1971 after the first skirmishes over coverage of Northern Ireland. Broadcasters' response then was to assure the government, in the words of Lord Hill, chair of the BBC, that 'as between the British Army and the gunmen the BBC is not and cannot be impartial' (Hill 1974: 209).

Direct censorship: the broadcasting ban

On 19 October 1988 Douglas Hurd introduced a Notice under clause 13 (4) of the BBC Licence and Agreement and section 29 (3) of the Broadcasting Act 1981 prohibiting the broadcast of direct statements by representatives or supporters of eleven Irish political and military organizations. The broadcasting ban, as it became known, is the first and, so far, the only use of this power since the beginning of British broadcasting history directly and overtly to rule out a whole class of political viewpoints. The minister responsible for broadcasting has the power to require the broadcasters in writing 'to refrain at any specified time or at all times from sending any matter or matters of any class'.[1] In principle this allows the government to prevail in any conflict with the BBC over editorial matters. Until 1988, however, its use had been limited to less controversial or general provisions.

The Notice was introduced after a year of confrontations between the government and the media and an increase in IRA attacks. The first major confrontation was over government attempts to gain access to small amounts of untransmitted footage of an attack on two soldiers who drove into a funeral cortege in West Belfast. The funeral was of an IRA volunteer killed at the funerals of the three IRA members who were killed by the SAS in Gibraltar. The Gibraltar killings also led to the next major row with the broadcast of *Death on the Rock* in Thames Television's *This Week* series, which suggested that three IRA members had been shot while giving themselves up and had been finished off on the ground. The government's prolonged attacks on Thames prompted Philip Whitehead to observe that *Death on the Rock* 'was enough to lose the IBA its remaining friends in government' (*New Statesman & Society*, 26 August 1988).

The 'last straw' for Margaret Thatcher (*The Times*, 22 October 1988) was the IRA bombing of a British army bus in which eight soldiers died, together with the aftermath of the bombing of the Co. Down home of Sir Kenneth Bloomfield, head of the Northern Ireland civil service. Following this latter attack, Gerry Adams was reported, by the *Sunday Times* (23 October 1988), as saying that civil servants working for the British government 'ran the risk' of attack.

These events provided the immediate rationale and trigger for direct censorship, but the shift in media–state relations from the period of 'cosy chats', through pressure and public intimidation, to overt censorship has a rather longer lineage. The skirmishes and rows over Northern Ireland starting in 1971 had meant a continual tightening of broadcasters' internal regulations, so that by 1980 the voice of armed Republicanism had successfully been banished from the screen (Curtis 1984; Schlesinger *et al.* 1983). The challenge to government policing of the media, which the rise of Sinn Féin represented, produced further attempts at control under successive Thatcher administrations. The logic of the attempt to remove Republican views from the screen was to stop Sinn Féin from being interviewed at all, but since they were a legal political party, such a step was hard to legitimize. This left the government in a bind, unless a way could be found to separate Sinn Féin as 'politicians' from Sinn Féin as 'terrorists'. In all the controversy around the *Real Lives* affair, this dilemma remained relatively obscure. But there is evidence that some top broadcasters were thinking this issue through to its logical conclusions. For example, the BBC Assistant Director-General, Alan Protheroe, had recognized the tendency:

Does the government therefore wish to prevent the expression on the air of views with which it disagrees from democratically elected supporters – at local council, Assembly or parliamentary level? Or does it wish to say,

'You can use Sinn Féin people on the air if they're talking about the drains in the Bogside or the state of the pavements in West Belfast – but you can't use them if they mutter a word about the need for the maintenance of the armed struggle?'

(Protheroe 1985: 6)

The former option would exclude all statements from people representing Sinn Féin and would have been more restrictive than the latter option which would allow Sinn Féin representatives to expound party policy on all issues except support for the armed struggle. The government eventually opted for the former, more stringent option.

The British Home Office Notice prohibits the broadcasting of 'any words spoken' where '(a) the person speaking the words represents or purports to represent' a specified organization; '(b) the words support or solicit or invite support for such an organisation'.

CONFUSION

The precise implications of this were not immediately clear and broadcasters spent the following weeks drawing up guidelines. Channel 4's original 'worst case'[2] interpretation was that the ban applied to a press statement 'read by a commentator with a view to casting contempt upon it' as well as to 'works of fiction'. ITN, though, interpreted the ban to mean that reported speech and fiction were allowable. Following a meeting between the BBC and the Home Office Broadcasting Department, officials elaborated further in a letter (also copied to the IBA) 'so that the BBC would be left in no doubt' (reproduced in BBC 1989b: Appendix V).

This letter stated that reported speech was allowable and that 'the Notice permits the showing of a film or still picture of the initiator speaking the words together with a voice-over account of them, whether in paraphrase or verbatim. . . . Programmes involving the reconstruction of actual events, where actors use the verbatim words which had been spoken in actuality, are similarly permitted.' It should be noted therefore that the government explicitly envisaged the use of interpreting techniques in its letter to the broadcasters. The use of such techniques cannot, therefore, be said (as they sometimes have been) to indicate that broadcasters are attempting to get round the Notice. A second confusion related to the meaning of the term 'represents' in the Notice. The Home Office confirmed that:

A member of an organisation cannot be held to represent the organisation in all his daily activities. Whether at any particular instance he is representing the organisation concerned will depend upon the nature of the words spoken and the particular context. Where he is speaking in his capacity as a member of an organisation which does not fall under the Notice (for example, an elected Council), it follows, from that interpretation, that paragraph 1 (a) will not apply.

(BBC 1989b: Appendix V)

BBC television news made use of this definition of 'represent' for the first time on 16 February 1989 when they interviewed Gerry Adams about jobs in West Belfast. Thirty seconds of sound on film was broadcast in Northern Ireland, with Adams speaking as MP for West Belfast rather than *Sinn Féin* MP for West Belfast. The *Media Show* (8 May 1990) took the definition of 'represent' to its logical conclusion when they interviewed Sinn Féin councillor Jim McAllister speaking about his role in Ken Loach's film *Hidden Agenda*. McAllister was speaking as an 'actor' rather than as a Sinn Féin councillor, even though his acting role in the film is that of a Sinn Féin councillor.

The Home Office clarifications still left some doubt in the minds of broadcasters, particularly about the lineage of some of the organizations covered and about the questions of historical and fictional coverage (Miller 1990). However, the government argument was that although the Notice imposed some restrictions on broadcast coverage, there was no provision in the text of the Notice which restricted television and radio from carrying as many interviews with Sinn Féin as before the ban. This was accompanied by a clear desire to remove Sinn Féin from the screen. However, this latter wish could not be made too clear in public since it would hamper the legitimation of the ban.

Confusion in broadcasting circles has been complemented by caution. Top broadcasters have been unambiguous in public about their opposition to the ban. John Birt (1989) has argued that the ban 'crosses a line that governments in democratic societies should not cross'. However, this has not meant that broadcasters have reported as fully as before the ban. The National Union of Journalists called off its one-day strike after assurances from BBC and ITV executives that 'health warnings' would be used to indicate the effect of the ban. But warnings were only used when Sinn Féin were interviewed, rather than to indicate the absence of a Sinn Féin interview.

Covering up censorship

The BBC's confidential Editorial Policy Meeting (EPM)[3] advised that the warning, or 'programme reference' as BBC executives preferred to call it, should be 'specific'. A 'blanket' warning should be avoided because it 'could sound propagandist' and 'It was important to avoid frivolous or point scoring references' (EPM, 15 November 1988). When health warnings have been used they have been woven into the text of reports by the journalist rather than being announced by the newscaster at the beginning of an item as has been the case with coverage from some other parts of the world. Here the principle of doublespeak is very important. At one end of the scale is 'censorship' and 'propaganda' which are practised by our enemies. Thus television reporters talk of IRA or Libyan 'propaganda' or Iraqi 'censorship'. At the other end of the scale we have 'reporting restrictions' and the 'fight against terrorism'. These are practised by our friends. Somewhere in the middle are those states allied to the west which, for one reason or another, have a blemish on their reputation. Countries such as Apartheid South Africa or pre-peace-deal Israel might be described as practising 'censorship' or the less shameful 'reporting restrictions' might come into play. This principle – you censor, we restrict for operational security – was used to great effect in the Gulf War of 1991 as ITN reporter David Mannion has revealed:

> We did use the word censored. We tried to be as accurate as we could in what we said in front of reports. In Iraq, in Baghdad we said reports were subject to Iraqi censorship. You notice that phrase. That is not to say that every report was censored, in fact some reports were not censored. But they were all subject to Iraqi censorship and we thought it right, even when they were not censored, to let viewers know we were working under those particular conditions. In Israel where reports were censored, we said they were censored. In Saudi Arabia where we had to leave out certain details for operational reasons, we said just that – we had to leave these details out for operational reasons. If you can't understand that, that's your problem.[4]

All broadcast coverage of Northern Ireland under the ban was subject to government censorship, and yet not a single news bulletin in the year after the ban was preceded by a warning. Indeed the BBC went further than this and introduced a ban on the use of subtitles in its news programmes. After BBC Northern Ireland subtitled an interview with Danny Morrison (*Inside Ulster*, 24 January 1989) the BBC decided that subtitles would no longer be used on the local news, because, in the words of one BBC Northern Ireland executive, 'it looked so dramatic – it looked like we were seeking to make a point'.[5] In the year following the ban the single occasion on which subtitles were used on BBC network news was an item on *Newsnight*.[6] The *Newsnight* report was shown at the next Editorial Policy Meeting and the BBC Northern Ireland decision was endorsed and extended to network news. On 18 April 1989 John Wilson, controller of editorial policy, was recorded as saying:

> The use of voice-overs in cases where supporters of the named organiza-tions could not be quoted directly was preferable to the use of sub-titles. This was the practice already followed in Northern Ireland. Sub-titles were odd and formed a further barrier in a restricted report between the audience and the speaker which was unnecessary. Robin Walsh agreed, and strongly favoured a moving, rather than a still picture in such cases, with a voice-over in the style of an interpreter.

Overall, subtitles were used on only five other occasions on network news in the year after the ban, all of them on *Channel 4 News*.[7] In the year following the ban, the most common way of dealing with the restrictions was to give a 'health warning', cut the sound of the interview and use the voice-over technique. One interview with Danny Morrison used an actor's voice (BBC 2, *Newsnight*, 27 January 1989).

The Editorial Policy Meeting also debated the finer points of what constituted an 'appearance' by a 'supporter' of 'terrorism'. In one example, BBC news broadcast footage which included shouting in Irish. The Editorial Policy Meeting noted that: 'The chanting had, in fact, been an IRA battle cry, and Chris Cramer warned all to get their Irish translators in before using material of this type' (EPM, 29 November 1988). By the next meeting the controller of editorial policy, John Wilson agreed that this type of material 'was undoubtedly covered by the restrictions' (EPM, 13 December 1988).

These discussions had the effect of tightening the already strict referral procedures for programmes on Northern Ireland. As BBC guidelines acknowledge, 'The need for referral and special consideration was increased by the Notice served ... in October 1988' (BBC 1989c: 38). John Conway, then editor of news and current affairs, at BBC Northern Ireland, has described the impact of the tightened-up procedure on working practices in Northern Ireland.

> The perception has grown up that we can still interview Sinn Féin about the state of the roads, blocked drains or other innocuous local issues. Not so. Every broadcast interview with a member of the party has to go through a much finer filter and that's what becomes so time consuming for editors and their journalists.... To ensure that an interview with [a] councillor could be broadcast, the news editor at [Radio] Foyle had to check with me in Belfast and I, in turn, had to consult with senior colleagues in London about potential legal and policy implications before the green light to broadcast was given. All that for the everyday voice of grassroots politics which local radio is there to articulate.
>
> (Conway 1989)

Under the ban it is in principle possible to interview representatives of any of the listed organizations as much or even more than had been the case before the Notice was introduced so long as their voices are not heard. However, in practice the broadcasters extended the ban well beyond its literal meaning. There are several reasons for this, such as the extra time it takes to get clearance for interviews with Sinn Féin and the time it takes to subtitle or voice-over an interview. Broadcasters also often argue that subtitling or lip-syncing don't make for 'good television'. On the other hand the confusion resulting from what John Birt has called the 'Byzantine' restrictions (Birt 1992) is often given as the excuse for any limitation in broadcasters' coverage. Whatever the merits of such arguments, they should not in principle be insurmountable. Yet it is clear that journalists on tight deadlines have

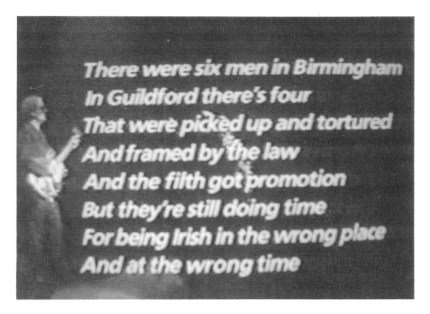

'Streets of Sorrow/Birmingham Six' shown on ITN.

frequently succumbed to the time-saving temptation to simply leave Sinn Féin out.

The caution of the broadcasters has meant that there have been very few attempts to test the limits of the ban. Among these are the responses of ITN to the banning of a song by the Pogues and a BBC documentary on the Maze prison. When the IBA banned the Pogues' song 'Streets of Sorrow/ Birmingham Six', ITN reported the IBA decision by showing footage of the Pogues in concert and rolling the words up on the screen. The reporter then recited them in an arguably more intelligible way than the Pogues' vocalist Shane McGowan:

> There were six men in Birmingham
> In Guildford there's four
> That were picked up and tortured
> And framed by the law
> And the filth got promotion
> But they're still doing time
> For being Irish in the wrong place
> And at the wrong time

(ITN, 17:45, 20 December 1988)

'Enemies within', made for the BBC's *Inside Story* series by Steve Hewlett and Peter Taylor, operated right up to the limit of the Notice. The programme featured extensive interviews with Republican and Loyalist prisoners in the H-Blocks of the Maze prison. When the prisoners were speaking in a personal capacity their voices were heard, but when they were

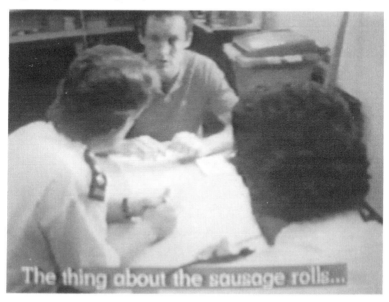

Subtitling of IRA spokesperson on food.

speaking as representatives of the IRA, the Notice was given maximum visibility. The interviewees were voiced over with an out-of-sync actor's voice, indicated by a caption at the top of the screen. Meanwhile at the bottom of the screen the words were also subtitled. This operation to the limits of the ban (but not beyond) allowed some prisoners to be heard giving a Republican political analysis in a personal capacity while others were subtitled when talking about innocuous topics in their capacities as representatives of the IRA. Thus the IRA spokesperson on food was subtitled when shown negotiating with prison officers over the size of sausage rolls served up in the prison.

The effect on coverage

Coverage of Sinn Féin prior to the ban was minimal and when interviews were broadcast the hostile interview technique was routinely used (Schlesinger *et al.* 1983; Curtis 1984). In the year leading up to the ban,[8] BBC network television news featured a total of 633 formal interviews on Northern Ireland. By far the largest category of interviewee was members of the Conservative Party with a total of 121 interviews including 50 interviews with the Northern Ireland secretary Tom King who was on more than anyone else. British politicians together with representatives from the army, RUC and civil service accounted for 172 interviews or more than 25 per cent of all interviews on Northern Ireland that year. By contrast other political parties had a much lower showing. The Labour Party was on 38 times (6 per cent), the Social Democratic and Labour Party (SDLP) and Ulster Unionist Party (UUP) exactly balanced at 36 interviews each and the DUP slightly trailed at 30. By contrast Sinn Féin was interviewed a total of 17 times in the entire year. Sinn Féin comments tended to be limited to short sound bites or single responses to journalists' questions.

Conducting an interview in the television studio is one indicator of the importance which broadcasters accord to an interviewee. It confers status and, especially on programmes like *Channel 4 News* and *Newsnight*, allows for exchanges of views between 'opposing' commentators or politicians and gives interviewees the opportunity to respond to points from journalists or other politicians (Henderson *et al.* 1990). In the year prior to the ban Conservative, Labour, UUP, DUP and SDLP MPs were invited into the studio but Sinn Féin were not allotted any studio interviews on British network TV news. Coverage of Sinn Féin in the year before the ban was very limited both in quantity and quality. Sinn Féin representatives appeared[9] on television, or their voices were heard, a total of 93 times. In the following year the number fell to 34, a drop of more than 63 per cent. It is also clear that when interviews with Sinn Féin did occur they were shorter and less informative.[10] Top broadcasters have acknowledged this point in private. The BBC's Editorial Policy Meeting was told by John Conway that when Sinn Féin councillor,

Francis McNally, was interviewed as a brother of a murder victim, the interview had 'said much less than it would have prior to the ban' (EPM, 29 November 1988).

The obvious corollary of this is that some news items are simply not filmed. This seems also to have been the case in relation to current-affairs and documentary programmes. Paul Hamman, the BBC producer who made *Real Lives*, went on to become head of documentaries at the Corporation. He has said that on taking up the post he 'had a couple of Irish films up [his] sleeve, new ways of looking at Northern Ireland, but since the [ban]...both of these films have bit the dust' (*Guardian*, 8 May 1989).

It is difficult to argue that 'confusion' is responsible for the steep decline in Sinn Féin interviews. The confusion arises in relation to the manner of covering Sinn Féin rather than in relation to covering them at all. In fact the result of the restriction has been largely to excise Republican sentiment from British television screens.

The most obvious and measurable impact of the ban has been on members of Sinn Féin, with a slight impact on the UDA. The second part of the Notice has had less obvious, though more far-reaching, effect. Interviews cancelled are the tip of the iceberg since it is difficult to tell which people and views are not even considered for inclusion. Whereas the Notice refers to words which 'support or solicit or invite support' broadcasters have interpreted it to cover attempts at understanding or explaining the conflict (Curtis and Jempson 1993; Irish Information Partnership 1990).

In November 1988 the IBA banned the song 'Streets of Sorrow/ Birmingham Six' by the Pogues. The song simply proclaims the innocence of the Guildford Four and the Birmingham Six, jailed for IRA bombings in the 1970s, but the IBA deemed it to be 'supporting or soliciting or inviting support' for a listed organization because it contained a 'general disagreement with the way in which the British government responds to and the courts deal with the terrorist threat in the UK' (*Observer*, 20 November 1988).

Ironically, the convictions of first the Guildford Four and then the Birmingham Six were finally acknowledged by the courts to be unsafe and all ten were released. The IBA would not lift the ban after the Guildford Four were released because in the words of one spokesperson, 'The Birmingham Six are still serving sentences as convicted terrorists' (*Sunday Correspondent*, 22 October 1989). When the Birmingham Six were released the Radio Authority revoked the ban. But the Independent Television Commission said only that 'it is highly unlikely' that they would intervene if the song was broadcast on television.[11]

That a popular song might 'contain a general disagreement with government policy' or make a 'political point' was now considered in some parts of broadcasting as being identical to supporting Sinn Féin or the IRA. This raises the key question of the acceptable range of opinion on the Northern Ireland conflict and how differing views are categorized. Margaret Thatcher posed the choice simply: 'Either one is on the side of justice in these matters, or one is on the side of terrorism' (BBC 2, *Newsnight*, 22:50, 22 March 1988). There is, however, no intrinsic reason why this view should be accepted by the broadcasters. As the ban became more entrenched in journalistic working practices so more decisions were taken which collapsed any critique of British policy into support for terrorism. This resulted in the category of prohibited views expanding markedly, yet almost imperceptibly. Irish Republicanism was joined by Irish nationalist and Left critiques, together with more centrist views, beyond the pale of acceptable broadcasting.

The most far-reaching decision resulted in the subtitling of Bernadette McAliskey, the former civil-rights activist and People's Democracy MP for Mid-Ulster together with members of a studio audience. 'Killing for a cause', part of a series titled *Nation*, used the examples of the conflicts in Northern Ireland and South Africa to ask if the use of political violence was ever justified. Bernadette McAliskey was one of a panel of three, including Conservative MP and former Northern Ireland minister, Peter Bottomley, and a member of the ANC. The moderator, Trevor Phillips, introduced McAliskey as a former supporter of 'the use of violence in the cause of Irish Republicanism'.

Asked about her current views on violence in the cause of Irish Republicanism McAliskey started by saying 'Well, I have to put it in context'. These were the only words directly broadcast. From that point on every word was subtitled. What she then said was:

> Quite honestly, if I supported it fully, if I could justify it, I would join the IRA. But since I am not a soldier, since I cannot within myself justify it, then I'm not. But I can understand it, I can explain it, I can articulate it and I can offer, what I believe to be a rational way out of it, which is discussion and negotiation, wherever it is in the world. But I don't think that a limited and emotionally packed statement like 'Do you support violence'.... No sane human being supports violence. We are often cornered into it by powerlessness, by lack of democracy, by lack of willingness of people to listen to our problems. We don't choose political violence, the powerful force it on us.

For BBC lawyers these were the key words which seemed to them to be sufficiently supportive of the IRA to fall within the terms of the Notice. The controller of editorial policy, John Wilson, who had been on holiday when the decision was taken, was apparently not happy. He wanted to offer McAliskey an apology, but he was overruled by the Director-General and a compromise reached.[12] This involved asking for external legal advice from an independent lawyer. David Pannick, the QC concerned, largely backed up the internal BBC advice, apparently making it difficult for the BBC simply to repudiate the treatment of McAliskey. Prior to this the BBC guidelines on what was covered by this part of the Notice maintained that 'generalised comments

Subtitling of Bernadette McAliskey on *Nation* series.

about or even in favour of terrorism in Ireland or about Irish Republicanism are not prevented' (BBC 1989c: 40). Following the Pannick judgement the controller of editorial policy rewrote the guidelines although he maintained that 'I will continue to apply the guidelines as narrowly as I reasonably can.'[13]

The central problem here is that understanding the actions of the IRA could apparently be construed by the broadcasters as being identical to support for the IRA. The BBC's difficulty in telling 'understanding' and 'support' apart was heightened by Peter Bottomley's public complaint that: 'If I had been asked to explain or give an understanding of the republican or loyalist killings, I could have done so.'[14]

Broadcasters and the ban

There is a long history of broadcasters accepting the official definition of Republican opposition. Lord Hill's 1971 declaration that 'as between the British Army and the gunmen the BBC is not and cannot be impartial' (Hill 1974: 209) set the pattern. The BBC echoed this view in the aftermath of the 1989 bombing of the Royal Marines at Deal in Kent. They dispensed with their signature tune and closed their main evening news bulletin with the Marines' band playing over slow-motion footage of a young boy in uniform laying a wreath to the dead (BBC 1, 20:55, 23 August 1989). When a contributor to Channel 4's *Right to Reply* complained that this was not news but 'pure emotionalism', the BBC responded that:

> The day before this item was broadcast ten Marine bandsmen had been murdered and around twenty injured. We are satisfied that the item properly reflected the feeling of many people in the aftermath of such an event.
>
> (Channel 4, *Right to Reply*, 7 October 1989)

This view remains strong in broadcasting. David Nicholas, editor of ITN, objected to the ban on the grounds that ITN interviews with Sinn Féin were conducted 'responsibly':

> Because we all understand what these extremist organizations stand for is abhorrent to many people. British public opinion has never been more resolute than it is now, in my opinion, in defeating terrorism and that owes a lot to the full and frank reporting that we've been able to conduct on Northern Ireland over nineteen years.
>
> (ITN, 22:00, 19 October 1988)

Here Nicholas claims to act 'responsibly' in the name of 'public opinion'. Opinion which, he maintains, the broadcasters have helped to create with their 'full and frank' coverage.

The close coincidence of the views of the broadcasters and the state on 'terrorism' helps to explain why much coverage of Sinn Féin has been directed at discrediting the party as part of the campaign to defeat 'terrorism'. One of the objections of the broadcasters has been that they no longer have control over their part of the campaign. This is to say that in part the caution of the broadcasters is not simply about being intimidated by the government, it also includes a strategy to defend their legitimacy to the outside world. Thus broadcasting executives are opposed to the Notice, but they are not in favour of free reporting. They would prefer the government to trust them not to be really impartial.

The rationale for the ban

It is essential that the British government present itself as acting within the rule of law so that it can claim that the conflict in Ireland is one of 'democracy' versus 'terrorism'. Many measures can be justified under the cloak of fighting terrorism. Let us now turn to a detailed consideration of the rationale given by the government for introducing the ban.

First, appearances by 'paramilitary organisations and their political wings ... have caused widespread offence to viewers throughout the United Kingdom, particularly just after a terrorist outrage' (Hansard, 19 October 1988, col. 893). Second, 'Those who live by the bomb and the gun and those who support them cannot in all circumstances be accorded the same rights as the rest of the population ... those who practice and support terrorism and violence should not be allowed direct access to our radios and television screens' (Hansard, 2 November 1988, col. 1074). Third, 'The terrorists themselves draw support and sustenance from access to radio and television. ... The government have decided that the time has come to deny this easy platform to those who use it to propagate terrorism' (Hansard, 19 October 1988, col. 893). Later Hurd said, 'direct access gives those who use it an air and appearance of authority which spreads further outwards the ripple of fear that terrorist acts create in the community' (Hansard, 2 November 1988, col. 1080). Fourth, 'We are dealing not just with statements that are offensive, but with the use of the media to deliver indirect threats' (Hansard, 2 November 1988, col. 1080).

John Birt, the then Deputy Director-General of the BBC, has stated that 'There is no evidence the BBC can uncover that our audiences are offended by responsible and relevant journalism' (Birt 1989). The IBA also claimed to have received no complaints (cited in Henderson *et al.* 1990). The Home Office did not commission their own research on this topic, nor, it seems, did they consult the research undertaken by broadcasters and academics. Although there are very few pieces of research in this area, they are consistent with each other. The last time British broadcasters interviewed a professing member of a Republican paramilitary organization in 1979, BBC audience research with members of the British public showed that 80 per cent of those sampled thought it right to broadcast the interview with a member of the INLA. Perhaps more importantly, from the government perspective, it also apparently increased hostility to the IRA and INLA and aroused sympathy for the police and army (BBC 1980).

This finding gains credibility from audience research carried out by David

Docherty and his colleagues. They conducted discussions with audience groups in Belfast and found that, far from being offended, most were opposed to broadcasting restrictions or censorship:

> the right of free speech is not impugned by the [audience] groups; the Protestants, with reservation, were willing to bite the bullet over the IRA, and the Catholics likewise the Protestant militants. But this is not enough for them; they want the debate to enter into complex areas where religion, politics and class fragment, and where real debates take place.
>
> (Docherty *et al.* 1988: 171)

Let us note that there is some evidence that public opinion on this issue is not nearly so conservative as is assumed by government, broadcasters and many others.

The tenor of the government case suggests that, before the ban, 'terrorists' and their 'supporters' constantly appeared on the broadcast media either urging the IRA on to victory or issuing some new threat against military personnel or others associated with the British government. As Douglas Hurd put it, 'What I used to hear, are supporters of Sinn Féin having the skill to stay just within the law and using the right of direct access to the media to glory in violence and death' (Hansard, 19 October 1988, col. 897). Furthermore it suggests in some places that both Sinn Féin and the IRA were continually able to gain *favourable* coverage on television. In fact, as we have seen, this was far from the case.

'The terrorists themselves' have not been able, as Douglas Hurd put it, to 'draw support and sustenance from access to radio and television', since interviews with active, professing Republican paramilitaries by British broadcasters have not been shown on television since 1979 and the IRA have not been interviewed since 1974. Let us remind ourselves that of 633 formal interviews on Northern Ireland on BBC network news in the year before the ban only 17 were with members of Sinn Féin. This compared with 121 with members of the Conservative Party, including 50 alone with Tom King, the then Northern Ireland secretary. This is already a very great imbalance, but in addition current BBC guidelines require that in interviewing 'terrorists' 'challenging questions should be used to get valid contributions to the examination of the issues' (BBC 1989c: 79). Journalists are also advised to 'take care not to show terrorists or people closely associated with them in an approving light' (ibid.: 80). The resulting coverage is hardly favourable to Sinn Féin. In the same year there were no interviews with members of the IRA. Indeed, it is doubtful whether any professing, current member of the IRA has been interviewed on British network television news in the entire period of the Troubles.

British government personnel have themselves occasionally acknowledged that representatives of Sinn Féin did not gain favourable coverage prior to the ban. One of the biggest news stories in the year before the ban was the

Enniskillen bombing, featuring eleven Sinn Féin appearances on British network news. The Chief Constable of the RUC at the time, Sir John Hermon, has commented on his view of the tenor of the coverage:

> Who could gainsay or forget the power of the poignancy of the images brought to us and to the whole world by the news media out of Enniskillen in 1987? Out of the coverage of that tragedy by the media came dignity, compassion, hope, and a powerful indictment of terrorism.
>
> (Hermon 1990: 41)

It is clear that much of the coverage of Sinn Féin was very negative for the party. Most Sinn Féin statements are not in fact about violence or the IRA nor could they in any way be construed as supporting the IRA. Sinn Féin have regularly complained that such statements are ignored by journalists in favour of questions about the IRA and violence (Morrison 1989). In fact were Sinn Féin never to make any statement which could be construed as supporting the IRA or 'terrorism' their words would still have been covered by the ban.

The fourth reason given for imposing the ban was that some statements were intended to be, and in some cases were, intimidating. The example used in Home Office affidavits before the High Court in Belfast and London (Scoble 1989, 1990) and in off-the-record briefings when the ban was introduced[15] is the aftermath of the IRA bombing of the home of Sir Kenneth Bloomfield, the head of the Northern Ireland civil service. The government alleged that Gerry Adams had said that civil servants working for the government 'ran the risk' of attack. However, in an extraordinary turn of events, the government then acknowledged that this example was simply inaccurate. In the High Court consideration of the ban in London, Lord Justice Watkins had challenged the example and Christopher Scoble, the head of the Home Office Broadcasting Department accepted that Adams' comments were 'not broadcast as a direct statement by a person covered by the notices' (Scoble 1990: 2). In fact Adams was referring to a statement by the IRA and his remarks were prefaced by the statement 'I'm not here as a spokesperson for the IRA' (BBC Radio Ulster, *Talkback*, 12 September 1988). However, in mitigation, Scoble claimed that the statement was issued through the Republican Press Centre. He went on to say: 'while I accept that the statement was not broadcast in a way which would have been caught by the notices, I nevertheless submit that the statement is evidence that terrorist organisations do make statements intended to intimidate' (Scoble 1990). Of course in the original submission the government had complained specifically about '*broadcast* statements'. The government have not been able to produce any evidence that Sinn Féin members have made such statements. Furthermore, the ban contained no provision which would stop the *reporting* of IRA statements that might be intended to intimidate.

In the year before the ban very few Sinn Féin appearances in the aftermath of IRA actions could easily be interpreted as intimidatory. There were a small number which related to distinctions between 'legitimate' and 'illegitimate' targets and the Republican contention that the war situation provides the context of IRA actions.

In summary, the access gained by 'terrorists' themselves on British television prior to the ban was virtually nil and in the year before the ban most Sinn Féin comments were not related to supporting the IRA. Let us remember, the ban was not aimed only at statements made by Sinn Féin which contained support for the IRA or the 'armed struggle'. It also applied to *any* statement made by Sinn Féin representatives.

British strategy

There has been little examination of the government's rationale for phrasing the Notice in such limited and vague terms. It is said that the government felt that it had to do something to react to the intensified IRA campaign of summer 1988 and the ban was the ill-thought-out result of that impulse. There may be some truth in this, but it seems clear that some careful thought was given to the precise terms of the ban for reasons of legitimation. It is remarkably convenient that the ban is phrased in vague terms and that, accordingly, broadcasters have to interpret its precise meaning. Because of the caution of broadcasting management in the face of government intimidation throughout the 1980s, Republican interviewees all but disappeared from network television news. The advantage of this from the government point of view is that the broadcasters can then be blamed for any over-zealous application of the Notice. In the case before the European Commission on Human Rights the government emphasized the limited nature of the Notice and tried to absolve themselves of responsibility for the actual implementation of the ban. Under the European Convention on Human Rights, a government may infringe freedom of expression so long as the infringement is strictly limited and corresponds to a 'pressing social need'. The fight against 'terrorism' is held by the government to be such a need and the limited nature of the ban means, they say, that it is precisely targeted and limited.

The strength of the official approach to the broadcasting ban is its conflation of the democratic activities of Sinn Féin with the political violence of the IRA under the single heading of 'terrorism'. If this view of 'terrorism' is seen as a political perspective rather than a simple truth, however, the official position is harder to sustain. The official position is also hampered by the fact that Sinn Féin remains a legal political party and by the government acknowledgement that Sinn Féin is not 'actively and primarily involved in terrorism' (Hansard, 2 November 1988, col. 1078). Nevertheless the British government's attempts to legitimate the ban paid off when the European Commission on Human Rights refused to refer the case to the European Court in 1994.

In the House of Commons Douglas Hurd had described the ban as applying to appearances by 'terrorists'. However, it is clear that 'terrorists' do not appear on British television. The government argument seemed to be that Sinn Féin and the IRA are so closely connected in the public mind that any statement by Sinn Féin is likely to increase the support for and legitimacy of 'terrorism'. This would be so even if the Sinn Féin policy on flood damage, maternity hospitals or post offices (all actual examples) were the same as that of the government. It seems clear then that the ban does not target statements which support terrorism (which are already illegal under the Emergency Provisions Act and would result in Sinn Féin councillors being disbarred from office under the Elected Authorities [Northern Ireland] Act 1989 [the 'oath of non-violence']); rather it is quite clearly directed against Sinn Féin as a party. It is part of the British strategy of attempting to marginalize Sinn Féin by managing public opinion in order to 'contain' the Troubles (O'Dowd *et al.* 1982; Rolston 1991).[16]

Legitimation

It is fundamental to the legitimation of a 'democracy' that there is the appearance of freedom of speech and of free elections. This is part of the reason why the ban is replaced during election times by the Representation of the People Act. Sinn Féin were able to make party election broadcasts and appear directly on television and radio in the same way as other parties pending the election. As Douglas Hurd noted in the House of Commons:

> I have always regarded the obligation of impartiality as an important part of holding free elections, and, in turn, the holding of free elections in Northern Ireland as a crucial part of our stance there. I did not want to do anything which undermined that.
>
> (Hansard, 19 October 1988, col. 895)

There were, however, other reasons for this exemption. To have prohibited direct statements in the run up to an election would have raised, as Hurd put it, 'significant legal difficulties' (Hansard, 2 November 1988, col. 1074).

When Douglas Hurd announced the ban he argued, 'This is not a restriction on reporting. It is a restriction on direct appearances by those who use or support violence' (Hansard, 19 October 1988, col. 893). Later he asserted, 'This is not censorship, because it does not deal with or prohibit the reporting of events' (Hansard, 19 October 1988, col. 898). The claim that the Notice does not amount to censorship is a key part of the attempt to legitimate the ban. Indeed, the distinction between a ban and 'restrictions' has been emphasized in British Public Relations in the US. In a letter to the *Washington Post*, a British Embassy information counsellor claimed that 'there is no "media ban" applying to terrorists or anyone else in the United Kingdom':

> There is no ban on terrorists and their supporters appearing on television. There is no ban on reporting what such people have said. There is no ban

on people criticising the government's policy. There is simply a requirement that television companies refrain from broadcasting the actual voices of anyone representing or soliciting support for either an illegal terrorist group or one of the three organisations with a history of apologising for terrorist violence.... The British government has made it quite clear that the interpretation of the restrictions is a matter for the broadcasters themselves. It is for them to decide whom they wish to interview.

(*Washington Post*, 26 November 1990)

Of course, this clearly does not relate to the actual effects of the ban on broadcasting, which it seems the government are quite happy with. They have at no stage complained about the broadcasters' over-enthusiastic implementation of the Notice. Indeed according to a Home Office press officer on the second anniversary of the ban:

> There will be grey areas and occasional isolated incidents where the prohibition might appear to be skirted, but generally we think it's been very effective and there are no present plans to change it.
>
> (*Washington Post*, 21 October 1990)

Did the ban work?

Critics on the Left and the Right and amongst civil-liberties organizations have suggested that the ban is 'stupid', 'risible' or 'silly'. On the Right there have been complaints that the ban is too limited. The journalist Herb Greer (1990) has argued that using an actor's voice to lip-sync Gerry Adams' words was a 'stunt engineered to circumvent the silly half-ban'. Calls for a total ban or for the outlawing of Sinn Féin are associated with this type of argument. From a different direction, amongst civil-liberties organizations there has been opposition to the Notice on the grounds that 'it is easily evaded and can operate in such a way as to add lustre to the arguments it is attempting to stifle' (Committee on the Administration of Justice 1991). Roy Hattersley, then deputy leader of the Labour Party, suggested the ban was stupid because it was:

> apparently perfectly legal to record an interview with a member of a banned organisation and broadcast it, *after dubbing with the voice of an actress or actor* ... – an example of how stupid the new regulations actually are.
>
> (Hattersley 1988: 19, his emphasis)

In this view there was no overwhelming reason to introduce the ban; indeed it is likely that the Notice would have a damaging effect on the fight against terrorism. As Hattersley argued:

> If censorship does not contribute to victory over terrorism, it is impossible

to justify the price to be paid for its introduction.... Abandoning our traditional freedoms in order to prevent Gerry Adams from appearing on our television screens is likely to have exactly the opposite effect to that intended by the censors.... The terrorists ... have been provided with a new weapon.

(ibid.)

The underlying theme of all these arguments is that the Notice is counter-productive. As Hattersley put it in the House of Commons, 'I cannot see what damage is done to terrorism and terrorists in Northern Ireland by the Government making themselves look ridiculous by imposing that sort of meaningless and pointless restriction on broadcasters' (Hansard, 2 November 1988, col. 1081–2). The evidence for this view is, first, that the ban is evaded by duplicitous broadcasters or that it is made to look stupid by the use of interpreting techniques.[17] Second, it is argued that the ban benefits Sinn Féin since it allows them to point out that they are being censored and to evade hostile questioning in the aftermath of IRA bombings.

As we have already seen, the Home Office explicitly acknowledged that voice-overs and actor's-voice techniques are allowable under the ban. Much of the evidence for the view that broadcasters are evading the ban rests not on actual evasions but on those instances where the limits of the ban have been tested by journalists willing to take the restrictions to their logical limit.

In fact there were few occasions on which broadcasters tested the limits of the ban. None actually broke it. Let us be clear about the second part of the argument; the ban allowed Sinn Féin to claim that they were being censored precisely because they *were* being censored. The logic of this argument is that only if no one knew that the censorship existed (or, in Hattersley's terms, if it worked) would it be acceptable. This is really a plea for broadcasters to be allowed to censor themselves. There is, however, some factual basis to the second part of this complaint. It is clear that Sinn Féin have used the existence of the Notice as a reason why they could not put forward spokespersons in the aftermath of some IRA actions (Birt 1992). But in the end the real question is the quality of information which people in Britain and Northern Ireland have access to in order to make up their minds on the conflict. The wider issue that this criticism of the ban raises is the proper role of journalism in a conflict like Northern Ireland.

THE EFFECT OF THE BAN

The ban does not appear to have been one of the catalysts which brought about the Hume–Adams process, the Downing Street declaration and an IRA ceasefire. Indeed it has been argued that cutting off what Margaret Thatcher has described as the 'oxygen of publicity' may have bolstered those sections of the Republican movement in favour of a more straightforward military strategy (Ó Maoláin 1989: 98). The ban has obviously made the democratic activities of Sinn Féin more difficult. In this respect it is no different from a number of government initiatives designed to marginalize the party, whether through the oath of non-violence, the refusal of officials to meet with Sinn Féin representatives, exclusion from Britain or raids on Sinn Féin offices. Such marginalization contributes to the general sense that Sinn Féin are not worthy of inclusion in news reports. Together with the ban this has an effect on the public-relations skills of Sinn Féin spokespersons. Sinn Féin director of publicity, Danny Morrison, has commented:

> It even has an effect on a person like myself. For example, when you're used to the cut and thrust of regular interviews – right – and very heavy interviews – it keeps you sharp. And I found that the first time the ban was lifted – as a result of the local-government elections and European elections in May and June 1989, I didn't feel quite up to it. I didn't feel as confident as I had been in previous times. So it has that effect.
>
> ('Politics', *Media Skills*, UTV, 2 February 1990)

There is little evidence, however, that the ban hampered the military activities of the IRA.

There is one criterion used by the government to justify the ban which has some validity. Appearances by members of the IRA have not had the effect of increasing the standing of the IRA since there have been no interviews with British broadcasters since 1974. On the other hand, Sinn Féin have been interviewed on British television, precisely because they are elected politicians. In a democratic society election to a properly constituted assembly of the state does mean that those so elected have a right to communicate through the public media. Such appearances, even though they were treated in a hostile manner by broadcasters, do confer a certain legitimacy on Sinn Féin politicians – the legitimacy partly earned by election to a council or to parliament. It is this which was adversely affected by the ban and which helped the government to marginalize Sinn Féin from the political process. In this sense, the ban was effective in helping to push Sinn Féin to the margins of political life and in helping to exempt state actions from effective scrutiny.

THE 'PEACE PROCESS' AND THE LIFTING OF THE BAN

So far, I have painted a general picture of ever tightening controls on the media and ever increasing journalistic self-censorship. But this all changed with the reappearance of Sinn Féin on British television screens in late 1993. Then, in September 1994, the ban was lifted by the government.

With the emergence of the Hume–Adams process, in which John Hume and Gerry Adams reached an agreement that John Hume called the 'best chance' for peace in twenty-five years, the basics of political reporting again required a glimpse of Republican perspectives. Sinn Féin's *de facto* exclusion from the news was ended and Gerry Adams and other Sinn Féin representatives appeared extensively. For the first time since the introduction of the ban and perhaps since the early 1980s Sinn Féin representatives were accorded status-conferring studio interviews, in many cases lasting some minutes. This so enraged some Tory MPs that Dame Jill Knight requested that John Major tighten the restrictions. The Prime Minister responded that 'I think many people felt that the [interviews] did stretch the present guidelines to the limit and perhaps beyond'. The criticism that the lip synchronization of the Sinn Féin leader's voice with the actor speaking his words was so close as to give the impression that Gerry Adams himself was speaking. Yet it is clear that such interviews are explicitly allowed by the ban. In any case, after a decent period had elapsed it was announced that a Department of National Heritage review had concluded that the ban should stay as it was. Sinn Féin continued to appear on the news, for example, on the question of clarification of the Downing Street declaration, as the peace process ebbed and flowed in news value. For the first time the ban began to look unsustainable.

It was the IRA ceasefire on 31 August 1994 which put the final nail in the coffin of the ban. On 16 September John Major announced in Belfast that it was being lifted. The development of the peace process and, in particular, the revelation of secret contacts between the British government and Sinn Féin, meant that broadcasters now felt able to interview Sinn Féin members more freely than previously. The fact that Sinn Féin were central to the change in political circumstances meant, additionally, that reporting the peace process required some accessing of Republican views. Sinn Féin were now harder to ignore.[18]

Sinn Féin interviews from the end of 1993 did comply with the restrictions. However, the frequency, length and depth of the interviews meant that, for the first time, the ban began to be counter-productive for the government. This was acknowledged by John Major when he lifted the ban: 'I believe the restrictions are *no longer* serving the purpose for which they were intended. Ways have been found to circumvent them' (emphasis added). In fact, as we have noted, the ban had not been circumvented. Major went on to state the other major reason for the lifting of the ban, which was the changed relationship between Sinn Féin and the government: 'Most importantly, we are now in very different circumstances from those of 1988 when the restrictions originally came in.'[19] The lifting of the ban was one indication of the process whereby Sinn Féin were brought in from the cold and the peace process advanced. This in turn meant that broadcasters had less cause to worry about government displeasure at their accessing of Sinn Féin. When John Major instituted an inquiry into the ban in December 1993 in the aftermath of the IRA bombing of the Shankill Road, the BBC reported Whitehall sources as dismissing the inquiry, as 'part of the Shankill backlash' (Miller 1993).

The greater leeway this has allowed broadcasters on Northern Ireland has been complemented by less hostility towards the BBC from the Conservative Party and by the weakness of the Major government in this period. In contrast, when the ban was introduced in October 1988, the Thatcher administration was at the height of its power. This difference has had an impact on the atmosphere in broadcasting organizations. The changing relationship between the government and the BBC has been described by John Naughton, the television critic of the *Observer*, using the example of BBC's flagship current-affairs programme, *Panorama*.

> *Panorama* functions as a weathervane indicating how the wind blows in the BBC. Under Alasdair Milne it was a cheeky, nose-thumbing, fuck you kind of outfit. Under the early Birt regime it was a spavined hack kept under a tight leash lest it offend Mrs Hacksaw. It is significant that virtually the only seriously embarrassing *Panorama* investigation to reach the screen in that period was [a] report on [Robert] Maxwell – a well-known Labour supporter who funded Neil Kinnock's private office. Anything which might have been embarrassing to the Tories ... was held back until the moment of maximum impact had passed. But now the wind has changed. The Charter is in the bag and the government is in disarray. After years of relentless sucking up to the Tories, John Birt is suddenly seen dancing the night away at Mrs Tony Blair's birthday party. Labour front benchers can henceforth look forward to an endless round of BBC boxes at Ascot and Wimbledon.
>
> (Naughton 1994)

It is the combination of these changed relationships among the government, the media and the Republican movement that resulted in the extraordinary sight of former Northern Ireland minister, Michael Mates, debating with Gerry Adams in a BBC 2 *Newsnight* interview in late September 1994. Mates was dispatched to the US to try to counter the perceived PR advantage gained by Adams on his two-week visit. Their appearance, sitting next to each other in the same studio (with a handshake as they walked into camera shot), was the first occasion in history in which a debate between Sinn Féin and a British government representative had been televised. Its significance was reinforced by the treatment of Adams by *Newsnight* presenter Peter Snow. Less than two weeks after the lifting of the ban the hostile interview technique used to control and direct interviews with outlaws had partially gone. Instead, when Snow tried to interrupt Gerry Adams early in the exchange, Adams responded by saying, 'Can I just make a point that I want to debate with Mr Mates not with you, Peter?' (BBC 2, *Newsnight*, 28 September 1994). Snow then more or less withdrew and Adams and Mates were left to debate with each other for over 4 minutes. Such an interview and the way it was handled by the BBC would have been unthinkable even a month before.

The change from the hostile interview technique towards the grilling of the 'legitimate politician' gathered pace in the remaining months of 1994 and early 1995. On television news Sinn Féin regularly appeared and were asked to contribute to bulletins almost as legitimate politicians. Jon Snow of *Channel 4 News* has explained the change in interviewing practice:

> I think we're now in a completely different circumstance from the one under which the ban operated. Then he [Adams] was linked with active terrorism, now he's part of a peace process ... Gerry Adams is amongst a number of people who have made a difference in Northern Ireland ... That's inescapable.
>
> (*Right To Reply*, Channel 4, 25 March 1995)

Meanwhile in current affairs programming, the boundaries of the permissible were also shifting. Extended interviews with IRA volunteers were broadcast in Ros Franey's 'Talking to the enemy' which was introduced with an acknowledgement of their previous impossibility: 'Four months ago this film could not have been shown. Now, with the ceasefire, the media can speak to the IRA' ('Talking to the enemy', *Network First*, 20 December 1994).

This was followed by *Panorama*'s 'The man we hate to love', in which John Ware profiled Gerry Adams of Sinn Féin. Ware had been behind a 1983 *World in Action* titled 'The Honourable Member for West Belfast', in which he described Adams as:

> the man whose following is set to crush, once and for all, any chance of reconciliation.... [This] is the story of a ruthless man and his rise through the ranks of the Provisional IRA. A man who has planned mass murder in Ireland and England and emerged victorious at the ballot-box.
>
> (*World in Action*, 19 December 1983)

Eleven years later the reporters' view had changed. The programme was introduced by Ware standing in a darkened studio in front of a bust of a bespectacled Adams: 'Tonight *Panorama* reveals how the man we hate to love has become the best hope for peace since Ireland was divided' (*Panorama*, BBC 1, 30 January 1995). Here was real evidence of the process of 'Mandelization' in which Adams was transformed in the manner of Nelson Mandela from 'terrorist godfather' to 'legitimate peacemaking politician'. Yet even here Sinn Féin are not being treated in the same way as other politicians discussing Northern Ireland. The long-standing Unionist practice of refusing to appear in the same studio as Sinn Féin continued and the broadcasters continued to accede to this restriction. According to Gerry Adams:

> The current situation is that broadcasters are bowing – perhaps not too reluctantly it must be said – to unionist demands that Sinn Féin spokespersons are interviewed separately from them. If this is not adhered to, unionists have threatened to withdraw from the debate.
>
> (Adams, 1995: 51–2).

CONCLUDING COMMENTS

The broadcasting ban was the only example of direct censorship in Britain since the beginning of broadcasting history. It was the furthest the British government has gone to control the media directly. The key effects of the ban were that, first, Sinn Féin appearances on television radically declined, second, broadcasters extended the ban to cover non-supporters of Sinn Féin or the IRA and, third, the ban helped to marginalize Northern Ireland in the British public sphere. The ban was very effective in limiting criticism of British government policy on Ireland.

However, the lifting of the ban does not mean that the media will suddenly take up the role of fourth-estate watchdog. Direct censorship may be gone but the three other main limits on reporting – public relations, intimidation and the use of the law, and self-censorship – remain to constrain the media.

But these limits are also affected by the lifting of the ban and more importantly by the developing peace process. Intimidation, the use of the law and even self-censorship have become less important as limits and the government has relied increasingly on public relations to manage media coverage. The shifts in political culture brought about by the peace process are exemplified in the glasnost which has started seeping into broadcasting as Sinn Féin have been brought in from the cold. The hard tactics of state censorship, intimidation and legal action are now less easy to legitimate and the pressure on journalists to censor themselves has somewhat dissipated. Instead we are faced with sophisticated political public relations tactics from the government as attempts are made by all sides to manage the political agenda and to negotiate in private and in public via megaphone diplomacy in the news media.

NOTES

1 Now clause 13 (6) of the Licence and Agreement (BBC 1989a: 112).
2 According to Liz Forgan, then director of programmes at Channel 4, the first C4 guidelines on the ban were made as restrictive as possible as a 'worst case' scenario in order to pressure the government by showing them how unworkable the ban was (conversation with Liz Forgan, *John Logie Baird Centre Seminar*, Ross Priory, Drymen, 14–16 June 1991).
3 Every two weeks the confidential BBC Editorial Policy Meeting (EPM) convenes to discuss editorial policy. We have obtained the minutes of these meetings for a nine-month period after the introduction of the ban. They show how the top people in the BBC dealt with the difficult issues which arose in the course of everyday coverage of Northern Ireland.
4 Quoted in *Free Press*, no. 63 (May 1991: 1).
5 Interview with the author, 28 July 1989.
6 BBC 2, *Newsnight*, 13 April 1989, using library footage from BBC Northern Ireland's current-affairs series *Spotlight*, broadcast on 27 October 1988. The item reviewed the effect of the ban.
7 14 November 1988, 21 November 1988 (twice) and 18 October 1989 (twice).

8   19 October 1987 to 13:00 hrs on 19 October 1988.

9   We looked at Sinn Féin appearances on network television news for a twelve-month period before and after the introduction of the broadcasting ban (19 October 1987 to 19 October 1989). Our statistics were compiled from computer printouts from BBC news and ITN databases, checked against our archive video tapes of news bulletins from the period. Where we found a Sinn Féin appearance on one bulletin we checked all other bulletins from that channel on that particular day. We took an 'appearance' to mean any occasion when the voice of a member of Sinn Féin or other Republican group was heard before the ban or was reported after it. Where two members 'appeared' on the same news we counted this as two appearances. Where the same footage was used on different bulletins we again counted these as separate appearances. Thus an 'appearance' would include any direct speech regardless of whether the words were spoken (a) in a personal capacity or as representative of a political party, or (b) in a formal interview or press conference, at a rally or simply heard on film at any news event. In this sense an 'appearance' is different from an 'interview'. Throughout this chapter the term 'interview' refers to a formal interview or statement whereas an 'appearance' also includes informal comments, press conferences, sound on film, excerpts from speeches at rallies and demonstrations and chanting at demonstrations. We have made this distinction because BBC and ITN computer records use it, but also because it is clear that the Home Office and the broadcasters have considered chanting and sound on film as covered by the ban.

10 See Henderson *et al.* 1990 for more details.

11 Letter to the author from Robert Hargreaves, deputy director of programmes, Independent Television Commission, 17 March 1993.

12 Information from a very senior BBC source in an interview with the author.

13 See John Wilson, 'Censorship and the BBC', *Guardian*, Letters to the Editor, 5 October 1992, in response to David Pallister, 'BBC to intensify gag on Ulster broadcasts', *Guardian*, 2 October 1992. See also Bernadette McAliskey's own account, 'Silenced', *Weekend Guardian*, 5 September 1992.

14 In David Pallister, 'BBC "put McAliskey's life at risk"', *Guardian*, 4 September 1992.

15 For example, in the *Sunday Times*, 23 October 1988.

16 I am not arguing that that strategy is either particularly well thought out or coherent or that there are not divisions over it within government. Douglas Hurd, for example, is said to have been uneasy with the Notice (Moloney 1991: 28). Nevertheless it clearly forms part of wider 'anti-terrorist' strategies.

17 For example, Mandrake, 'What are they doing about Gerry Adams?', *Sunday Telegraph*, 15 April 1990; Robert Shrimsley, 'BBC shows Sinn Féin MP interview despite ban', *Daily Telegraph*, 2 October 1990.

18 This does not mean that broadcasters suddenly dropped the hostile interview technique reserved for political outlaws or that they felt particularly able to note the contradictions of official policy (which maintained that there would be no talks with Sinn Féin until the IRA stopped its campaign, at the same time as secret talks were in fact continuing) (see Miller and McLaughlin 1994 for an analysis of some of this coverage).

19 The full text of Major's statement is in 'Referendum will guarantee honest outcome says Major', *Irish News*, 17 September 1994: 3.

REFERENCES

Adams, Gerry (1995) 'Speaking of peace', *Index on Censorship*, 24 (2), March/April: 50–3.

BBC (1980) 'The INLA interview on Tonight: 5 July 1979', *Annual Review of BBC Broadcasting Research Findings 1978/79*, vol. vi, London: BBC: 88–106.

—— (1989a) *Annual Report and Accounts*, London: BBC.

—— (1989b) *BBC Producers Guidelines*, London: BBC Information.

—— (1989c) *Guidelines for Factual Programmes* (December), London: BBC.

Birt, John (1989) 'Time to tell the whole Ulster story', *Daily Telegraph*, 16 October: 18.

—— (1992) 'Let us hear their apologies', *Independent*, 19 October: 19.

Charters, David (1977) 'Intelligence and psychological warfare operations in Northern Ireland', *RUSI Journal*, vol. 122: 22–7.

Committee on the Administration of Justice (1991) 'Human rights in Northern Ireland, Submission to the United Nations Committee Against Torture', (February), Belfast: CAJ.

Conway, John (1989) 'Pressure and practicality', *Aerial*, 24 January: 7.

Curtis, Liz (1984) *Ireland: the propaganda war*, London: Pluto.

—— and Jempson, Mike (1993) *Interference on the Airwaves: Ireland, the media and the broadcasting ban*, London: Campaign for Press and Broadcasting Freedom.

Docherty, David, Morrison, David and Tracey, Michael (1988) *Keeping Faith: Channel Four and its audience*, London: John Libbey.

Greer, Herb (1990) 'When television gets away with murder', *Sunday Telegraph*, 22 April: 24.

Hattersley, Roy (1988) 'Read my lips', *Listener*, 15 December: 18–19.

Henderson, L., Miller, D. and Reilly, J. (1990) *Speak No Evil: the British broadcasting ban, the media and the conflict in Ireland*, Glasgow: Glasgow University Media Group.

Hermon, John (1990) 'The police, the media and the reporting of terrorism', in Y. Alexander and R. Latter (eds), *Terrorism and the Media: dilemmas for government, journalists and the public*, Washington, DC: Brassey's.

Hill, Charles (1974) *Behind the Screen*, London: Sidgwick & Jackson.

Irish Information Partnership (1990) *Irish Information Agenda*, 6th edn, London: Irish Information Partnership.

Miller, David (1990) 'The history behind a mistake', *British Journalism Review*, vol. 1 (2) (Winter): 34–43.

—— (1993) 'Lip Service', *Fortnight*, no. 323 (December): 10.

—— (1994) *Don't Mention the War: Northern Ireland, propaganda and the media*, London: Pluto Press.

—— and McLaughlin, Greg (1994) 'Reporting the peace in Ireland', paper for *Turbulent Europe*, European Film and Television Studies Conference, London, 19–22 July.

Ministry of Defence (1969) *Land Operations*, vol. III: *Counter Revolutionary Operations*, London: Ministry of Defence.

Moloney, Ed (1991) 'Closing down the airwaves: the story of the broadcasting ban', in B. Rolston (ed.) *The Media and Northern Ireland: covering the Troubles*, London: Macmillan.

Morrison, Danny (1989) *Ireland: the censored subject*, Belfast: Sinn Féin Publicity Department.

Naughton, John (1994) 'Rolling heads and contracts', *Observer Review*, 2 October: 25.

O'Dowd, Liam, Rolston, Bill and Tomlinson, Mike (1982) 'From Labour to the Tories: the ideology of containment in Northern Ireland', *Capital and Class* 18 (winter): 72–90.

Ó Maoláin, Ciaran (1989) *No Comment: censorship, secrecy and the Irish Troubles*, London: Article 19.

Protheroe, Alan (1985) 'Wanted – more thought, less rhetoric', *Listener*, 15 August: 5–6.

Rolston, Bill (1991) 'Containment and its failure: the British state and the control of conflict in Northern Ireland', in A. George (ed.) *Western State Terrorism*, Cambridge: Polity Press.

Schlesinger, P., Murdock, G. and Elliott, P. (1983) *Televising 'Terrorism': political violence in popular culture*, London: Comedia.

Scoble, Christopher (1989) 'Affidavit in the High Court of Justice in Northern Ireland, Queen's Bench Division (Crown Side). In the Matter of an Application by John Mitchell McLaughlin for Judicial Review of a Decision dated 19 October 1988 by the Secretary of State for the Home Department', 25 May.

—— (1990) 'Affidavit in the High Court of Justice in Northern Ireland, Queen's Bench Division (Crown Side). In the matter of an Application by John Mitchell McLaughlin for Judicial Review of a Decision dated 19 October 1988 by the Secretary of State for the Home Department', 14 February.

Whitehead, Philip (1988) 'The age of Mogg and Murdoch', *New Statesman & Society*, 26 August: 12–13.

Chapter 5

The Falklands War
Making good news*

Glasgow University Media Group

ORDINARY JOURNALISM

'Corrupting', 'pernicious', 'a cosy conspiracy', 'appalling': these are all words used recently to describe the 'lobby system' in British journalism. They were spoken both by people who have used the system to help their political employers, such as Joe Haines (press secretary to Harold Wilson), and by journalists who were subjected to it.[1] It is a system in which favoured correspondents are given private and confidential briefings, mainly by the Prime Minister's press secretary and by other ministers. The journalists do not reveal where the information has come from.

The largest group of 'lobby correspondents' are the 140 political journalists based at Westminster, who have their own rules and 'officers' to supervise the system. There are also smaller groups covering areas such as education, industry and defence. Lobby correspondents have other privileges such as access to White Papers and government documents before they are released to the general public. Any who break the rules may have their lobby privileges withdrawn. The system has been attacked by some journalists, especially American, since instead of encouraging investigation it produces a reliance on the government to provide pre-packaged information. This theme was taken up by a government policy adviser in a recent television programme:

> It's very tempting on the government side to use it to hand out little goodies of information like sweets to children on the assumption that the recipients will be good boys and handle the information in a nice way.[2]

Another advantage for the government is that they can make statements without anyone being held responsible – even if they are wrong. This is the origin of phrases in journalism such as 'Whitehall sources have revealed tonight'. On this aspect of it, Joe Haines commented:

---

*This chapter was originally published in 1985 in *War and Peace News*, Milton Keynes: Open University Press.

What we get is a cosy conspiracy which is convenient for the government – they can make statements without attribution – it's [also] too cosy for journalists; they can just go up and be spoon fed.[3]

The lobby system is not the only or even the central problem in British journalism.[4] But it is symptomatic of the key relationships within which the media are organized. Political authorities can assume a consensus amongst most journalists on the range of views which are to be featured in any 'serious' fashion.[5] Perhaps more crucially, they can assume that a limited number of people have the right to speak in an 'authoritative' way. Journalists tend to take such hierarchies for granted – this part of practical journalism has become 'normal' and routine through arrangements such as the lobby briefings. Such 'normal journalism' carries with it the assumption of a class society that some people are more important than others. We made this point in our earlier work, pointing out that it seemed 'natural' to journalists to take information largely from senior civil servants and ministers. We were criticized for saying this by Richard Francis, the director of news and current affairs at the BBC. He simply reaffirmed the truth of what we were saying when he wrote:

> The BBC's journalists do indeed find it natural to ask 'an important person' – a senior civil servant or government minister, for instance – for they are the people whose decisions largely determine how things will be run in our democracy.[6]

If such exhaustive consultation limits other opinion, then the media are also helping to determine how things will be run in our democracy.

Not all journalism is so respectful. A degree of criticism is acceptable and is good copy for newspapers, just as the critical interview makes 'good' television. Journalists may, for example, question the activities or competence of particular ministers, but do not usually question the nature of the political and social system.[7]

Where journalists do touch areas which are deemed too 'sensitive', the authorities have an array of controls which they can add to their informal briefing of journalists. David Leigh in *The Frontiers of Secrecy* lists the Official Secrets Act, contempt of court, libel laws and 'D notices'. The 'D' in these stands for Defence and they are basically a set of rules held by news editors, agreed between them and the Ministry of Defence. They involve voluntary censorship in a range of areas from 'defence plans' through to 'anti-interrogation techniques' and the whereabouts of Soviet defectors. The basic 'notices' can be supplemented by 'private and confidential' letters on particular issues, sent to editors from the 'D notice' committee. This is composed of government officials from the MoD, the Home and Foreign Offices, together with eleven 'responsible' journalists, and its secretary is at present a rear-admiral.

Of all these formal constraints, the Official Secrets Act[8] is potentially the most wide-ranging, since it means in effect that all government information is secret unless an 'official' statement is made about it. Although prosecutions are rare, in practice no journalist or citizen has free access to government information (even about themselves), and civil servants may not release it unless express permission is given to do so.[9]

There are, then, two ways of looking at the constraints on information in the media. One is from the point of view of 'official' sources and attempts at control. The second is from the point of view of the journalists and the extent to which they will accept these pressures. The two groups meet most often in the middle ground of private briefings and the lobby system. The heavy hand of control is rare but journalists are none the less integrated into the club-like atmosphere of the privileged. The book of rules which governs lobby briefings was drawn up by the journalists themselves. The rules are private and confidential and state that the workings of the lobby system should be kept completely secret. Journalists are not to talk about lobby meetings before or after they are held, especially in the presence of those not entitled to attend them (rule 3). The rule book includes 'general lists' on behaviour, and correspondents are told that they must never run after a minister, never crowd together, never use a notebook in the members' lobby and never in any circumstances make use of anything 'overheard' at Westminster. Finally they are instructed that they must not 'see' anything in the members' lobby.[10] If one MP should punch another (as has happened) they would not report it. The most extraordinary feature of the lobby system is the manner in which journalists 'police' each other to secure confidentiality for the government. The system is so confidential that information gained from one lobby shouldn't be used to ask direct questions in a different one. A journalist is not supposed to go to a defence lobby meeting and say to a minister, 'I heard this morning from Downing Street information that directly contradicts what you are saying.' An ITN correspondent gave us this story of his own experiences at the time of the Falklands conflict:

> Information had come from a lobby briefing at Downing Street. It came to me from the ITN newsdesk. I decided to check it out and asked a question on it at the defence correspondents' lobby. Three journalists who were 'officers' of the parliamentary lobby jumped on me and said they would make a formal complaint to the political editor of ITN.

Lobby journalists now provide a great part of what becomes news, but the price of joining such clubs is dependence on 'official' sources. As David Leigh writes:

> Deprived, in theory at least, of independent right of access to information about public affairs, the journalist depends on what he is told as a favour. The frequent reason for claiming secrecy on power-holders' operations is

to allow them to present their own unchallenged version of reality: the obverse of the secrecy coin is always propaganda. From the point of view of a politician, the ideal journalist is one who will accept misleading statements and disguise their source.[11]

Many journalists contest this view – as professionals they tend to see themselves as independent and critical. But our earlier research on television news[12] did show that it tended largely to follow 'official' explanations and to justify these in its reporting. There are, of course, exceptions, where journalists in areas such as foreign reporting have departed radically from official policy. For example, some news reports on El Salvador and Nicaragua have been extremely critical of US policy there. The conditions which make this possible are probably that Britain's immediate interests are not seen as threatened; and the sheer distance from which reports are being sent gives the journalist some latitude. This contrasts sharply with the strictures placed on journalists over the reporting of Northern Ireland. There is now a large number of documented cases of programmes being censored, delayed or banned.[13] For these to emerge at all into public debate meant often that journalists jeopardized their careers. Many have spoken of the process of 'self-censorship' which more often characterizes reporting in this controversial area.

Defence news is highly sensitive and tends to be conservative, especially at times of crisis. Where defence is an issue in a news story it may override normal journalistic values. For example, television, operating as it does from within generally liberal and social-democratic principles, has a positive commitment to 'democracy'. Yet as we showed in earlier work[14] some television reports of a military coup in Turkey overrode this in favour of the 'defence' angle. The BBC reported:

Turkey has a long border with the Soviet Union on the southern flank of NATO, and the West have been watching with gloom the troubles building up there. So *putting aside a few crocodile tears about democracy*, most western observers are quietly pleased that the region looks that much more stable tonight than it did last night. Particularly since it may improve the prospects of Greece returning fully to the NATO fold. The Russians, inevitably perhaps, suspect the Americans of a hand in this coup. Apart from the former Turkish government, Moscow is probably the most aggrieved by it all.

(BBC 1, 21:00, 19 September 1980)

After the military take-over, there were a stream of reports of torture and the violation of human rights,[15] yet the struggles of people in Turkey have received scant attention, especially when compared with those of a country such as Poland. Attitudes to the Soviet Union are crucial here: the fall of democracy in Turkey is related to how 'aggrieved' Moscow will be. The rise of free trade unions in Poland is again often linked to the aggravation it is causing behind the iron curtain – and this is one of the reasons for the saturation coverage it has received.

We should not be too cynical, since television does have a record of featuring 'human rights' stories, especially in countries such as South Africa. Yet even here defence interests are sometimes a priority. On the same night as the report on Turkey, the BBC featured a story on a military base in Simonstown. The reporter stresses only the advantages of the British using it:

> JOURNALIST: Until five years ago, the South African naval base of Simonstown *played a vital part* in Britain's defence thinking. The Labour government ended that link.... Simonstown has been in the past, and traditionally, *a marvellous base*, for other navies as well, but has it still got that potential...?
> SOUTH AFRICAN NAVAL OFFICER: Well, I think, at the moment it's a fantastic base for our navy....
> JOURNALIST: It's these resources, plus the recreational opportunities for sailors after periods at sea, that South Africa appears to be offering.
> (BBC 1, 21:00, 12 September 1980)

The conservatism of defence reporting is intensified by the extreme sensitivity of the government, and by the intense lobbying that accompanies each issue. Recently, Duncan Campbell described the 'selling' of Trident missiles:

> The Ministry of Defence is making a mighty effort to massage public opinion into accepting the Trident submarine missile system – at a cost which even its enthusiasts reckon to be not less than £8 billion.
>
> Defence Secretary John Nott is now lavishing secret briefings on the national press. Two weeks ago, he leaked details of 'offset' arrangements for British firms to work on Trident, and got a front-page lead in the *Sunday Times*. On Wednesday last week he invited a group of Fleet Street editors to a private dinner at his London home, on 'lobby terms'. They were Harold Evans of *The Times*, and editors of the *Guardian*, *Financial Times*, *Daily Express*, and *Sunday Telegraph*. The government team consisted of Nott, Sir Frank Cooper (Permanent Secretary, Defence) and Admiral Sir Terence Lewin (Chief of the Defence Staff). Ian MacDonald, acting head of MoD Public Relations, was in attendance.[16]

Some writers have pointed to the close affinity between some news staff and the military. James Bellini had this to say about the BBC's Assistant Director-General:

> 'Colonel' Alan Protheroe, as he is known to his colleagues, received the MBE in 1980 – for his services to the territorial army. He was one of a number of senior BBC TV news staff who had connections with the

military. Defence Correspondent Christopher Wain is a former major; Managing Editor Tony Crabb was an officer in Military Intelligence.[17]

Critical TV journalism does exist, but those who tread in the most sensitive areas risk much. For example, *The Friday Alternative* was a weekly programme on Channel 4, set up to give the 'other side' of the news. On 7 January 1983 a programme examined television coverage of the Falklands. It was based on research by the Glasgow Media Group and was the first time there had been any sustained account of its work shown on television. According to a later *Sunday Times* report, this was a major factor in the series being terminated. The report describes a meeting between Jeremy Isaacs, the chief executive of Channel 4, and David Graham, the programme's editor:

> But without doubt, the programme which got *The Friday Alternative* into deepest water was one, broadcast on January 7 this year, about the media coverage of the Falklands War. This claimed that, during the war, journalists had allowed themselves to be manipulated by the government.
> (*Sunday Times*, 28 August 1983)

The Falklands conflict raised special problems for 'ordinary journalism', and we turn to these now.

TELEVISION AND THE FALKLANDS: MAKING GOOD NEWS

The Falklands conflict will not be remembered as a highpoint of 'open news' and free information. The restrictions on what could be reported fell into three broad areas: (1) the limits imposed directly by the Ministry of Defence in the form of censorship and controls on journalists; (2) the restraints of the 'normal' system of lobby briefings; and (3) controls which the broadcasters imposed upon themselves in the name of 'taste' or in deference to what they saw as public opinion.[18]

The most obvious limit from the MoD was that only British journalists were allowed to go with the Task Force. Even these had no facilities for sending satellite pictures and experienced extreme difficulties in sending back copy. After the conflict, broadcasters continued to believe that it had been deliberate policy to stop the transmission of television pictures, while the MoD maintained that the failure was merely technical – that it had not been possible to arrange it. Both ITN and BBC believed that there had been an 'absence of will' on the part of the military authorities to make television pictures possible.[19]

There was a climate of opinion in military circles which regarded television as a potentially dangerous weapon in lowering morale. Rightly or wrongly, it had been blamed for the US public's increasing disillusionment with Vietnam. As early as 1970, an MoD director of defence operations had gone on record as saying: 'We would have to start saying to ourselves, Are we going to let television cameras loose on the battlefield?'[20] At the same time, Air Vice Marshall Steward Menaul[21] had commented: 'Television had a lot to answer for in the collapse of American morale.'

When it came to the Falklands battlefields, the public had to make do with film which was weeks old. There were no pictures of casualties from the land fighting until after the final ceasefire. It is difficult to know whether more immediate visual coverage would have had much effect on public opinion. The crucial issue is not whether there were pictures, but what kind of pictures were shown and how they were used to comment on the war. This is seen in the case of still photographs from the Falklands, which were in fact transmitted. They were not allowed out by the MoD with equal speed. After the conflict there was an inquiry by a Parliamentary Defence Committee on the handling of the press and public information. On this issue it commented:

> Was it just by chance that the celebrated picture of a San Carlos villager offering a Marine a cup of tea achieved such instant currency, whilst others such as the one of HMS *Antelope* exploding suffered considerable delays?[22]

The MoD was anxious to control reporting about the Falklands, for what it called 'operational' reasons and the safeguarding of life. But it was argued at the time that its censorship extended beyond this to the 'management' of news to secure a favourable impression of the war. Copy from journalists with the Task Force was censored at two levels: by MoD officials on the Falklands and then again by public relations staff at the Ministry in London.[23] There were many examples recorded at the time of this process going beyond the needs of 'security'. The BBC complained of being told not to use a picture of a body bag and to remove the phrase 'horribly burned'. Brian Hanrahan of the BBC sent back a report of the Argentine bombing at Bluff Cove, but it was delayed until this sentence was removed: 'Other survivors came off unhurt but badly shaken after hearing the cries of men trapped below.'[24] On HMS *Hermes*, Michael Nicholson of ITN and other journalists were so annoyed by the conduct of the military authorities that they sought to prefix their reports as 'censored'; but the word was itself censored. After the ceasefire, Robert Fox of the BBC made a remarkable statement about a conversation with an MoD official. It is recorded in the BBC's confidential News and Current Affairs minutes: 'Robert Fox recalled that one press officer, following the attack on the *Sir Galahad*, had said, "We only want you to print the good news."'[25]

So many complaints were made that the BBC's Assistant Director-General referred to the period as 'open season on the Ministry of Defence'.[26] For their part, there were many in the Services and Ministry itself who were intensely suspicious of journalists even with the strict controls which applied. One senior BBC producer told us that in his view there were some good reasons for this. He argued that experienced journalists could deduce new information from even the barest of Ministry statements. For example, in the early stages of the Falklands conflict on 25 May a British helicopter had ditched into the sea with serious loss of life. He commented that reporters had immediately realized that an SAS group was involved by looking at the spread of military units from which the casualties came.

The apprehension with which some in the MoD regarded the media led to strange conflicts.[27] At the onset of the Falklands crisis, the acting head of the Ministry's public relations department was Ian McDonald. He was a civil servant in the traditional mould of the well-rounded non-specialist. By many accounts, there were major strains between his approach and that of the public relations specialists employed within the Ministry and within each group of the Services. McDonald's initial response to dealing with the media was to hold them at arm's length. Defence correspondents had been accustomed to 'unattributable' briefings from Sir Frank Cooper who was the top civil servant at the MoD. At the beginning of the crisis these were stopped, and British and foreign journalists now had to make do with short, formal statements from McDonald. He would not speak privately with the media and instructed all his staff to do the same. His intention was to develop the 'D notice' system of voluntary restraint by editors. McDonald was worried that 'off-the-record' briefings were difficult to control and might violate security needs. There was also in his attitude perhaps a basic lack of sympathy with the thrusting demands of the media, especially television. He explained to us a decision to announce the final sinking of HMS *Sheffield after* the television cameras had been switched off. It would not have been right, he thought, to do it in front of all the lights and cameras – it was like announcing the death of a child'. This was a different world from that of a professional PR.

McDonald's general approach to the media was strongly challenged by the man who had been designated to take over his job later that year.[28] This was Neville Taylor, a PR specialist and one of a new generation of 'professionals' in the Ministry. The new attitude was that the MoD should meet the demands of the media by giving them 'hot' news, pictures, etc., but should organize and limit what was given in order to meet its own needs.[29] By the middle of May 1982, Taylor's ideas had begun to dominate the MoD's approach, and 'off-the-record' briefings were re-established.

Here we find the second major limit on information – one which was acceded to by the British media. Robert Harris, a BBC journalist himself, argues that the period in which unattributable briefings were stopped left some journalists 'gasping for information, like patients whose life-support systems had been switched off'.[30] When the briefings were restarted, the effect was to make journalists more reliant upon them and less likely to criticize. The government, for example, had no difficulty in planting the story on 20 May that there would be no 'D-Day style' landing on the Falklands and instead giving the false impression that the Task Force would engage only in small 'hit and run' raids.[31]

After the war foreign journalists, particularly those from the US, were very critical of the lobby system. Leonard Downie, the national editor of the *Washington Post*, wrote:

This was the system used by the British Defence Ministry to control through the lobby of defence correspondents most information about the Falklands war. Only these correspondents were allowed into secret briefings held throughout the war, while the rest of the large body of newsmen covering the conflict from London were told little in public statements and Press conferences.

Few British newsmen sought to find out more from officials or senior politicians outside these government-controlled forums [lobby briefings]. The leading political correspondent for a respected British Sunday newspaper said he would not even try to contact members of Thatcher's inner 'war cabinet' because he doubted they would talk to him and he wanted to avoid 'doing anything that might endanger our boys'. As a result of such self-censorship, it was left to an American newsman to report from sources in the war cabinet that it had unanimously made the decision to sink the Argentine cruiser *General Belgrano*, one of the most important military and political events of the war.[32]

What dismayed the Americans was that the media's reliance on 'official' sources had become so routine. It was the 'normal' way in which things are done. This quality of British journalism might explain in part why television was so reluctant to criticize the authorities during the war, and to indicate to viewers at home that material was in fact being censored.[33]

Where information is given as a privilege and controls normally operate, censorship might be seen simply as an extension of what already exists. This change could perhaps occur without there being a special point where anyone notices the difference. Could this be why broadcasters did not put the label 'censored' across news bulletins? David Nicholas, ITN's editor, was asked about this on *The Friday Alternative*:

Looking back on it I wish we had; because we certainly put 'censored material' – a 'censored' superimposed caption [on material] from Poland and in the later stages of Zimbabwe. In a sense the censorship aspect of the Falklands sort of crept steadily on. . . . I think it would have been better had we as a practice regularly put up, 'This report was censored.'[34]

There is a final postscript to the 'briefings' system, revealed by Robert Harris. When the House of Commons Defence Committee was conducting its inquiry, it discovered that the 'non-attributable' briefings had all been recorded by the MoD. This would have enabled a direct comparison to be made between what was said by the Ministry and what appeared in the news. But, according to Harris, by this time Neville Taylor was:

'mending fences' and 'trying to establish better relations and a better understanding' with the media, [he] consulted the defence correspondents concerned, and *they* voted by nine to seven not to give the committee access to the tapes.[35]

The third limit on information was imposed by broadcasters within their own organizations. The broadcasters were not against censorship as such, but they did not wish the control to lie with outside agencies. They were afraid that their own credibility would be undermined if they were not 'seen' to be independent. Consequently, they were prepared to cut material themselves on grounds of 'taste' or what they saw as the 'public mood'. For example, we were given an account of an NUJ meeting in the BBC which had discussed the editing of a script by Brian Barron. He had used the words 'tragic incident' in relation to the sinking of the *Belgrano*, and these were cut before transmission. Similarly, when film of British casualties began to arrive, both BBC and ITN engaged in their own selection and editing. Some very harrowing shots of the wounded at Bluff Cove were shown on the BBC 1 *Nine O'Clock News* on 24 June, but these were edited or cut completely from all the other news programmes on both channels that day. The reasons for such internal decisions lie in part in the complex relations between the broadcasters and the government. The BBC, in particular, was under attack at this time.

WHAT THE BBC REALLY THOUGHT

The following account is based largely on minutes of the BBC's News and Current Affairs (NCA) meetings for the period of the Falklands crisis. Each week, the top thirty producers joined the Director-General and/or his aides at confidential meetings. The minutes of these were circulated at senior levels within the BBC. Where possible, we have confirmed or added to information within them by interviewing participants. The minutes are an important source of what was being thought and said at the time, but they are not the whole story. There is always a potential gap between what senior staff desire and what occurs at the level of programme makers. Also, the minutes tend to act retrospectively – as a series of comments on past programmes. One very senior member of the NCA meeting gave us his view of how the system worked: 'There are rarely hard rules laid down at the meeting. An atmosphere is generated and people act within the prevailing climate'.

At times the minutes contain suggestions and warnings about future actions; sometimes on how language is to be used. For example, on one occasion we hear from Alan Protheroe, the Assistant Director-General: 'To describe a successful British assault on the Falklands, [he] favoured 'repossession', and objected to the use of 'invasion' ... [but] discretion of editors was required to determine the most apposite word or phrase' (NCA, 18 May 1982).

The crucial issue which these minutes help resolve is how the BBC saw its own relations with the government. The BBC approached the crisis with its normal view of 'balance'. That is, it saw itself as giving access to the views of 'authoritative' and 'legitimate' sources from each side.[36] On 6 April, the Director-General spelled out the issues:

> he anticipated that the BBC would come under pressure, as it had during the Suez crisis, to 'conform to the national interest'. There was a legitimate point in this: the difficulty was to define precisely the 'national interest'. Clearly the BBC should be careful not to do anything to imperil military operations or diplomatic negotiations, but it should report accurately and faithfully the arguments arising within British society at all levels. For example, Mr Benn might be advancing views which were unpopular even with most of his Tribune group colleagues, but he was entitled to be heard.

The speaker's view of arguments 'at all levels' came down to a division of opinion between MPs. As the conflict developed, even this definition of balance was to come under attack. A section of the Conservative Party sought to outlaw any criticism of sending the Task Force as being 'subversive'. Some prominent Tories such as Cecil Parkinson distanced themselves from this, seeing that attacks on the BBC might imply that the party was against free speech. But for a time the Corporation was under ferocious attack from the Tory back benches leading what turned out to be a minority of public opinion.

The biggest row was over a *Panorama* programme broadcast on 10 May, which featured Conservative and Labour opposition to the war. It was branded an 'odious and subversive travesty' by Sally Oppenheim MP. It brought to a head a number of other complaints such as the BBC's refusal to use the words 'we' and 'us' when talking about the British. In the words of John Cole, the political editor, 'the knives had been out in the House' (NCA, 11 May 1982). A few days later, the Chairman of the BBC and the present Director-General were verbally savaged at a packed meeting of the Conservative Party Media Group in the House of Commons. This meeting was described by David Holmes (chief assistant to the Director-General) as 'an exercise in intimidation' (NCA, 18 May 1982).

The BBC refused to apologize for *Panorama* but the Corporation was deeply shocked by the attacks. Voices were raised in the NCA meetings on the need to meet the 'emotional sensibilities of the public', rather than simply journalists' criteria of 'impartiality' and 'balance':

> It was vital that BBC reporting was sensitive to the emotional sensibilities of the public. The truth had been well told so far, especially by those on the ground, but there had been some mistakes – the BBC was not infallible. The Director General advised that, with the public's nerve endings raw, the best yardstick to use would be *the likely general susceptibility*.
>
> (NCA, 18 May 1982, our emphasis)

One week earlier, another senior broadcaster had 'reminded the meeting that the BBC was the *British* broadcasting Corporation. It was now clear that a large section of the public shared this view and he believed it was an unnecessary irritation to stick to the detached style' (NCA, 11 May 1982). On the following day, the BBC 1 *Nine O'Clock News* ended with shots of a group of people singing 'There'll always be an England'. The subsequent *Panorama* programme featured extensive support for the government position.[37] It is not clear whether such items can be attributed simply to the political attacks. It is probable that, in any event, the weight of coverage would have featured government policy. But it appears from the NCA minutes that the effect of the new climate in the BBC was to make it more difficult than usual for those who wished to pursue alternative views.

A series of directives came down via the meetings on key issues such as interviews with relatives of those who died in the conflict. A senior broadcaster told us that there was considerable disquiet in government circles about the effects of such interviews on morale, and he believed that this had been conveyed to the BBC. This issue first emerges in the minutes, the day after the *Panorama* storm. The present Director-General encouraged editors 'to be extremely self-critical with regard to items such as interviews with the bereaved, and invitations to Argentine diplomats to contribute to programmes in one-to-one interviews' (NCA, 11 May 1982). Over the next three weeks, the pressures against interviewing the bereaved hardened into an absolute ruling. On 1 June, Alan Protheroe, the Assistant Director-General, announced: 'there had been a firm Board of Governors ruling that there should be no such interviews under any circumstances' (NCA, 1 June 1982).

Under pressure from the editor of *Nationwide* and others, a few exceptions to this rule were made. But the records of the meetings show that, to gain even these, an extraordinary number of hoops had to be gone through. One interview from *Nationwide* had been shown first to Chris Capron, the head of television current affairs. He stated:

> it had given him no concern on any score. He had referred to the Assistant Director General, and had then discussed it with the Director General, and had been given the go-ahead. He had not been unhappy with this procedure, though he conceded that a more emotional interview might have provoked greater problems.
>
> (NCA, 8 June 1982)

What was the source of these 'problems'? Andrew Taussig took up the point and said that 'there was a danger that, by broadcasting an emotional interview, the BBC would be charged with undermining national will' (ibid.). Alan Protheroe stated that he did not see it in these terms and that 'the issue was intrusion into private grief, compounded by mindless questions' (ibid.). However, this argument begins to look a little thin when it is apparent from the minutes that the relatives themselves were striving to get on. Earlier in this meeting we hear of an interview with the mother of someone missing from the *Sheffield*. It had been recorded and then stopped from going out and one producer complained that 'it had been a marvellous interview largely because she had been keen to give it'. A week later we hear that 'The only difficulties that local radio had experienced had been caused by the ruling against bereaved relatives: many had wanted to participate in phone-in programmes (NCA, 18 June 1982).[38]

The general ban was sustained, but on 29 June we hear that some relatives have been approved for interviews. Alan Protheroe 'confirmed to Robin Walsh that there would be no restrictions on interviews with the relatives of those granted posthumous awards ... providing those interviews were done with taste, discretion and elegance' (NCA, 29 June 1982).

The departure from journalists' criteria on who should be interviewed was justified by an appeal to the public interest and public sensibilities – even though a section of the public was actively striving to depart from this definition of what is wanted. The words of Lord Reith at the time of the 1926 General Strike rise up irrepressibly: 'Assuming the BBC is for the people and that the government is for the people, it follows that the BBC must be for the government in this crisis.' In the name of such 'public' opinion, journalists were advised to avoid the sensitive areas and the 'difficult' questions. On 15 June at the NCA meeting the BBC's director of public affairs gave his views. He sensed that 'public opinion remained volatile, and he suggested special caution, in the weeks ahead, over the question "has it all been worth it?"'

With such a vision of the public, it is difficult to see how the BBC fell out with the government at all. Some programme makers, mainly in BBC current affairs, had taken the 'balance and impartiality' argument seriously and had dipped the Corporation's toe in the waters of dissent. When these waters proved too hot, the BBC withdrew, while attempting to preserve its apparent independence from the government. This was vital since the broadcasters believed that their own credibility was at stake and that they could not be seen to bow to outside pressure. Many regarded the rows as having a beneficial effect. The Director-General is reported as agreeing that 'one benefit to come out of the savaging of the BBC had been the clear proof it provided to outside countries of the BBC's independence from government' (NCA, 18 May 1982).

Yet these broadcasters were in no doubt where the weight of their coverage had been directed. This is seen most clearly in the manner in which they defended themselves. They believed that they were wrongly accused. In the meeting on the day after the controversial *Panorama*, a clear statement was made: 'the weight of BBC coverage had been concerned with government statements and policy. In their vilification of the BBC, the government seemed to have entirely overlooked this. The meeting endorsed this point' (NCA, 11 May 1982). The defence against all the individual charges is the same. The producer of *Panorama*, George Carey, protested to the meeting that 'the introduction to the programme had emphasised that the British cause was utterly right' (ibid.).

In a *Newsnight* programme on 3 May, Peter Snow had used the phrase 'if the British are to be believed' and had been criticized for doing so. But Chris Capron, the head of TV current affairs, reassured the meeting that 'the comment had been quoted out of context; the script as a whole had made it absolutely clear the British claims were far more reliable' (NCA, 11 May 1982). Had there been too much from Argentina? Not according to Larry Hodgson: 'There had been the accusation that the BBC had been pumping out Argentine claims: this was manifestly untrue – the vast majority of Argentine claims had *not* been reported: others had been nailed as propagandist lies' (NCA, 11 May 1982). This is hardly the language of the liberal dissident; those at the meeting seemed quite clear where the BBC stood.

WHAT DID THE MEDIA WANT?

After the conflict the BBC joined the rest of the media in attacking the information policies of the government and MoD. There were four main areas of criticism. The most common complaint was that the inefficiency of the MoD in providing information and clearing material meant that journalists simply could not do their job. At the NCA meeting on 8 June the Assistant Director-General asked what difficulties were being experienced in general coverage. He was told: 'clearances by MoD were still taking a long time ... the previous day had seen some particularly bad delays ... these were more the result of inefficiency than the desire to censor' (NCA, 8 June 1982). At an earlier meeting, we hear that there were perhaps other purposes behind the delays. The editor of radio news commented:

> the MoD seemed, on occasions, to be indulging in brinkmanship by delaying clearances until just before air-time, even though the BBC had made it clear it was prepared to use reports if clearances were not given in time.
>
> (NCA, 1 June 1982)

The professional needs of journalists raise here the prospect of defying the MoD. In their evidence to the Defence Committee the BBC commented that the delays were effectively increasing the credibility of Argentine information, at the expense of the MoD's.[39] The delays and paucity of visual material also enraged the press. One newspaper editor summed up the limits of the briefings given by Sir Frank Cooper:

> Whenever it got a bit hot, he'd drag up 'the national interest'. Here are you screaming, 'Where's my bloody pictures?' and he says, 'It's my job to safeguard lives.' There's not much of an answer to that.[40]

A second area of criticism was that the services and the war effort could have been portrayed better if the MoD's media operation had been organized by PR professionals. This belief was particularly strong in the army following their years in Northern Ireland. It found supporting echoes in the BBC where it was thought by some that the dominance of the administrative civil servants was doing less than justice to the forces. The army, navy and air force all have directors of public relations. Their work was effectively suspended – in the opinion of Alan Protheroe, the BBC's Assistant Director-General, the 'practised machine was shunted into a siding by the mandarins'.[41] His views were drawn to the attention of the NCA meeting on 8 June:

> The Assistant Director General said members of the meeting would be aware of the piece he had written for the *Listener* which called for an enquiry into the MoD's handling of information dissemination. He had received a great deal of support for this call from within the government information service, but the reaction from administrative civil servants had been 'sniffy' ... there should be adequate provision of information throughout a crisis. ADG knew that the Army supported this view strongly and that the Air Force also subscribed to it, though the Navy had yet to make up its mind where it stood.

(NCA, 8 June 1982)

ITN was also clear about the direction that its news coverage should take. In its evidence to the Defence Committee[42] it said the inadequacies of the MoD had meant that 'great opportunities were missed for the positive projection of single-minded energy and determination by the British people in their support of the Task Force. For example: 'ITN sought permission to report how dockyard workers were completing tasks in record time.' The BBC *had* managed to give such an impression of a dockyard in Glasgow – although in fact 40 per cent of this workforce had voted against lifting an overtime ban to speed up work on the Task Force ships.[43] This raised the crucial question of to what extent the British people were of a 'single mind' about sending the Task Force. ITN believed that the Falklands issue was not socially divisive and contrasted it with Vietnam: 'Vietnam divided American home opinion: the polls in Britain showed a consistent majority support for the Task Force action.'[44]

The best that can be said of such a view is that it represents the 'tyrrany of the majority' and says nothing of ITN's duty to represent the approximate one-quarter/one-third of the population whom it believed to be against the action. The worst is that ITN had a completely inaccurate analysis of what the British people thought of the conflict. The polls showed that attitudes were very complex.[45] Until well into the crisis a majority thought that the issues did not merit losing British life. Crucial escalations of the conflict such as the British landings on the Falklands received majority support only on condition that diplomatic negotiations and other non-violent actions were impossible. A poll on this, just before the landings, also showed that 76 per cent of the population wished the United Nations to administer the islands pending a diplomatic solution. Little of this appeared on ITN. The 'nightly offering' the ITN desired was quite different: 'Flair in high places could have led to a nightly offering of interesting, positive and heart-warming stories of achievement and collaboration born out of a sense of national purpose.'[46]

In an interview with us, two senior ITN journalists summarized what they saw as the prevailing attitude at this time:

> We're a national news service. We reflect the nation and the mood of the nation. The nation trusts us. We reciprocate that trust by giving people the truth including the bad things, unless that would undermine morale; then we wouldn't put them on.

In both ITN and BBC there were many who apparently believed that the 'British people' and the 'public' as a whole were unreservedly behind the war. None the less the broadcasters would not accept the outright fabrication of stories to secure or increase this support. They were afraid that, if they carried false information, their credibility would be undermined. The editor of BBC radio news put this clearly:

> the BBC had made it clear there were some things it could not reveal. If at the end of the conflict it had to confess to the public that it had deliberately misled it, rather than withheld certain information in the interests of safeguarding life, the BBC's credibility would be gone.

The defence of the Corporation was a paramount concern of the NCA meetings and was a further source of the criticism directed at the authorities. Many bitter words were spoken on the duplicity of politicians:

> The Assistant Director General said he was most disappointed by the calculated misrepresentation of the BBC by some MPs. The prime example was Lord———'s accusation against [a journalist]. The ADG noted the special position of politicians, but felt a good many of them had exceeded the latitude even Parliamentarians could expect and had made fools of themselves: he recognised there was no requirement on politicians to be either accurate or truthful.
>
> (NCA, 18 May 1982)

Later we hear that 'he had copied the BBC's response to the Prime Minister's office as a precaution against more MP chicanery' (NCA, 8 June 1982).

These attitudes left the BBC caught in a contradiction. In practice they were helping the government and MoD construct a particular image of the war. But as professionals they could not be seen to take part in manipulation or no one would believe them in the future. Even those in the BBC with the greatest affinity with the forces still felt this problem. There was an extraordinary exchange at the House of Commons Defence Committee when Alan Protheroe, the BBC's Assistant Director-General, was giving evidence. He was challenged by one of the MPs[47] to give an example of 'manipulation' by the MoD which was different from what the BBC normally did when it 'co-operated' in 'suppressing news'. Protheroe gave the example of an MoD statement that there would only be 'raids' on the Falklands rather than the full-scale landing which actually took place. This was referred to by the *Daily Express* as 'the most blatant piece of misinformation' of the war.[48] Yet Protheroe was ambivalent:

> I would find it, frankly and honestly, very difficult to condemn the Ministry of Defence for putting out that statement in the way that they did because clearly you can interpret that as being operationally required, that the publication of that intention is to confuse the enemy.... I am still very troubled by a feeling that there is something wrong when a government department is seeking to manipulate and manage the news. That I find a matter of immense professional personal concern.

The MP deftly pulled the rug from under him:

> Mr Protheroe, I am not seeking to embarrass you, but after several minutes of questions you have failed to give me a single example of where you think the Ministry of Defence did wrong in this area, in contradistinction from the way you performed precisely the same way in principle.[49]

There was a further source of criticism from journalists and others who sought outrightly to condemn the government's information policy as well as the conduct of much of the media. With the exception of the *Daily Mirror*, the popular papers had largely supported the war, and even relished it. Kim Sabido, the Independent Radio News reporter with the Task Force, was sharply critical: 'We have all been acting to a smaller or larger degree like overblown egos auditioning for parts in some awful B war movie.'[50]

In the NCA meeting there were serious criticisms made of the BBC's own coverage. Some voices were raised against the too ready acceptance of MoD claims and against decisions such as the banning of bereaved relatives. On 25 May, there was a surge of dissent:

> Rick Thompson said the Television News foreign desk had been in a dilemma over the *Antelope*. The MoD had been very strong against disclosure and had confined their own reference to 'one of our frigates has sustained some damage' at the tail-end of a statement. But since the ship was on fire and the Argentines were unlikely to be in any doubt that she had been seriously damaged, it was hard to think of an operational reason for delaying disclosures. It was difficult to eliminate the suspicion that news was being delayed because naval losses were politically sensitive. Endorsing this point, Roger Bolton [editor of Nationwide] asked if the BBC had too readily accepted the MoD claim that 5,000 troops had been landed.

(NCA, 25 May 1982)

But the dominant trend in television news and the popular press was to support government policy and many journalists embraced the heady mix of patriotism and fascination with war.

This appetite for conflict on the part of those who were in no danger was commented on by David Tinker, a naval officer who eventually died on HMS *Glamorgan*, three days before the end of the war. He wrote:

> The newspapers just see it as a real-life 'War Mag' and even have drawings of battles, and made-up descriptions entirely from their own imagination! If some of the horrible ways that people died occurred in their offices, maybe they would change their tone.[51]

This was not true of all reports and some from television journalists with the Task Force made no effort to disguise the horror and carnage of battles such as Goose Green. Against this must be set the comic-book version of the war and those fighting it which was more typical of the media as a whole. These cardboard images disguised the real thoughts, fears and beliefs of a huge number of different people. For example, the war-comic view does not permit the admission that any of the Task Force were less than perfect. After the war, Robert Fox, the BBC radio reporter in the Falklands, did make such a brief acknowledgement, while writing in the *Listener*:

> I cannot pretend these men are angels. In Port Stanley when the tension of battle was over the amount of 'proffing' by British troops was considerable – some understandable, some not, such as the thieving of a collection of gold coins from a young vet who had just lost his wife in the final bombardment.[52]

But the mass audiences received largely the overblown images of war – a tendency which extended into television, with headlines such as 'How the SAS dared to win' (ITN, 4 June 1982); and 'grandiose' descriptions from the BBC, as David Tinker recorded:

> The BBC were on board and grandiosed everything out of all proportion (Antarctic wind, Force 9 gales, terrific disruption done, disrupted entire Argentinian war effort, etc.). Mostly, they sat drinking the wardroom beer and were sick in the heads: the weather was in fact quite good.[53]

This was not how the BBC saw its coverage. On 15 June, the Assistant Director-General

> asked for his thanks and congratulations to be extended to everyone involved with the BBC's Falklands coverage. He had never been prouder of BBC journalism. . . . When others tried to claim (as they frequently did) that fine war reporting had died at the end of World War Two, ADG hoped his colleagues would shout aloud, in their rebuttal, the names of such as Hanrahan and Fox of the BBC and Nicholson of ITN. They had behaved

in exemplary fashion, with courage and professionalism. ADG said the BBC's coverage of the Falklands crisis was a shining chapter in the history of the BBC's journalism.

(NCA, 15 June 1982)

In the period after the conflict the glow faded and many in the BBC and ITN expressed unease about the quality of the coverage. A strong impression from our interviews was that journalists believed they had been 'had' by the MoD and, worse, had fallen too readily for the atmosphere generated by Fleet Street. One very senior member of the NCA meetings revealed his opinion to us: 'The whole atmosphere in Fleet Street did somehow affect broadcasting. I accept privately that the news responded too enthusiastically ... in its writing and presentation, it was a bit over the top.'

WHAT SORT OF BROADCASTING DO WE HAVE?

Broadcasting is not a simple tool of the government. It is incorrect to see the state itself as a single unified apparatus able to transmit its views at will, via subservient broadcasters. To begin with, there are divisions within the state – between, for example, the 'administrative' civil servants and the new PR professionals. While one sought to close down on contacts with the media, the other sought to provide certain types of information and meet the 'needs' of journalism. More crucially, there were major divisions between sections of the state – as between the government and the military and between different parts of the armed forces. There was intense jealousy and rivalry between these, particularly since they saw their 'profile' in the Falklands War as affecting their own future. Max Hastings, in an article published after the conflict, commented on the divisions between the army and navy:

> The land forces staff were infuriated by newspaper reports – presumably inspired by the Ministry of Defence in London – commending [Admiral Woodward's] judgement for choosing San Carlos Bay as the landing zone. In reality the Navy had favoured a landing on the featureless Plain of Lafonia to the south, and it was Thompson's staff [Army Command] who insisted otherwise.[54]

Decisions on who should be featured affected the MoD's thinking on censorship. ITN were asked to remove a passage about the Second Parachute Regiment: 'The ITN representative could see no security objections. When challenged, the MoD man in London said that 2 Para had received too much publicity already.'[55] One effect of this tension between the Services was to make the policy of limiting contacts with the media difficult to enforce. As one senior BBC editor told us: 'If the Navy thought the Army was getting too much coverage, then they would leak stories about what they were doing.'

There was also tension between the government and military, since one of the government's priorities was to announce 'victories'. There are many hints in the NCA minutes that this sometimes clashed with military priorities such as the need to keep troop positions secret.

One BBC journalist who was with the Task Force revealed his suspicion that 'political pressures in London had led to premature release of information' (NCA, 29 June 1982). There were other divisions between the 'political' and the 'military' which had direct effect on broadcasting. Decisions over cuts in defence budgets and over the allocation of resources were extremely sensitive. The broadcasters were effectively caught in the middle of these arguments. Alan Protheroe commented in one NCA meeting on the loss of the *Sheffield*. He believed that 'accountants in the MoD had effectively sunk the *Sheffield* by denying the ship anti-missile capability: the story of delays over Sea Wolf would develop and it was bound to anger the government' (NCA, 11 May 1982).

There is no absolute unity of interest among the media, the government and the military. As we have seen, conflicts arose from the professional and commercial needs of journalism for pictures and 'news'. None the less, there were some general values which linked most of the media and the various sections of the state – specifically a desire to win the war and to be seen as supporting 'our' patriotic effort to the maximum. It is not hard to see why a right-wing press should so readily embrace these values and lend support to the government during the conflict. But why should this be so for broadcasting?[56] There were three reasons important at this time. First, many journalists relished the experience of war reporting. A senior ITN correspondent told us that as the conflict was essentially a local affair it carried none of the overriding fears of a major conflagration. Reporting from London, if not from the Falklands, was perfectly safe. In his words: 'There was never any danger that this good wonderful war could escalate into anything like *The Day After* [the nuclear war film]. It was a good gutsy war but it was a safe gutsy war.'

Second, the broadcasters had a professional interest in speaking on behalf of what they hoped was 'the people'. Both BBC and ITN seek the authority and prestige of being a 'national' news service. ITN especially began to deviate from the normal format of news. It included, after its main bulletin, small homilies intended to catch the 'national' mood. On 25 May, Alastair Burnett gives his views on 'willpower': 'It is usually willpower, plain people's willpower, that wins wars' (ITN, 22:00, 25 May 1982).

Finally, the 'normal' manner in which broadcasters represent opinion and the sources which they use meant that they would tend to support and mainly feature 'official' views. In a sense, it was dangerous for them to do anything else given the pressures they were under, but it is probable that their normal procedures would have led them in this direction irrespective of the rows with the government. Public broadcasting does not see its main function as being to feature the views of 'the people'. Rather it shows those of the people's 'representatives', reflecting the authoritative points of view which emerge via the official channels. As we have seen, government sources tend to dominate such channels, but there was a further problem which affected the coverage of the Falklands conflict: the official opposition was divided on its approach to the war, even though a substantial section of the population was against it. In the absence of a clear lead from the political apparatus, television was unable to feature anything like the public debate which existed. In the early stages of the conflict some broadcasters were clearly aware of this absence. John Cole, the BBC's political editor, commented:

> [The BBC] was most vulnerable to criticism over its limited coverage of the internal debate in the country, though many Tories would regard any coverage of this as pure speculation because the dissenting views were being kept so private.
>
> (NCA, 11 May 1982)

Although there was apparently dissent from the government's policy on both sides of the House of Commons, much of this remained muted. Politicians were using the system of 'unattributable' quotes to avoid the dangers of making a firm stand against the war. This is the sense of John Cole's reference to 'dissenting views being kept private'. It does not mean they were private in the country as a whole. In practice, however, *because* the BBC could get its 'normal' and 'official' channels to work, the debate in the country went largely unreported. It is clear from the NCA discussions that those present knew much more than they would allow to be said on the air. We hear in the same meeting that the 'Government machine' is stressing one line while 'ambassadors and, in private, members of the war cabinet were saying different things' (on the need for negotiation). Consequently, 'the basis for reporting anything in addition to the official line was insubstantial' (ibid.). Again, in the case of the row over *Panorama*, the editor, George Carey, stated that its 'misinterpretation' owed much to the fact that the extensive support for the Crouch–Meyer view [the dissent] among Conservative MPs was only expressed in private' (ibid.).

On another occasion the BBC was attacked for allegedly revealing information on troop positions to the detriment of the British forces. According to the BBC the information had actually been released by the MoD or by senior politicians. The argument surfaced over reports on the Goose Green attack:

> The countryside in the area was completely open and 2 Para had been desperately vulnerable to air attack. The Argentines had brought up reinforcements during the night and Brigadier Thompson had considered calling off the attack. Col Jones had discussed steps he might take on his return to the UK to protest against this: he had threatened to sue a senior MoD person, and had decided on an open letter to *The Times*. David

Holmes said it appeared it had taken the ground forces some time to accept that the information about the Goose Green attack had been released by the MoD.

(NCA, 29 June 1982)

It was widely believed in the BBC that the information was being released for 'political' reasons – from the desire to announce early victories. If British troops were being endangered because of such political priorities then this was surely a very hot news story, but one not destined to see the light of day. A journalist with the Task Force gave the details:

> Brian Hanrahan suspected that political pressures in London had led to the premature release of information. He knew the surrender of the Argentine garrison at Goose Green had been announced semi-officially in London on the night of Friday 28 May; the surrender had not in fact taken place until the Saturday morning. A more glaring example was the report of the recapture of Darwin: the Task Force commanders believed this had been accomplished without the Argentinians being aware that it had happened, but any advantage that could have derived from this had been lost by the statement in London from MoD.

(NCA, 29 June 1982)

The most significant feature of these arguments is that they all took place behind closed doors. The BBC would rather suffer the attacks on itself in silence than betray its self-imposed 'confidences'. In part the silence from the broadcasters on the issue of Goose Green may be explained if they wished to defend their own information sources. It is less understandable when the issue is the premature release of military information for political reasons. The result of this style of journalism is that information which is familiar to politicians, civil servants and broadcasters is kept from the public. It is only for the ear of the 'privileged'.

DOES BROADCASTING MATTER?

As the war progressed the broadcasters became less concerned with the problems of featuring dissent and used a crude notion of 'public opinion' to limit their coverage. But even if all the public had supported the war, the broadcasters must still face the problem that such support is in part conditional upon what people hear both about the war, and chances for peace. The information given about UN peace attempts varies between news services and to some extent between different countries. For example, in the United States there were reports early in June that the Argentines were contemplating a ceasefire and unilateral withdrawal. But the television news in Britain gave mainly the 'official' view that the peace plans 'would have left the Argentines on the Falklands'.

Some broadcasters believe that their coverage did have an effect in shaping public opinion. Barry Cox, the head of documentaries at London Weekend Television, criticized the role of the MoD in this:

> They [the MoD] were making optimistic assertions – for example of the success of the blockade and the bombing of the runway and the poor quality of the Argentine soldiers' equipment and morale. Had we as journalists not all reported in quite the way we did at the time the Peace Party would have had a better chance of turning the Task Force round and the war in the Falklands of not taking place.[57]

When the journalists use 'public opinion' as a justification for limiting coverage they create a closed circle in which information that makes dissent credible is excluded in the name of such dissent not existing. Stuart Hood was editor of BBC television news between 1958 and 1961 and was a senior broadcaster at the time of the Suez crisis. He compared for us his own experiences then, with the BBC's performance over the Falklands:

> At Suez where the country was split down the middle, and this split was reflected in management, a decision had to be taken on editorial policy – on whether to broadcast those [views] which reflected that split.[58] There is evidence from highly placed officials that Eden was prepared to commandeer the BBC overseas services. The immediate question was, should the overseas services continue to broadcast these programmes (which could be heard by troops going into Suez) – or should they censor the views?
>
> Hugh Greene decided that as journalists we had a duty to continue the services. He decided to continue and relied on a public outcry if they were stopped. In the case of the Falklands, there was certainly a split of opinion in the BBC, but they decided eventually that they had to keep in step with 'public opinion' as they perceived it – a public opinion that they had very largely created.

There is an argument which suggests that distortion in the media does not really matter – that people do not care about being misled if the 'war effort' is enhanced. This is one of the conclusions of the House of Commons Defence Committee:

> Many principles, supposedly regarded as sacred and absolute within the media, are applied in a less rigid and categorical way by the public as a whole when it is judging its government's conduct of a war. In our judgement the public is, in general, quite ready to tolerate being misled to some extent if the enemy is also misled, thereby contributing to the success of the campaign.[59]

It is not clear how the exaggerated accounts of British successes, as in the bombing of Port Stanley airfield, could have been expected to deceive the Argentines. Such stories were presumably meant for home consumption. The

Committee may, however, be correct in its conclusion if the intention of the deceit or censorship is to preserve life. Very few would argue that 'freedom of information' should extend to revealing troop positions. But there are other conditions under which deceit might not be so acceptable: if the intention was to 'manage' public opinion into accepting the high casualties of war, or to prolong a conflict by avoiding chances for peace. The public might not be so ready to accept these, and perhaps even less the possibility that politicians might reveal what the military regard as 'secret' in the cause of winning swift political victories at home. All these raise quite different questions about what the public 'thinks' and what it has the right to know.

NOTES

1   On BBC, *Panorama*, 8 March 1982.
2   Dr Bernard Donoughue (Prime Minister's Chief Policy Adviser 1974–9): ibid.
3   Joe Haines (press secretary to Harold Wilson): *ibid.*
4   Two other key factors in routine journalistic practice are the general reliance on the press to define the parameters of an 'acceptable' story plus the reliance on news services such as the Press Association to supply a large amount of basic news material. Journalists in television news to whom we spoke complained of the difficulties of initiating news stories unless something like them had already appeared in the press. Attempts by journalists to initiate new themes were met by the question, 'where are the press cuttings on this?' The use of 'standard' news material as provided on the wire services of the Press Association acts as a substitute for investigative or innovative reporting. It also favours those institutions with extensive publicity and public-relations departments, who routinely provide the news rooms with 'their side' of a story. One such organization which has recently used this system effectively is the National Coal Board. It is no accident that, during the 1984/5 coal dispute, television news programmes were so frequently introduced by statements on the number of miners returning to work. Such practices in normal news productions are important in understanding news content. We focused attention here on the additional effects of the lobby system since it highlighted the importance of the special relationship between broadcasters and official sources which was used to such effect during the Falklands crisis.
5   It is too trite to say simply that most newspapers and television tend either to the political Centre or the right wing. They vary over particular issues and in relation to their own audiences. Still, support for the political Left is largely absent in the national media (e.g. for the Left of the Labour Party). The recent sharp move to the Right in politics and 'Thatcherism' produced misgivings among many television journalists and also among some normally 'conservative' newspapers – especially over the rise in unemployment. The 'success' of the Falklands conflict largely eclipsed the fears of the right-wing press, and the general dominance of right-wing politics has ushered in some more stringent controls in television – though not in all areas. See, for example, the pressure of *The Friday Alternative* on Channel 4 and the evidence in this book on the coverage of the Falklands conflict.
6   Richard Francis, letter to *New Statesman*, 20 April 1979.
7   For example, the popular newspapers and television news had a hard time explaining the 1981 riots. The popular press focused mainly on violence and

destruction, and some on the 'racial' angle. The *Daily Mail* had a headline on 'Don't Their Parents Care?' The *Daily Mirror* stood out in that it sent a journalist who was from Toxteth to report on what people there were saying about the causes of the trouble. But much explanatory journalism was on the level of the search for 'agitators', and one television programme featured an 'expert' talking about the effects of lead fumes in the air on people's behaviour. There were few headlines suggesting simpler explanations such as that people were helping themselves to what they couldn't normally afford.

 8 As David Leigh notes, section 2 of the Act carries the notorious anti-press clause asserting that: 'the uttering or receipt of any information learned by a civil servant in the course of his job is a crime' (*The Frontiers of Secrecy*, London: Junction Books, 1980, p. 50).

 9 A recent case of its use was in January 1984, with the prosecution of Sarah Tisdall for releasing a Ministry of Defence memo to the *Guardian*.

10 Quoted in *Panorama*, 8 March 1982.

11 Leigh, *The Frontiers of Secrecy*, p. 33.

12 See *More Bad News*, London: Routledge & Kegan Paul, 1980.

13 Liz Curtis lists more than forty such incidents between 1963 and 1983 in *Ireland the Propaganda War*, London: Pluto, 1984.

14 *Really Bad News*, London: Writers & Readers Co-operative, 1982, p. 14.

15 Sometimes these were sent directly to us as the people concerned could not attract much attention from the media.

16 Duncan Campbell, *New Statesman*, 12 March 1982.

17 James Bellini, *Rule Britannia*, London: Jonathan Cape, 1981, p. 210.

18 The research in this volume features mainly the second and third 'limits' – since the first has been extensively commented on elsewhere.

19 See their evidence to the House of Commons Defence Committee on the *Handling of Press and Public Information during the Falklands Conflict*, London: HMSO, 8 December 1982.

20 Brigadier Caldwell. Spoken at a seminar on *Defence and the mass media*. Quoted in P. Knightly, *The First Casualty*, London: Quartet, 1983, p. 379.

21 Air Vice Marshall Menaul was later a resident military expert for ITN during the Falklands conflict.

22 House of Commons Defence Committee, *The Handling of Press and Public Information during the Falklands Conflict*, vol. II, p. xxxviii.

23 In their evidence to the Defence Committee, ITN noted that at times stories had to pass through *six* separate layers of screening; from (with the forces) the local military authority and the MoD press officer, to (London) the Director of Public Relations, Chief PR Officer, the Clearing Committee and the Secretary of State; ibid., vol. II, pp. 66–7.

24 Quoted in Robert Harris, *Gotcha! The media, the government and the Falklands Crisis*, London: Faber, 1983, p. 61.

25 BBC, NCA minutes, 28 June 1982.

26 *Ibid.* 27 July 1982.

27 For more detailed account of this see the evidence given to the House of Commons Defence Committee, op. cit., vol. II, pp. 254–74.

28 This was a formal change in appointment which had been agreed before the conflict began. Although his replacement arrived in April 1982, McDonald initially retained responsibility for public relations concerning the Falklands.

29 This approach to public relations has been most fully developed by the army, following their experience in Northern Ireland and the Falklands. In October 1983 a full-scale operation was organized to give a fifty-strong group of journalists accreditation as war correspondents and take them on a military

exercise. In the words of the army's director of public relations: 'Self-censorship is what we are trying to preach' (reported in *Soldier*, 14 November 1983).

30 Robert Harris, *Gotcha!*, p. 110.
31 Complaints were made afterwards about this to the House of Commons Defence Committee, and many regarded incidents such as this as having done lasting damage abroad to the image of statements from the British government.
32 Leonard Downie, *Washington Post*, reprinted in *UK Press Gazette*, 6 September 1982.
33 Journalists who were with the Task Force had wished to indicate this, but the feeling was apparently not shared by the programme controllers in London.
34 David Nicholas, speaking on *The Friday Alternative*, 7 January 1983.
35 Robert Harris, *Gotcha!*, p. 150.
36 In practice, it does not do this – as we showed in *Really Bad News*. It tends, for example, to report the views of the right wing of the Labour Party more than the left and to endorse the views of the right in interview questions.
37 See chapter 6.
38 There is an extended discussion of 'relatives' on the news and 'public opinion' in chapter 6.
39 BBC evidence to House of Commons Defence Committee, vol. II, p. 43.
40 Derek Jamieson, quoted in Robert Harris, *Gotcha!*, p. 109.
41 *Listener*, 3 June 1983.
42 Op. cit., vol. II, pp. 76–7.
43 See chapter 6.
44 Evidence to Defence Committee, op. cit., vol. II, p. 72.
45 For a detailed analysis of the polls and public opinion see chapter 6.
46 Evidence to Defence Committee, op. cit., vol. II, p. 77.
47 Dr John Gilbert.
48 Evidence to Defence Committee, op. cit., vol. II, p. 100.
49 *Ibid.*, p. 61. The BBC were so taken aback by this exchange that they made a second submission to the Defence Committee later in 1982, giving further evidence.
50 Kim Sabido, quoted in *UK Press Gazette*, 14 June 1982.
51 His letters home were published as *A Message from the Falklands*, ed. H. Tinker, London: Junction Books, 1982, p. 189.
52 Robert Fox, *Listener*, 15 July 1982.
53 H. Tinker, ed. *A Message from the Falklands*, p. 182.
54 Max Hastings, 'How the Admiral upset the Army', *Evening Standard*, 23 June 1982.
55 Evidence to Defence Committee, op. cit., vol. II, p. 67.
56 Broader issues are involved, including the relationship of broadcasting to the state, and broadcasting neutrality in the face of class and cultural interests. We give a fuller account of these in *Really Bad News*.
57 Barry Cox, speaking at the Edinburgh International Television Festival, 1982.
58 The point at issue was broadcasts which reviewed what was being said in the newspapers – including those which were against the war.
59 Evidence to the Defence Committee, op. cit., vol. II, p. xiii.

Chapter 6

The Falklands War: the home front
i Images of women in wartime
ii Public opinion

> Mrs Thatcher said it made us realize we are all really one family.
>
> (BBC 1, 21:00, 21 May 1982)

This chapter analyses the image television news constructed of the nation at war. The bulk of TV news reports on the 'home front' were about the relatives of the Task Force waiting at home. We look at this coverage in detail, finding that the Task Force families – the women in particular – were mainly presented as models of support for the war but were largely denied the possibility of expressing their own opinions and doubts.

TASK FORCE FAMILIES

The relatives and friends of those serving on the Task Force had a crucial part to play in reporting the home front. Although the viewing public was assumed to have an insatiable appetite for Falklands news, and the Prime Minister insisted that the Falklands 'were but a heartbeat away', most British people were not directly involved. Few had previously heard of the Falklands; the fighting was invisible, thousands of miles away, and (in the judgement of the *Financial Times* of 7 April 1982) 'no vital national interest in any material or strategic sense' was at stake. But friends and families of men and women on the Task Force were 'deeply involved in the current events' (BBC 2, 22:45, 5 May 1982); reports on their plight became a familiar item on the news, appearing three or four times on each channel in the first week of the fighting. Their experiences were part of the national experience of the war; their human reactions and emotions were offered up to the rest of us via television, to provide the Falklands story with a 'human interest' angle, allowing us to share a surrogate personal involvement in the distant and confusing campaign. As

---

*This chapter was originally published in 1985 in *War and Peace News* (Milton Keynes: Open University Press).

one serviceman's wife put it: 'Ordinary people with no military involvement felt it was *their* lads out there, fighting for what they believed in' (Sara Jones, *Options* magazine, April 1983).

We analysed a total of 141 items relating to Task Force families from 390 bulletins recorded over the period 1 May to 14 June 1982. Seventy-one dealt with families waiting at home (23 of these concerned the royal family), 51 with partings and reunions, and 18 with memorial services. In some cases the views of relations were highlighted, in reports on the first deaths of British servicemen: 'The father of a Sea Harrier pilot who also died has said, "I'm proud to have a son who died for the country he loved"' (ITN, 13:00, 5 May 1982).

When the *Sheffield* sank, one bereaved mother appeared, saying: 'I'm proud of him, I'm extremely proud of him, and if he's gone to war and fought for his country, and died for his country, I'd like everybody to feel that it's not in vain' (BBC 1, 21:00, 6 May 1982). But during the whole period of the fighting we found only one case of a bereaved relative's doubts over the campaign being quoted – in this report on the casualties of HMS *Sheffield*:

Twenty-year-old Neil Goodall had planned to get engaged at Easter. Instead he sailed with the Task Force.... His mother who lives in Middlesex said, 'My son never joined the Navy to die for something as wasteful as this.'

(ITN, 22:00, 6 May 1982)

We found only two interviews with relatives suggesting that the loss of life might not be worth it: in one late-night bulletin on BBC 2, a naval wife says:

I didn't want them to go out there.... I feel now I'd like to see it go to the United Nations.... I feel there has been too much bloodshed already and I feel that if there is any more the nation is going to turn against the government.

(BBC 2, 22:45, 5 May 1982)

While in an interview on a lunchtime bulletin two naval wives give their opinion:

I just think neither of them want to lose face, do they?

Just give it back to them.... I mean it's our men that's out there, if they can blow up one ship, how many more are going to go? It's ridiculous.

(BBC 1, 12:30, 5 May 1982)

In the main bulletins on the same channel later in the same day, these less-than-supportive remarks are edited out and replaced with an interview with the wives of two survivors, in which the only question raised is: 'How did you pass the time?' (BBC 1, 17:40, 5 May 1982).

Apart from these exceptions in the first days of fighting, the Task Force families appeared only as supporters of the campaign; and as the losses mounted and their suffering increased, they disappeared from our screens, not to be readmitted until afterwards on the return of the survivors, to display what TV journalists described as 'the indescribable joy of knowing that a loved one is safe' (ITN, 22:00, 11 June 1982).

If this was the TV image, what was the true experience of those at home who were close to someone on the Task Force? Obviously it is not possible to measure or summarize all the varied attitudes and reactions of people who lived through the war knowing that someone close to them daily faced death or disablement. It is hard to imagine the full cost of war in human terms, the impact on people's lives when men were killed or injured. The Task Force friends and relatives, however, had no choice but to face up to and bear the human costs – this was precisely what made them such an important group for the TV coverage of the war at home. From this perspective, their views on the war understandably varied. Many remained loyal to the Task Force whatever happened. One bereaved mother said:

> I miss him terribly. Sometimes I would have felt better if I had gone to war. If I could have laid down my life for him I would. I loved him so much. But it was such a worthwhile thing. They went because they were needed. It wasn't a waste. I wouldn't ever accept that.
>
> (Pamela Smith, mother of a corporal killed at Mount Harriet, *Sunday Times*, 3 May 1982)

Without denying the strength of such loyalty and pride, or the personal conviction that the British cause was just and 'it wasn't a waste', it is important to realize that not all relatives reacted in the same way. It would be facile to try to draw a line between 'supporters' and 'critics' of the campaign – relatives could feel both anger and loyalty:

> I'm bitter he went through Ireland and then got killed for an island nobody had ever heard of. They should have blown it out of the sea. But I knew he'd like it this way because he was so proud of his country.
>
> (Jean Murdoch, mother of lance-corporal killed on the Falklands, *Glasgow Evening Times*, 8 July 1982)

However, many expressed definite opposition to the war in the light of their own experiences:

> We probably all thought it was worth it at the time . . . but when you finally do lose someone, it makes you wonder then whether it was worth it. I probably would've thought it was if my brother hadn't been lost in it, but it makes you look at it completely differently when you lose someone.
>
> (Ben Bullers, brother of a sailor killed on *Sir Galahad*, Channel 4, *The Friday Alternative*, 7 January 1983)

> I think it should never have happened – this government virtually invited Argentina in. . . . Throughout this whole crisis the only ones who really feel

it are those who have actually lost someone or had someone injured. It just doesn't hit home with the rest of us, and that's the unpleasant reality – that's why they can yell and cheer on the quayside.... There's no glory to war, and despite what's being said about patriotism really – what's there to be proud to be British about?

(Brenda Thomas, wife of a caterer on a Task Force aircraft carrier,
Spare Rib, August 1982)

I am proud of my son, but not proud of the fact that he died for his country in a war which was not necessary. I accept that it's a serviceman's duty to fight, but in a futile situation like this, I think it's evil to put men's lives at risk when negotiations around a table can save so much heartbreak.

(Mrs Samble, mother of a sailor killed on HMS *Glamorgan*,
Bridport News, 18 June 1982)

David had to die because of crass error, and weakness disguised as boldness in high places.

(Hugh Tinker, father of lieutenant killed on HMS *Glamorgan*[1])

He did not die for his country, he died because of his country. There were men in charge of that strip who were paid to know better.

(Mrs Gillian Parsons, mother of a Welsh Guard killed at Bluff Cove,
BBC Wales, *Week in Week Out*, 25 March 1983)

So there was a clear current of opinion among the Task Force relatives against the conduct of the campaign. It could have been expressed, and might possibly have had some impact on the views of the 'ordinary people with no military connection' who felt 'it was their lads out there'. But the TV news representation of the Task Force relatives' emotions was carefully controlled. The relatives' support for their loved ones was used to obscure their real thoughts about whether they should have been sent to war at all.

Soon after the sinking of HMS *Sheffield* on 4 May 1982, the BBC Board of Governors issued a firm ruling that the relatives of the dead would not be interviewed at all. The official grounds were those of 'privacy' and 'taste', but the *effect* was to silence those who could have told us most directly about the human costs of the fighting,[2] and to censor any doubts they may have had about whether the fighting was worthwhile. The BBC did make certain special exceptions. At a News and Current Affairs meeting where fears of 'undermining the national will' were discussed, the chief of current affairs programmes mentioned that:

Nationwide had shown one [interview with a bereaved relative] which was impeccable and had given him no concern on any score. He had referred to ADG [the Assistant Director-General], had then discussed it with DG [the Director-General], and had been given the go-ahead.

(NCA minutes, 8 June 1982)

Nationwide's 'impeccable' interview featured a widow, who worked for a naval wives' self-help organization, saying, 'I certainly don't feel bitter', and talking about another woman whose husband was killed on the same ship – 'she's absolutely marvellous ... coping fantastically' (*Nationwide*, 4 June 1982).

A number of assumptions were made by the TV reporters about the role that relatives were to play on the screen. The BBC Assistant Director-General's justification of the ban on interviews with the bereaved is interesting here:

> Put brutally, interviewing a widow was an 'easy' story and he was strongly against an opening of the floodgates when restrictions were eased. The answers that the bereaved would give were, after all, largely predictable.
>
> (NCA, 8 June 1982)

The journalistic consideration (an 'easy' story) is put above the right of people directly affected by the war to express their views. He dismisses as 'largely predictable' the whole variety of reactions among people struggling to understand and judge a controversial war in which they had to sacrifice a close relative. Most revealingly, reporting on the bereaved has to mean 'interviewing a widow'.

WIVES, MOTHERS AND SWEETHEARTS

This last assumption reveals one of the main preconceptions structuring the coverage of the Task Force relatives; that those left behind are all women. Although those serving on the Task Force had men and women close to them – fathers, brothers and lovers were left behind as well as wives and mothers – the TV news framework evidently sees that it is *women* who wait while the men go and fight; 'widows' who are left when they die. In a total of forty-eight interviews with relatives at home during the period of the fighting only four men appear: three 'proud' fathers, and Prince Charles who says that Prince Andrew is 'doing the most important job' (ITN, 21:15, 26 May 1982).

All the remaining relatives are wives, mothers and fiancées. The conviction that waiting is the *women*'s role is so total that 'wives' seems interchangeable with 'families' in the journalists' vocabulary:

> These remarks highlighted a particular problem for the *families* of servicemen, of which reports to believe and which to discount. [Our reporter] has been finding out how naval *wives* in Portsmouth have been coping.
>
> (ITN, 17:45, 5 May 1982)

> The calls from distressed *families* for news about their men went on all night. But in the large naval estates around Portsmouth the grief is being shared by all the *wives*.
>
> (ITN, 17:45, 5 May 1982)

The company has invited *wives and families* of the crew of the *QE2* to a meeting.... The *wives and mothers* of merchant seamen have found the waiting war a lonely one.

(BBC 1, 17:40, 3 May 1982)

A further indication of the way the news treated waiting at home as a 'women's affair' is that women reporters were more visible here than in any other area of the Falklands coverage. Over half the reports on families at home were done by women reporters, who covered only a small minority of the diplomatic, political news, and only one military story (on the Red Cross 'safe' zone in Port Stanley).

It is very unusual for married women in the home to appear on the news. An underlying assumption is that serious news stories should be about public events – government proposals, stock market movements, etc. The lives of women at home are taken as a sort of steady background, only 'newsworthy' in this case because the men are absent, and because the men are making news. Having selected 'ordinary' married women's thoughts and lives as an issue in these extraordinary circumstances, the TV journalists present them in a traditional women's role, which does not include expressing dissident views. Reports on the relatives are approached as 'human interest' items, 'soft' news stories where the issue at stake is how wives and mothers, sitting at home with emotions rather than political opinions, cope with the waiting. Given the rare chance of reports from naval housing estates to present an area of life that the news normally neglects, the TV journalists find themselves falling back on the old-fashioned stereotypes of women's role and family life.

According to the 1980 General Household Survey, conventional family units – couples living with children – make up only 31 per cent of households.[3] Households where the woman is dependent on the man and stays at home to look after the children represent only 13 per cent. Altogether, two-thirds of married women have paid jobs outside the home. This is not to cast doubt on the genuine warmth, security and family solidarity that the TV cameras captured, or the depth of joy and relief felt in reunions with survivors after the war. The point is that the TV news portrait of the nation at war was *selective*, and that it selected images of unity and families, concealing much of the real conflict and true attitudes within the country. This is as true of the image of family life as the image of broader public opinion.

The news reports present the conventional stereotypes. Women are shown in relation to men, and not at all as individuals in their own right. In the coverage of Task Force wives, mothers and fiancées, we do not hear any details of their jobs, for instance, or any activity at all apart from waiting for their men.[4] These are typical introductions to interviews with two women:

Karen Murphin's only source of information was on news bulletins. She last saw her husband in November. Since then Kevin, who is a stoker, and his shipmates were in the Mediterranean before going to the Falklands.

(ITN, 22:05, 5 May 1982)

He was the ship's NAAFI manager, although he had in fact served previously in the army. His employers, the NAAFI, say they're proud of him; so are his family.

(BBC 1, 21:00, 24 May 1982)

In one fairly long interview with a naval wife, the woman is not even named; instead the camera zooms in on her 2-year-old son as she feeds him, and the reporter begins:

Peter Goodfellow's father is a sailor too. He was the engineering officer aboard the frigate HMS *Antelope*. Commander Goodfellow was injured. When the news was first broken to his wife, the navy still had no idea of the extent of his injuries. She had to wait.

(BBC 1, 18:00, 4 June 1982)

He tells us about the man's job, and even the 2-year-old boy's name is given, but we learn no details about the woman.

The women are most commonly interviewed with babies or young children on their knees. Every report from naval married quarters estates includes a shot of women with children, used as 'wallpaper footage', while the reporter's voice-over reminds us, 'But for the women and children life must go on' (ITN, 13:00, 5 May 1982). We are shown close-ups of weeping widows at memorial services, but they only kneel and weep, they are given no chance to speak. When they are picked out of the congregation they are identified only in relation to their men:

Wives of Acting Chef Michael Till and Petty Officer Anthony Norman. Both men died when an Exocet missile hit the *Sheffield*.

(ITN, 20:45, 9 May 1982)

Early arrivals were the widows of two of the men who perished, Petty Officer Anthony Norman and Acting Chef Michael Till.

(BBC 1, 21:30, 9 May 1982)

Since so few *male* relatives were featured, it is not possible to make a properly representative comparison with TV's presentation of men left at home in the same position; but one was Prince Charles whose life is detailed elsewhere in the news; another is referred to by name and occupation:

A second man that died as a result of the explosion that destroyed the frigate HMS *Antelope* on Sunday. . . . Today his father Mr Stanley Stevens, who's a miner, said . . . Stevens had died for a good cause.

(ITN, 17:45, 27 May 1982)

A third male relative appeared after his son was awarded a DSC. He is filmed at his radio as the reporter begins, 'At his home in Anglesey, Keith Mill's father Alan, who's a keen amateur radio enthusiast, has already passed the news to radio hams in Montevideo'; and is then interviewed declaring, 'I'm absolutely delighted ... and obviously very very proud to be his father' (BBC 1, 13:00, 4 June 1982).

Female relatives, by contrast, are shown without occupations or interests outside the home, waiting anxiously for their men, listening to the news, looking after children and weeping for the dead. This is not confined to women in Britain: a report on a Falkland Islands woman who had escaped to Chile to have her child identifies her husband by his job and shows the woman, as usual, 'waiting':

> In spite of worries about the safety of her husband on the Falklands, the birth went beautifully, a fine 8 lb baby girl, Zoe Alexandra, born here in Chile, but nationality British Falkland Islander. And her lucky father is *Alex Betts, an accountant* in Port Stanley.... In the next days Rosa will leave hospital to *wait* for her island home's liberation.
>
> (BBC 1, 17:05, 25 May 1982)

As well as being shown only within and in relation to their families, women are portrayed, not as active members of society, but more as vessels of emotion. TV reporters seem scarcely interested in what they think or what they do, but only in what they *feel*. There are only two cases in the period when any relatives are invited to speak for themselves about the political implications of the Falklands War:

> Now that Ian has been hurt, how do you feel about the Falklands crisis and Britain and Argentina? Do you still support Britain's stance?
>
> (ITN, 20:45, 2 May 1982)

> What have been your thoughts since the Task Force left? Have you had any thoughts about what the government should be doing in all this?
>
> (BBC 2, 22:45, 5 May 1982)

On both occasions the women showed themselves perfectly able to give cogent answers. There were no intrinsic reasons to stop asking this sort of question, but none the less it is not raised again in the other forty-six interviews. Instead, we endlessly hear the question, 'How do/did you feel?'[5]

Whenever men are interviewed, there is a marked sex difference in the questioning, as if men are *not* expected to have feelings. For example, in a *vox pop.* on Londoners' reactions to the sinking of HMS *Sheffield* (ITN, 13:00, 5 May 1982), the interviewer asks seven men in the street what they 'think' or 'believe' – the main question being, 'Do you *think* it was inevitable?' Only one woman appears, and for her the question is, 'Can we just ask you how you *felt* when you heard about HMS *Sheffield*?'

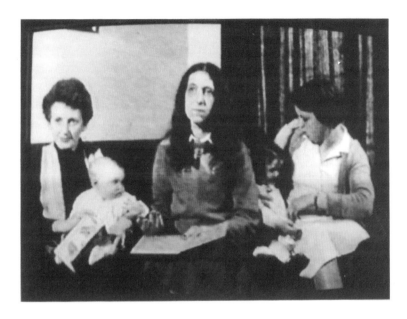

BBC 2, 22:45, 5 May 1982.

BBC 2, 22:15, 3 May 1982.

BBC 1, 17:40, 5 May 1982.

In a 'human interest' end-of-bulletin story about the wedding of a lieutenant commander who was about to leave for the Falklands ('Despite the crisis, wedding celebrations went ahead this afternoon at a country church ... for all concerned the timing has proved exactly right' – BBC 1, 22:10, 8 May 1982), the bridegroom is asked whether his marriage is 'going to make things more difficult for you if it comes to action?', while the bride is asked how she *feels* about being separated so soon. Reporters sometimes see the answers as very 'predictable' in this sort of questioning:

> REPORTER: How were you feeling as the *QE2* came up. Did you glimpse him up on the deck. Did you see him?
> WOMAN: No, I didn't have my glasses on.
> REPORTER: Through tears probably.
>
> (ITN, 22:00, 11 June 1982)

The reporter assumes, even before he asks, that the woman should feel like crying; although in the same report, an interview is broken off in embarrassment when a *man*, the captain of a sunken ship, understandably distressed, bursts into tears.

The same ideas of a woman's role are revealed elsewhere in the Falklands TV coverage, in casual remarks by journalists, treating women as 'sexual interest', marginal to the real business of the news. For instance, a woman at the dockside in black stockings delivering a singing telegram as the troops embark is picked out and described as 'some cheeky light relief' (BBC 1, 21:00, 12 May 1982); and over close-ups of women dancers a reporter comments: 'Hot Gossip gave the troops something of what they'll no doubt want to see' (ITN, 20:45, 30 May 1982). Women actually involved in the campaign can receive the same sort of treatment: the caption given to the Ministry of Defence photograph of soldiers talking to women in Port Stanley is '42 Commando met the more decorative of the Islanders'; while the commentary for film of nurses working in a military hospital is 'but now it's over and there's time to chat up a nurse' (both ITN, 22:15, 17 June 1982).

An interview with the parents of a stewardess on the requisitioned *QE2* concentrates on her being surrounded by 3,500 men, and the journalist suggests that 'she might have got a taste for it by now ... [*laughs*]' (BBC 1, 11:40, 11 June 1982). This sort of innuendo is mild and respectful compared to the coverage in the popular press at the same time. 'Sexy Capers on the Ocean Rave! Buxom blonde Jane Broomfield yesterday spilled the beans on saucy antics that turned the *QE2* into a floating love-nest,' began the *Sun*'s story on the *QE2* stewardess (12 June 1982). But although the TV news is more dignified and restrained, it does share similar, very limited preconceptions about women's roles. When the first women soldiers were sent out to the Falklands garrison after the British regained the islands, the news story (ITN, 22:00, 19 July 1983) was about what *clothes* they would wear (evening dresses for off-duty and wellington boots for the mud).

'42 Commando met the more decorative of the Islanders' (ITN, 22:15, 17 June 1982).

THE WAITING WAR

The basis of these stories is that the families are having a difficult time, and reporters made serious attempts to capture the shock and suffering. For instance, these items on the reaction on naval estates to the sinking of HMS *Sheffield*:

> There was a deep feeling of shared grief.
>
> (BBC 1, 12:30, 5 May 1982)

> Today was the day the reality of the conflict in the South Atlantic came home; the reaction was naturally one of shock.
>
> (BBC 1, 17:40, 5 May 1982)

> There was no mistaking the feeling of desolation here.... And the anxious wait goes on, with the fear that tomorrow might bring news of more deaths, more injuries. The war that seemed such a long way off is real enough now.
>
> (ITN, 22:00, 6 May 1982)

At the same time, reporters seem anxious to point out the positive side, the benefits of the experience, to maintain the picture of high morale instead of exposing any doubts that might have been raised about British policy. In the BBC 2 *Newsnight* item on 3 May 1982 on how 'naval wives have been getting together to cope with the strain', all the interview questions are up-beat ones about plans for a summer ball on HMS *Invincible* when it comes back. The coverage of families on HMS *Sheffield*'s crew focuses on the relief of women hearing their men have survived:

> One Faslane woman described how she at last got good news of her son. Chief Petty Officer Steven Ball is one of the lucky ones, his wife cannot believe he is coming home.... For Karin Murphin the long wait for information ended suddenly . . . he has been picked up.
>
> (ITN, 22:05, 5 May 1982)

There is an interview with one of the bereaved (newsworthy because 'in the confusion' the MoD told her that her son was missing, then that he was safe, and then that he was lost). The reporter's only comment during the interview is: 'you, if I may say so, seem to be holding up very well indeed' (BBC 1, 17:40, 21:00, 6 May 1982).

Family and community solidarity in the face of adversity are repeatedly underlined:

> The crisis has brought wives and families together in a way that they've never known before.
>
> (BBC 2, 22:45, 3 May 1982)

> The grief is being shared by the families.
>
> (ITN, 13:00, 5 May 1982)

The grief is being shared by the wives.

(ITN, 17:40, 22:05, 5 May 1982)

In a community as close as this, their grief is a common one.... Many know their men are safe, but everyone helps unreservedly. There is a feeling here that they are all in this together.

(ITN, 17:45, 6 May 1982)

The coverage of meetings for isolated Task Force relatives is again about home-front morale being kept high:

The launch of a club to help families ... they'd felt isolated, and this was a way of overcoming it.

(BBC 1, 13:00, 27 May 1982)

... invited wives and families of the crew of the *QE2* to a meeting to reassure them that the ship was in no danger.... The morning proved that *a trouble shared is a trouble halved.*

(BBC 1, 17:40, 3 June 1982)

The only interview questions in these reports reveal the priority of morale:

Is the meeting a morale-booster do you think?

(BBC 1, 13:00, 27 May 1982)

So you're happier now?

(BBC 1, 13:00, 17:40, 3 June 1982)

WHO SPEAKS?

Every single report on reactions the day the *Sheffield* was hit shows an anxious wife sitting by the radio or zooms in on newspaper billboards or front pages. The BBC reporter opens with: 'The local newspaper calls it the city of anguish', over a close-up picture of the headlines (BBC 1, 17:40, 21:05, 5 May 1982). 'The copy of the local paper says it all', commented *Nationwide*'s reporter (BBC 1, 18:00).

The items on Londoners' reactions (ITN, 13:00, 5 May 1982) start at a station news-stand, again with the camera scanning the headlines while the reporter tells us how the commuters studied them. Later when HMS *Coventry* sank, the TV turns to the press again showing film of papers piling off the press:

This was how the news was rushed on to the city street.

(ITN, 17:45, 26 May 1982)

Civilians and servicemen's families were once again faced with the grim headlines.

(BBC 1, 18:00, 26 May 1982)

Thus the TV news uses other media literally to mediate: we hear of 'anguish' first via the newspaper, instead of direct from the anguished themselves; this sets up a closed circle in which the media refer to one another instead of directly to the public.

This reluctance to give access to the participants (unless they have a very high status) is common – journalists seem happier turning to accredited 'experts' and 'sources', professionals like themselves. This was prevalent in the coverage of the Task Force families, with journalists repeatedly finding someone else to speak for them, since it was assumed that wives and mothers can contribute only individual emotional reactions, and not any objective or political overview. For instance, an ITN evening report, supposedly on the families at a Gosport naval estate, shows film of the estate, a woman pushing a child on a swing, a family at home and a naval chaplain arriving to visit. The reporter's voice-over tells us about how much the families help each other, but she selects just one person to speak about their experiences: the naval chaplain.

CHAPLAIN: It's been marvellous to see the amount of support that these families have had . . . really remarkable, their resilience is superb.

(ITN, 17:45, 6 May 1982)

Or again, a report on a memorial service for the *Sheffield* shows weeping widows in their pews; but the only words we hear are from the provost, speaking about the men 'who had given their lives for Queen and country'. According to the newscaster, he 'summed up the feeling of the city' (ITN, 20:45, 9 May 1982).

By failing to give a voice to the relatives themselves, TV news controlled not only the picture of their opinions about the war, but also the image of the navy at home. They broadcast the official MoD news release about information centres for next of kin, assuring us that 'they will be able to provide information for relatives'. This kind of assurance has to be seen against the experiences of many relatives, who reported that the information was grossly mishandled, that the navy itself made the waiting much harder to bear by consistently being rude and unhelpful, and refusing to give information, and that the emergency lines were rarely obtainable in emergencies. One woman with a husband in the Task Force wrote in July:

I heard nothing at all from the Navy the whole time.... The Navy still haven't contacted me and I have no idea when he will get home, it could be months. And that's so typical. Wives and families – the ones they say it's all for – have never been taken into consideration.

(Brenda Thomas, quoted in *Spare Rib*, August 1982)

Such dissatisfaction was never investigated by the TV news until it was forced to their attention by a group of forty navy wives speaking out publicly on 26 May, demanding that their MP raise with the navy their complaints about information centres. The women's action presented the TV news with something of a contradiction – it did not fit in with their image of loyal wives waiting quietly at home, nor their image of a super-efficient naval machine.

ITN did not cover the issue at all until the story was given formal legitimacy by being raised in parliament on 26 May 1982 (when the Secretary of State for Defence himself admitted that he could have been wrong about releasing some information). Even then the relatives' anger and their charges against the naval information service of inefficiency and rudeness are not mentioned. ITN gave us a single sentence: 'Wives of other men serving with the Task Force have also spoken of the distress caused by waiting to hear exactly which ship has been hit' (ITN, 21:15, 26 May 1982).

The BBC does cover the complaints, sending a film crew down to the meeting between the wives and their MP. On the main news we hear: 'Sailors' wives from Gosport in Hampshire where many naval families live are unhappy about the flow of information from the Task Force' (BBC 1, 21:00, 26 May 1982). There are three clips of women speaking, two suggesting to the MP that a list of ships hit could be released after next of kin have been informed. The angry woman mentioned a naval information officer telling her, 'I don't know what's wrong with you wives, you're all hysterical', was edited out after the first lunchtime report; and, ironically in a report of an occasion when women are specifically speaking out for themselves, none is interviewed or given a chance to articulate her complaints. Instead the camera zooms in on the small children in their arms and at their feet, while we hear the authoritative tones of the reporter describing the constituency's connections with the navy and reminding us of, 'The difficulties facing Ministry spokesmen and the Navy's information service' (BBC 1, 17:40, 21:00, 26 May 1982). The person who is interviewed to sum up the women's views is the MP who speaks about announcements in the media and says kindly of the women that 'they're grown up and they want to be kept informed'.

The next night the story of relatives' complaints is followed up (BBC 1, 21:00, 17 May 1982) but by now the mediation of their views is so complete that they are not featured at all. The newscaster introduces the report with:

> The Royal Navy's been answering criticisms that they take too long giving relatives and dependants information after radio and TV broadcast news of sinkings and casualties. The Navy invited the BBC to see for itself the welfare operation it has mounted.

The women's stand in making their complaints has now been written out of the story: 'the Royal Navy's been answering criticism', but it is disembodied criticism, we are not told who it comes from – moreover, it has already been answered, this is established right at the beginning. The nature of the criticisms is limited to the point that the navy takes too long to contact relatives. The complaints about release of information to the media and about what the women termed the insulting way they were treated have been dropped. Then 'the Navy invited the BBC to see for itself', and it came when invited: the Navy obviously has less trouble getting a platform than the women do.

The report opens at the naval information centre at HMS *Nelson* in Portsmouth, with film of busy officers at their desks as the reporter explains how they arrange 'for welfare personnel to call on the families of both survivors and casualties'. The starting point then is the naval operation rather than the experience of the families. Next we move out to the naval estate. The camera takes in the playground, then pans to follow a naval social worker through the door of a flat where two wives are waiting, while the reporter goes on:

> This afternoon Marie Powell, who's a naval social worker, visited two wives who learned last evening that their husbands aboard the HMS *Coventry* were safe. They were very happy about how they were kept informed.

So relatives do appear, but as usual they are female relatives, getting good news, defined only by the name of their husbands' ship. According to the reporter they are 'very happy', with no awkward opinions and, above all, they do not speak. Finally we get to the criticisms, but none of the dissatisfied relatives are introduced to explain the problem themselves; instead the reporter speaks for them – 'They were very happy about how they were kept informed, but a lot of wives are not' – and returns to HMS *Nelson*, where a naval captain is shown giving a speech on the problems caused by the Argentines, the media and 'security'. He fails to address the charges of naval incompetence, secretiveness or rudeness, assuring us: 'What I would say above everything else is that if we have time then we can get in touch with people quickly.'

This 'follow-up' story is no more than the Navy being given a right of reply to the criticisms which surfaced in a very controlled way on the previous night's news. It is a typical case of broadcasting 'balance'. The 'wives express concern' story is formally balanced by the 'navy welfare service' story, but the navy speaks from a position of power, has official status and is granted preferential direct access.

A DISAPPEARING ACT

That a story about the plight of the families waiting at home should become a story about the problems of the Royal Navy information centres is an effective illustration of how much the coverage changed during the course of the fighting. In the early days, the personal grief and anxiety of those directly affected were at least covered, albeit in the limited framework of 'wives and mothers showing their support' and by presenting them as individual tragedies. When HMS *Sheffield* was lost, there were two days of news items about reactions among families and on the naval estates (thirteen items in all) claiming to show how 'the reality of the conflict in the South Atlantic came home' (BBC 1, 17:40, 5 May 1982). But as the losses mounted, the suffering families disappeared from our screens. Two weeks later a second ship went down, HMS *Ardent* at San Carlos. Twenty-four men were killed and 30 injured, but their friends and families did not receive the same attention, and the reports of the grieving at home port were brief and impersonal: 'In Plymouth, home of HMS *Ardent*, flags were at half mast and there was thirty seconds silence before this year's city marathon got under way' (BBC 1, 17:45, 23 May 1982).

One family at home connected with the *Ardent* was selected by the television news: 'And we go back to the Falklands for our final story, about a remarkable hero from the tragedy of the *Ardent*' (BBC 1, 21:00, 25 May 1982). He was 'remarkable' because he manned the gun although he was a civilian NAAFI manager. The BBC 1 report begins with the newscaster telling his story over a still picture of his face, then moves on to film the women at home. First we see his mother, inevitably asked 'how do you feel?', replying: 'Well, we were ever so proud of him, because well we just didn't know what was happening you see, and we were glad that he'd done something for his country.' Then his fiancée, filmed sitting at the garden gate, is asked: 'If somebody told you that your John was going to be sitting there machine-gunning low-flying jet planes that were attacking his ship, would you have believed them?' She is asked what she *thinks*, not what she thinks about the war, or the loss of the ship, but:

REPORTER: What do you think about John now?
FIANCÉE: I think he's marvellous. I always thought he was marvellous anyway.

ITN carried a similar report. After the newscaster's introduction we see the hero's mother leafing through a family photo album during the reporter's voice-over account of what happened. She is then invited to give a mother's view: 'In a way it surprised me but I can understand it now because he was always a bit of a lad and he liked to scrap, and well I think he's really proved himself.' The reporter gives more details of her son's career, showing still photographs; then the item closes with a shot of the family grouped in front of their house as the reporter concludes: 'Now his fiancée in Plymouth and big family in Birmingham are waiting to give a hero's welcome for the man who forgot he's now a civilian' (ITN, 22:00, 24 May 1982).

Coverage of the families at home had been reduced from a guarded attempt to capture some of the personal grief involved to up-beat 'human interest' stories of 'remarkable' heroism while mother and fiancée are at the sidelines, 'waiting to give a hero's welcome'.

Following the sinking of HMS *Sheffield*, the direct reporting of the impact of the war on families at home dried up almost completely after 26 May. We found one reported statement of support from a relative: 'Today his father, Mr Stanley Stevens, *who's a miner*, said Stevens had died for a good cause, and he was 100% behind the battle to retake the Falklands' (ITN, 17:45, 27 May 1982). Apart from this, their experience is mediated once more by safer, official sources. For example, the 'special problems facing the families of servicemen' are referred to again (BBC 1, 21:00, 24 May 1982) but the item does not feature any families directly; it reports only Defence Secretary Nott's speech in the House of Commons about the 'tragic loss of life' and the 'deep sympathy of the whole nation to the relatives and friends of those killed and injured'; so that it is Nott's view of the relatives as objects for sympathy and his comments about 'the whole nation' that are covered rather than the families' own opinions or experiences. Similarly both channels' reports on where 'the loss of the *Coventry* is being felt particularly sharply' (BBC 1, 21:00, 26 May 1982) turn out to be about the *city* of Coventry rather than the families or friends of the crew, the 20 dead or the 20 seriously injured. For both the initial reaction and the memorial service, those interviewed as 'spokesmen' are the Lord Mayor and a Royal Navy lieutenant commander.

The language of family involvement is still seen as appropriate: the Lord Mayor of Coventry describes the sailors as 'like sons', while the SAS are described as 'one of the families' in Hereford where 'the entire city mourns' eighteen SAS men killed when a helicopter ditched (BBC 1, 20:55, 23 May 1982). But by now Task Force families themselves are referred to only in passing: 'Apart from leading figures in the community, the cathedral was packed with families of men aboard HMS *Coventry*, and shoppers' (ITN, 22:00, 28 May 1982). The city's formal and official mourning rituals – the memorial services and the flags at half-mast – are covered, instead of the immediate impact of the deaths and injuries or the relatives' reactions.

Later still, when 51 lay dead and 46 injured after the daylight raid at Bluff Cove, or 23 killed and 47 wounded in the battle for Mount Longdon, there were no news items about their families or the families or friends of those who were waiting to hear whether their men would be next.

PARTINGS AND REUNIONS

The Task Force families shot back into prominence at the quayside and on the airport tarmac when the survivors returned from the Falklands. Suddenly their voices were heard again, with as many as thirty-eight interviewed on a single programme (BBC 1, *News Afternoon Special*, 11:40, 11 June 1982). For the coverage of families waiting at home, indeed the war itself, was framed by emotional scenes of families parted and reunited:

It was an emotional departure.

(BBC 1, 22:00, 12 May 1982)

The dockhead swelled with people and emotion.

(ITN, 22:00, 12 May 1982)

... these joyful, tearful reunions.

(ITN, 22:00, 11 June 1982)

Then the moment they'd all been waiting for, as fathers, sons and husbands poured onto the tarmac.

(BBC 1, 21:30, 27 May 1982)

As soon as they pour onto the tarmac, the 'marvellous fighting forces' are transformed into 'fathers, sons and husbands', instantly integrated back into television's idealized image.

Earlier in the war, on 12 May, ITV had covered the departure of the *QE2*. This helps show how this image is built up. The reports from the Southampton docks concentrate on the soldiers: 'without doubt', exclaims the reporter, 'it was the troops' day!' She interviews soldiers embarking on the *QE2*, and in the early report at lunchtime she interviews two wives as well:

REPORTER: How do you feel about him going?
WIFE: Well, upset, disappointed, but it's his job, he's got to do it, so it's just one of those things really.
2ND WIFE: He knows his job, so long as he keeps his head down and one hand on the lifeboat, that's good enough for me.

(ITN, 13:00, 12 May 1982)

Then the report finishes with shots of soldiers waving from the ship's deck. However, by the evening the opening footage of 'the troops' day' remains, but the interviews with the wives are edited out. Instead of hearing them speak for themselves (and admit to being 'upset, disappointed') the camera focuses on their tearful faces as they wave Union Jacks on the quayside, while we hear the reporter's account of that day's emotions:

The carnival atmosphere built up both on the quay and on the ship. The dockhead swelled with people and emotion. There was a lot of jollity and some cheeky light relief. As one well-wisher looked on, another's bra was hoisted aboard.... [The *QE2*] slipped her moorings, leaving the crowd and the razzmatazz behind her.

(ITN, 22:00, 12 May 1982)

Comparing the two bulletins, we can see the newsroom's interpretations of the event being constructed. In order to put across the final image of the 'carnival atmosphere ... jollity ... razzmatazz', the true feelings of the women left on the quay are excluded, leaving only the image of their tearful faces and brave smiles on the screen as the men sail away. The significance of television reports did not pass unnoticed at the time: the BBC's NCA meeting of 25 May was told by the Assistant Director-General that 'there had been thanks and praise from the MoD for the coverage of the departure of the *QE2* for the South Atlantic'.

While the interviews recommenced when the troops came back, the journalists still limited what should be discussed, asking mainly, 'How do you feel?', 'How would you feel about him going back?' and 'What are you going to do now?': The question of 'Was it worth it?' was put firmly behind us[6]:

> The ordeal is finally over – they're about to be reunited with their families.
> (BBC 1, 13:00, 27 May 1982)

> This evening the tragedy was all but forgotten – his friends and neighbours were just glad to see him alive.
> (BBC 1, 21:30, 27 May 1982)

> As the *QE2* approached the quayside, the time for reflection seemed to be over, and the feeling was mostly one of relief at being home, and delight at seeing loved ones.
> (BBC 1, 21:00, 11 June 1982)

> The memory of those three weeks and more ago, when those three ships were lost, is today being *erased by happy family reunions*. The moment for meeting relatives, kind words and smiles, though *not erasing the resolve*. Many signs from the *QE2* this morning and on the dockside, slogans that read, 'Falklands First, World Cup next!'
> (BBC 1, 11:40, 11 June 1982)

And there is a deeply conventional image of the return to normality when the men get home:

> They made their way home to find peace and privacy ... one man, asked what he'd do tonight, said simply, 'I'm going to be waited on'.
> (BBC 1, 21:30, 27 May 1982)

Although survivors are given some opportunity to talk about their experiences during the war ('Oh dear, what happened to you?' a reporter asks a burn victim from HMS *Coventry* – BBC 1, 11:40, 11 June 1982), what is emphasized in the commentary is the families' emotions:

> ... their job at today's reunion.
> (BBC 1, 12:30, 27 May 1982)

> ... unconcealed joy.
> (ITN, 22:00, 29 May 1982)

> ... great many emotional hugs and kisses on the tarmac ... an amazingly joyful occasion.
> (BBC 1, 21:00, 7 June 1982)

The joy is directly tied to the family being brought back together. '*Back with their families*, the survivors from HMS *Sheffield'*, ran the BBC 1, 21:30 news headline on 27 May. When the *QE2* returned, ITN covered two reunions beyond the quayside: one survivor was filmed at a street party outside his Plymouth home; another, from HMS *Antelope*, was picked out because his wife had given birth while he was away, and the local TV company had intervened to give him his first sight of the baby from a studio in Newcastle before he returned home.

It was perfectly accurate to report that the homecomings were very emotional – the hugs and kisses and street parties were not invented by TV. The problem is the selection involved: the emotions of the joyous home-coming are news, whereas the less morale-boosting emotions of the friends and families waiting anxiously at home or suffering bereavement are excluded. For example, the excitement of the survivor returning to his family and seeing the new baby is celebrated on TV, though nothing was heard at the time about the experience of his wife who had gone into labour when she heard his ship had been hit. The Task Force homecomings are treated as major media events, extensively covered, often rather in the style of a royal wedding – the return of the *QE2*, for instance, was the subject of an 80-minute special news programme on BBC 1, using eight on-the-spot reporters, and a 50-minute special on ITN. It was advertised on five separate occasions during the previous day's ITN bulletins ('Don't forget the *QE2*'s return on ITV tomorrow morning!'), probably helping to draw the crowds which TV cameras could then film. This enthusiasm and these resources were never devoted to covering the equally important but unhappier feelings on the home front. As a senior ITN reporter pointed out to us later:

> You compare the return of the *QE2* and the *Sir Bedivere*. When we did the *QE2* it was a big megalopolis special. When the *Sir Bedivere* came home, with the bodies – what was it? – a minute, 20-second quickie. In strictly moral and human terms we should have honoured the return of the dead.

Instead, we find the experience of the Task Force relatives deployed to include the entire nation in a surge of pride and support.

'Where better than here to catch the mood of the nation?' asked a reporter at Southampton as the *QE2* left, over film of troops holding up an enormous Union Jack (BBC 1, 12:30, 12 May 1982). Then, later, on its return:

> HEADLINE: They waved, they kissed, they talked of heroism, the *QE2* is home.
> NEWSCASTER: One banner on the Southampton quayside said it all: 'Welcome home lads,' it said. 'We're so very proud of you.'
> (BBC 1, 21:00, 11 June 1982)

There is one day's outburst of cynicism and irony, one homecoming that is described as a 'carefully organized hero's welcome', (BBC 1, 22:45, 6 May

'Where better than here to catch the mood of the nation' (BBC 1, 12:30, 12 May 1982).

1982), an 'elaborately staged welcome' (BBC 1, 21:00, 5 May 1982); but this was the return of the *Belgrano* survivors to Argentina.

WOMEN AT THE TOP

The TV news coverage of Task Force relatives, then, shows a very traditional image of women, and it is interesting that even those women who are already public figures in their own right, specifically the Prime Minister and the Queen, are not totally immune. Some references to the feminine stereotype are made only casually and in passing, for example, in this report on the Prime Minister's meeting with the US President at Versailles: 'The President didn't seem to mind one bit that she exercised a lady's privilege and was late' (BBC 1, 21:00, 4 June 1982).

Looking at these women at the top, the significance of assumptions about the nation and the family becomes clearer. The Prime Minister has considerable control over her media image, unlike the Task Force relatives, and she also has a special interest in fostering traditional pictures of family life. She frequently describes herself in 'typical housewife' terms; for example, in one interview on how she dealt with the Falklands crisis she says: 'It's like when you have a family crisis. Someone has to stay in control and keep going' (*Women's Own*, 28 August 1982). Mrs Thatcher's preferred image of the nation as a whole, and specifically the nation at war, leans heavily on the idea of the family as an ordered unit, all its members pulling together. This was made explicit in her speech at Finchley on the day of the British landings on the Falklands: 'The Prime Minister said today that the courage and skill of the men in the Task Force had brought a new pride to this country. Mrs Thatcher said it made us realise we are all really one family' (BBC 1, 21:00, 21 May 1982).

The TV news goes beyond reporting Mrs Thatcher's words: in its own structuring of news from the home front it shares and endorses her views. Thus the nation is seen to be made up of families; within the family women are dependent on men and occupied with the home, the heart, and the children; women in the family are proud of their men fighting for the nation; the nation is united like a family is united; and the nation is united behind the men (and women) of the Task Force. The Queen is also shown as fitting into women's allotted position, as if the national crisis produced an equality overriding the divisions in society, reducing even the Queen to just 'one of thousands':

> The Queen is one of thousands of worried mothers with a son in the fleet.
> (BBC 1, 17:05, 26 May 1982)

> For a moment, we were not looking at a Pope and a Queen, but rather at a concerned priest and an anxious mother.
> (ITN, 17:45, 28 May 1982)

She is also accessible to the 'normal world' of television viewers, as ITN news stressed in their story about the Queen visiting the *Coronation Street* set in Manchester:

> HEADLINE: And in the normal world of Coronation Street, the Queen meets the neighbours.
> JOURNALIST: An out-of-work school leaver asked the Queen in Manchester today, 'How's Andrew?' and got the answer, 'I hope he's alright.' The actor Peter Adamson also had his thoughts on the Falklands; he told the Queen, 'Our hearts are with you.'
> (ITN, 22:05, 5 May 1982)

This suggestion of equality is significant, as the Royal Family is often presented as a model family, a family that represents the nation, in itself a symbol of national unity and social solidarity.

The royal family can be seen as offering the viewer 'personal' identification: 'For the royal family it's a *personal* anxiety: Prince Andrew is a helicopter pilot with the Task Force' (ITN, 21:15, 26 May 1982). Messages from royalty are used to frame stories about other families, as if to set the appropriate tone. An item on the families of HMS *Sheffield* survivors in Faslane and Portsmouth begins:

> As friends and families connected with six different naval bases waited for

news today, the Queen sent her own message to the Chief of Naval Staff.... And the Prince of Wales, whose brother Andrew is a helicopter pilot on HMS *Invincible*, joined the Princess to send 'our very deepest sympathy to the wives and families of those who gave their lives so courageously'.

(ITN, 22:05, 5 May 1982)

(ITN's news that day closed with a piece of film from the archive showing the Queen launching HMS *Sheffield* in 1975.)

There is nothing new in the TV's concern with the words and activities of the royal family. As Alastair Burnett put it: 'The royal family ... has very many plain people who watch its activities with great affection and interest. It is, I think, something that adds a sense of continuity and coherence in their lives' (*Guardian*, 19 December 1983). In fact their position as a constant background to the turbulence of daily news was underlined during the Falklands crisis: a report on the Queen and Prince Philip at the Chelsea Flower Show began: 'Despite what's happening abroad in the South Atlantic the yearly pattern of life here seems to be unchanged.... The Royal Family are traditional visitors to the Chelsea Flower show' (BBC 2, 18:50, 23 May 1982).

There is nothing new either in the TV news pretence of giving the viewer access to some sort of personal contact with Royalty. The same tendency can be seen for instance in the advertising for ITV's *National Salute to the Task Force* on 18 July 1982; the *TV Times* cover showed a Union Jack and an engraved card with a picture of Prince Charles below the words, 'Your invitation to join the Prince of Wales', as if watching TV really puts the viewer in his company.

What is remarkable is the unusually explicit political content of the comments of this 'one of thousands of worried mothers', given to us as much more than 'personal anxiety'. Take the use made by BBC 1 of the Queen's speech at Keilder Dam on 26 April:

HEADLINE: The Queen speaks for the nation.
NEWSCASTER: The Queen spoke today for the whole nation ... she said her thoughts were eight thousand miles away and she prayed for the success of the Task Force.

(BBC 1, 17:05, 26 May 1982)

Or take ITN's use of her speech, during President Reagan's visit, in the prominent positions of headline and closing summary:

HEADLINE: The Queen says we're standing up for freedom.
SUMMARY: The Queen said that Britain was standing up for freedom in the Falklands. The conflict was thrust on us by naked aggression, she said, and

we are naturally proud of the way our fighting men are serving their country.

(ITN, 22:00, 8 June 1982)

BRITISH HISTORY

Even routine coverage of royal pageantry is drawn into the Falklands net. When the Queen is filmed walking into Westminster Abbey in formal robes, the newscaster points out:

> The Queen looked pensive this morning when she attended a service at Westminster Abbey for the Order of the Bath. Yesterday she said her thoughts and prayers were with the servicemen in the South Atlantic. They of course include Prince Andrew.
>
> (ITN, 13:00, 27 May 1982)

At the Chelsea Pensioners' founders' day ceremony:

> As the Queen arrived to take the salute, nobody needed reminding that once again British servicemen are fighting for their country.
>
> (BBC 1, 13:00, 10 June 1982)

And with more royal/military spectacle at the Trooping of the Colour: 'Things weren't totally normal ... everyone conscious of the situation in the South Atlantic.'

> (ITN, 21:00, 12 June 1982)

When Prince Charles presents new colours to the 15th Scottish Volunteers battalion of Parachute Regiment, his face appears behind the newscaster under the 'Falklands Conflict' logo, and we are reminded: 'Soon too Falklands may be added to the battle honours. . . . Servicemen, said the Prince, were among the first to make the ultimate sacrifice in defence of principles and values' (BBC 1, 17:40, 21:00, 28 May 1982). An important part of the Royal Family's role is to keep alive links with British tradition and history, even on the Task Force itself: 'The ships of the Task Force weren't too busy to forget naval tradition when they crossed the Equator on their way south. . . . And who better to play the King of the Sea than Prince Andrew?' (ITN, 21:45, 15 May 1982). The Queen is always shown surrounded by reminders of her family history and the nation's history, as in this report on President Reagan's visit to Windsor. The news slips into potted history tones:

> She led him through the Waterloo Chamber, pointing out the delights created by her ancestor George IV to commemorate Napoleon's defeat. . . . Their cheerful steps led them to St George's Hall, a great chamber built by Edward III. . . . Especially for the occasion, Queen Victoria's dining table had been installed.
>
> (ITN, 22:00, 8 June 1982)

In the Falklands coverage, journalists carried their sense of historical occasion beyond the royalty stories, slipping historical references into reports about ordinary mortals as if to heighten awareness of Britain's historical traditions at a time when the armed forces were defending them. For instance, interviews with commuters crossing London Bridge include shots of a naval relic – 'In the Thames sat the old seadog HMS *Belfast* looking sombre' – and refer to older victories too: 'above the tourists towered Britain's greatest naval hero, Lord Nelson' (ITN, 13:00, 5 May 1982). Reports from Portsmouth naval estates seize on street signs as an opportunity to make historical links (Normandy Road, etc.), as the reporter intones: 'The people are not strangers to famous sea battles' (ITN, 13:00, 17:45, 22:05, 5 May 1982).

A common historical parallel is 'people haven't known anything like it since World War II' (BBC 1, 19:40, 5 May 1982). It is debatable whether the Falklands were actually like World War II at all, since national security was not threatened, and most people were not directly involved. But it is as if an attempt is made to incorporate the Falklands into the flow of British history and legend, by injecting historical references wherever possible and appealing to selected folk memories of the last war – Vera Lynn, for instance, who did actually release a record during the Falklands campaign. The BBC not only treated this as news, but also gave us a historical introduction, an interview with Vera Lynn, and extracts from her song accompanied by wartime stills of the 'forces' sweetheart' and current film of her wandering through an English country garden:

NEWSCASTER: Dame Vera Lynn has recorded a patriotic song for the men of the Falklands Task Force. Dame Vera became the forces' sweetheart in the Second World War, with songs like 'We'll Meet Again' and 'The White Cliffs of Dover'. Her new record, on sale shortly, is called 'I Love this Land'. . . .

SONG: I love this land,
       I love her hills and rivers and trees. . . .

DAME VERA: . . . I was very happy to be able to do something. . . .

SONG: These memories of home, when my memories roam,
       Bring England near at hand.
       It will stay that way for ever.
       Which is why I love this land.

(BBC 1, 18:00; BBC 2, 19:15, 29 May 1982)

Meanwhile, other popular songs released especially for the Falklands War such as Crass's 'How does it feel (to be the mother of 1,000 dead?)', which lack the patriotic element of 'Love This Land', do not make news in quite the same way.

When British military action began with the bombing of the Port Stanley runway, it was given a place in Britain's record by being compared to World

War II air attacks. A reporter 'interviews' World War II hero Sir Arthur Harris:

> NEWSCASTER: The man who organized Britain's air offences during the Second World War, 90-year-old Marshal of the RAF Sir Arthur Harris, attended a special service for the Air Crew Association.... Afterwards he gave his own views on the Falklands conflict.
>
> REPORTER: Although this was a dedication service, there was a discernible spirit of buoyancy among the congregation, typified by Sir Arthur 'Bomber' Harris, Marshal of the RAF. After the service I asked Sir Arthur about the air assault on the Falklands.... What sort of action would you be recommending should be taken now if you were involved?
>
> SIR ARTHUR: Exactly that, keep the runways out of order so that our enemy, if he's worth calling that, can't use them.
>
> (BBC 1, 17:50, 2 May 1982)

On another occasion, a Harrier pilot on the Task Force is asked in an interview: 'Do the dogfights compare with those in the Second World War?' (ITN, 18:15, 14 June 1982).

The ships of the Task Force itself are also wreathed in history. On the day of the *QE2*'s departure ('the biggest single troop embarkation since World War II', BBC 1, 21:00, 12 May 1982), ITN's main bulletin shows a long sequence of archive film of the *Queen Mary* leaving New York in 1943: 'The *Queen Mary*, Cunard's former flagship, was also requisitioned for the war, in 1943.... Churchill later said the use of the *Queen Elizabeth* and *Mary* shortened the war by nearly a year' (ITN, 22:00, 12 May 1982). Churchill appears again later, in a comparison with the present Prime Minister: 'Mrs Thatcher has to go on saying it's business as usual in Downing Street.... In war, a real war, a Prime Minister is protected, as Churchill was' (ITN, 21:00, 19 May 1982).

Another favoured memory was D-Day. Before the British landing on the Falklands, a defence correspondent suggests the parallel: 'Now to what extent would an operation like this be a re-enactment in miniature of the day that changed the course of the last world war?' (BBC 2, 22:55, 19 May 1982). The bulletin goes on to show lengthy clips of film from 1944, complete with the original commentry ('Then we hit the beach, and we were there!'), only to follow it with the current MoD account: 'Now the re-invasion of the Falklands, if it does happen, will look very different.' The reports from San Carlos return to the theme: '4,000 men of the 5th Infantry Brigade have now completed the second Falklands D-Day landing', evidently assuming a common stock of memories and images: '*it would have reminded anybody* of British Tommies landing on D-Day in 1944' (BBC 2, 23:25, 6 June 1982) – as if all generations of viewers would be keeping alive these memories of forty years ago, although none of the harsher memories are rekindled, nothing is said for instance about the victims of the war or those left to mourn for them.

Instead our thoughts are directed to moments such as the liberation of Jersey from the Nazis. Both the BBC and ITN take the opportunity of Jersey's donation to the Falklands campaign to show film of crowds lining the streets and women kissing soldiers as the British march in. The link is made explicit:

> Jersey is planning to give the British government £5 million to help free the Falklands and re-establish the islanders in their homes. ... The Channel Islanders may well know better than any Britons how the Falklanders are feeling, as British troops bring about their liberation.
>
> (BBC 1, 21:00, 4 June 1982)

The sense of historical occasion can be seen at its height in the BBC coverage of the Falklands remembrance service, sweeping beyond World War II to embrace 'more than 1,000 years of fire and pestilence':

> And so, on so many occasions of joy and sadness, a thanksgiving and remembrance, through more than a thousand years of fire and pestilence, peace and war, the nation turns again to London's cathedral church, with its golden cross lifted high above the City and Ludgate Hill. ... Not for today the pageantry that brought Nelson home to St Paul's or Wellington to his marble tomb.
>
> (BBC 1, 21:00, 26 July 1982)

THE NATIONAL INTEREST AND DISSENT

The TV news reference to British history finds a close parallel in government speeches which appeal to our history and heritage in order to justify, interpret and celebrate the campaign. For example, Mrs Thatcher's widely reported speech at Cheltenham on 3 July presents Britain as:

> the nation that had built an Empire and ruled a quarter of the world. ... We rejoice that Britain has rekindled *that spirit which has fired her for generations past* and which today has begun to burn as brightly as before. Britain has found herself again in the South Atlantic and will not look back from the victory she has won.

She comments in an ITV documentary: 'I was very upset at the people who lost their lives in the Falklands and then I thought of Wellington after the battle of Waterloo' (ITV, *PM, The Woman at No. 10*, 29 March 1982). And to the *Daily Express*: 'I had the winter at the back of my mind. The winter ... down in South Georgia, the ice, what will it do? It beat Napoleon at Moscow' (*Daily Express*, 26 July 1982).

The TV news broadcasters would rarely use such openly partisan rhetoric as the Prime Minister's. The question of their independence from the government was hotly debated at the time of the Falklands, and the broadcasters were self-consciously defending their integrity. They apparently believed that they were successful. In a speech at the International Press Institute, in May 1982, a BBC managing director, Richard Francis, insisted: 'Our contribution to national morale relies on telling the truth. We are not in the game of patriotism. We are dealing with the job of finding out facts.' The BBC in particular took great pride in presenting 'all sides' of the story in a 'balanced' way. One journalist asked in a news interview:

> It is not a vindication of the way in which broadly the media, and God knows the range of opinion has been broad enough, has treated it that when the public are faced with such a wide range of opinion, they still say 'yes we have seen it all' – and *I think they probably have seen it all* – 'and still we back the government'? Now isn't that an enormous source of strength?
>
> (BBC 2, 22:45, 12 May 1982)

However, as we have seen, the coverage was not 'neutral' and the viewers did not exactly 'see it all'. The problem here was not simply direct government manipulation, but that by basing justification of their policy on appeals to national unity and the 'rekindled' national spirit, the government hit broadcasting neutrality in a very weak spot.

In this case the government managed to define the national interest as the prosecution of its own policy against Argentina. This put the broadcasters in a painful position: while the liberal, centrist values of many journalists and their loyalty to the national 'consensus' were probably not in sympathy with the government's radical conservatism, they did share a view of the nation, a belief in national interests which can override the divisions and conflicts in our society. As one reporter put it:

> The broadcasting authorities have themselves felt as though they're on a desert island which the sea is gradually eating away, and have moved more and more to the centre of the island.... At precisely the time when the conflicts in our society demand a greater degree of courage to interpret the realities of what is going on ... it's very easy to get caught in the web of the Establishment's perception – I find it happening to me.
>
> (Jonathan Dimbleby, *Stills* magazine, November 1982)

The broadcasters' idea of 'national consensus' can lead to a blindness to social conflict – leaving the coverage open to the government's use of the concepts of 'national unity' and the 'national interest'.

The routines of 'balance' were not enough to produce impartial coverage. In fact it can help to *create* the very national unity and consensus of opinion that it relies on to establish its supposedly impartial position. Oddly enough, British broadcasters seem to recognize the role of the media in creating national unity in Argentina more readily than in their own case:

Argentine President General Galtieri has also been preparing his people for war through the medium of broadcasters and newspapers.... The newspaper headlines sum it all up in Buenos Aires as the military junta prepares the nation for war and drums up patriotism.

(BBC 2, 18:50, 2 May 1982)

NEWSCASTER: Argentine television has been rallying the country's 27 million people for war using rather bizarre methods....

CORRESPONDENT: Argentine television presents a lunchtime magazine of pure propaganda.

(ITN, 13:00, 5 May 1982)

Untranslated clips from the Argentine programme are shown, then the newscaster comments at the end: 'You'll have noticed the British television's approach is rather different' (ibid.).

This is not to suggest that the British government or British TV are the *same* as those in Argentina,[7] but the free criticism of Galtieri's junta for 'drumming up patriotism' by manipulating the media underlines the British broadcasters' own uncritical assumption of 'national unity' at home. During the Falklands War the general problems of broadcasting independence were sharpened, because keeping public morale on the home front high was seen as part of the war effort, so the 'national interest' demanded that the TV news should paint a picture of national support, and isolate opposition to the war. Too much questioning of the government's policy and the precise interests it served was thought by some to be unpatriotic.

The most spectacular case of the limits put on acceptable expression of dissent on TV was not about the news but about the *Panorama* programme *Can We Avoid War?* on 10 May 1982. It led to immediate outbursts in the House of Commons the following day, with Conservative front-bencher Sally Oppenheim branding it as 'An odious subversive travesty in which Michael Cockerell and other BBC reporters dishonoured the right of freedom of speech in this country' (House of Commons, 11 May 1982). This opened a bitter debate on TV coverage of the crisis in general and *Panorama* in particular. The BBC's Chairman had to reassure the Prime Minister that 'the BBC is not neutral' (BBC press statement, 11 May 1982), and he and the Director-General designate were summoned to a stormy meeting of the Conservative backbench Media Committee to face calls for their resignation. *Panorama*'s presenter Robert Kee first publicly disowned the controversial programme, then left the BBC. The press soon joined in the row, with cries of 'traitors' – the *Sun* commented: 'The *British* Broadcasting Corporation needs a shake-up. Too many of its studios are infested with arrogant little know-alls ready to serve up their loaded version of "truth" to viewers' (*Sun* leader, 15 May 1982).

It was an impassioned episode, important if for nothing else in reminding us how self-conscious the BBC is of its degree of independence, and how mistrustful the Conservative right-wing is of the BBC's liberal centrist 'neutrality'. As one MP who spoke out against the programme reflected: 'The Conservative Party has long been suspicious of the BBC because of the undeniable fact that its trainees always seem to be recruited from those with extreme left-wing motivation' (Alan Clark, *Washington Post*, 27 May 1982). Our own analysis of the programme shows that it contained more statements in support of government policy than against. None the less it was probably the clearest articulation on television at that time of alternative views. Its effect on the rest of programming was probably to make it more difficult than usual to feature these views.

In *Panorama* the following week there was a report from the constituency of David Crouch, one of the dissenting MPs, using interviews at his Conservative club which showed that he did not represent local views. The *Panorama* team then went to the Yarrow shipyard in Glasgow to interview workers who supported the Task Force and were stepping up work on frigates for the South Atlantic. This interviewing was carried out on a Sunday afternoon and did not feature the Yarrow workers who were rejecting overtime. (Forty per cent had voted *against* lifting an overtime ban for the sake of the Task Force frigates.)

In news programmes there was some coverage of dissent within the Labour movement, but it was mainly in the traditional mould of coverage of internal disputes between MPs: 'Mr Denis Healey had launched a thinly veiled attack on Mr Tony Benn for breaking away from the party in his views on the Falklands crisis' (ITN, 17:45, 12 May 1982). *Attacks* on the breakaway views rather than the views themselves often make the news:

> Barnsley's Labour MP Mr Roy Mason has criticised his local party and the miner's president Mr Arthur Scargill, who voted to recall the Task Force. Mr Mason said, 'I can't think it right that we should give in to a damnable military junta.'
>
> (ITN, 22:00, 17 May 1982)

Roy Mason's words about not 'giving in' are put on the screen with his picture – his local party and the miner's president appear only as objects of his criticism, and not with their own views in their own right. This is the nearest we get to coverage of 'grassroots' Labour views, though of 66 resolutions on the Falklands from constituency Labour parties, 6 backed the front-bench line of support for the Task Force, and 60 dissented. There were no news items on dissension in the ranks of the Conservative Party, for instance the splits discussed on *Panorama*, or the Prime Minister's policy adviser Ferdinand Mount's call for a ceasefire in the *Spectator* on 6 May. Doubts about the military escalation came from various quarters but did not receive much TV news coverage, and were not offered the same treatment as official policy.

ACCESS

If some views are less acceptable on TV than others, who *did* appear on the news about the Falklands? Our breakdown of studio interviews reveals a rather limited choice.

Table 6.1 Studio interviews – Falklands items, all TV news, 1 May to 14 June 1982 (390 bulletins)

Politicians	Conservative MPs	74
	Labour MPs	22
	Alliance MPs	15
'Experts'	military	72
	academic	9
	industry	6
	other	4
Falkland Islanders		22
Media	British	16
	USA	3
Diplomats	British	15
	Argentine	13
Britain	serving military officers	8
	church leaders	6
	shipping industry	5
Argentina	civilian	7
	military	1
World	Chile	2
	USA	1
	Commonwealth	1
	International Red Cross	3

Figures for interviews given in the TV studios do not reveal everything about who appeared on the screen. We exclude some familiar faces like the 'family' interviews in the home and on the quay, the 53 MoD statements (featuring the new screen personality Ian McDonald, who *never* gave televised interviews), the 43 appearances of the UN Secretary-General on his way in and out of meetings of the UN, and even 52 of the Prime Minister's own appearances (at news conferences, in recorded reports from parliament, interviews outside No. 10, etc.). But since studio interviews are a prestigious form of appearance, and normally provide the best opportunity for putting across a point of view, these figures give an important indication of whose views are given the best airing on TV news. They show a clear 'hierarchy of access' which it would be hard to justify as 'balanced'.

The single highest-scoring group is Conservative MPs with 74. Of these, 50 interviews are with the four members of the 'war cabinet', and none featured the most extreme 'hawks' or 'wets', ensuring that the official government view was dominant. This compares with only 22 studio interviews for Labour, almost half of them with Denis Healey, and a total of 3 for the Parliamentary 'Peace Party' (out of the 73 who signed the Early Day Motion on 4 May 1982 calling for an immediate truce in the South Atlantic). The only other group to appear in anything like these numbers is the military 'experts' – at 72 – who mainly discussed possible military tactics and analysed past military exploits. It is noticeable that taken together 'our experts here in the studio' make up the second biggest group after MPs, reflecting once again the tendency of TV news to pull away from people immediately involved in events and give pride of place to the 'expert' who can make 'authoritative' comments as if s/he (usually he) was outside and above the action. This is part of the ritual of TV 'balance and impartiality'; but in fact the experts are *not* always impartial or disinterested. The military experts were almost all retired military officers, in general retaining their military outlook. No other group was as fully represented: a glaring example is the very low figures for world opinion – a touchy subject for the government (since world support declined as British action was thought to escalate).

The Falkland Islanders themselves (whose views or interests were said to be 'paramount') receive a respectable 22 appearances. Seventeen of these interviews were with a single member of the Falkland Islands council; but the broadcasters could hardly give access to a wide range of Falklanders in the circumstances. It is interesting to note that the Islanders get roughly the same total number of studio interviews as the Argentines (21 including the diplomats). Allowing for this, the general picture given by the studio-interview figures remains one of strictly controlled access, with over-whelming preference given to the government and the military, and a TV voice for only a very narrow range of views.

'Revolutionary Communists Supporting Argentina' (BBC 1, 17:45, 23 May 1982)

Although we argue that public attitudes to developments in the South Atlantic were more complex and flexible than the 'pro-war'/'anti-war' caricatures, there was a section of the population which clearly opposed the military operation and when the fighting started called for a ceasefire and serious peaceful negotiations. It is hard to judge the size of this minority, especially without putting too much trust in opinion polls – although there are polls taken *after* the British victory showing 22 per cent against the war 'given the cost in lives and money' (*Economist*, 22 June 1982) and 25 per cent seeing it as Britain's 'greatest mistake' of the year (*Observer*, 2 January 1983). Furthermore, the anti-war minority was not an isolated fringe; many of those in the 'middle' who did not condemn the war outright did not give it unconditional support either. While backing the troops, they shared much with the anti-war group, as can be seen in the unwillingness to sacrifice life and the support for UN administration (see the polls analysis, p. 143). This was uncovered again much later in a Gallup poll commissioned by the *Daily Telegraph* in which two-thirds of those questioned thought the war was not inevitable:

> The government should have done more to prevent a war over the Falklands.
>
> Agree   67 per cent
> Disagree   25 per cent
> Neither, don't know   8 per cent
>
> (*Daily Telegraph*, 4 February 1983)

During the days of the fighting, there was a network of active groups throughout Britain demonstrating their opposition. Activities included a Saturday morning leafleting campaign by a Plymouth women's group:

> There was some hostility of the 'what a cheek, giving out such a leaflet in Plymouth of all places' type, plus the usual shouts of 'you couldn't do this in Argentina/Russia'. But there was quite a lot of positive response too – many people coming up and asking for one when they realised what it was about, saying that they agreed. And we noticed that many older women supported us, recalling the horrors of previous wars, and their loss of friends and relatives.
>
> (Plymouth Women's Centre report, *Spare Rib*, August 1982)

There were also marches, meetings, pickets, fasts and vigils organized by forty-nine different *ad hoc* Falklands peace committees up and down the country. One local committee reported:

> More than 500 people sent letters of protest to the government protesting at the escalation of the conflict in the sinking of the *General Belgrano*, and urging an immediate ceasefire.... This activity was followed by a hastily convened public meeting on May 15th. Over 200 people representing a broad cross-section of the community attended, clearly united in their concern ... on 21st May a 24 hour vigil and fast started, calling for peace, which was maintained by 20 people and supported by several hundred others.... It was decided to maintain a presence for peace from 1.00 to 2.00 p.m. each day until the war ends ... the response to the Bangor Ad Hoc Campaign suggests that in this part of Britain at least, the military 'solution' commands much less than the 80% claimed by the media.
>
> (*Output*, local Bangor paper, June 1982)

The forty-nine local committees linked to a National Peace Committee in London – which had the formal backing of eight MPs and some thirty national bodies (mainly peace groups and churches) presented the Foreign Secretary, Francis Pym, with a ceasefire petition bearing 26,000 signatures on 8 June.

In other words there was a small but active movement opposed to the war, demanding a ceasefire and the reopening of negotiations, supported by perhaps one in four of the population, with many more apparently open to its arguments. How was this reflected on TV news? None of the activities outlined above was mentioned. There was some coverage of the three rallies and marches in London, although the BBC ignored the 3,000 people marching down Fleet Street on 16 May protesting about media coverage of the crisis.

Another interpretation does surface: the late-night BBC 2 news item on a Falklands peace march on 23 May reports that the march attracted 5–10,000 people and that:

> they represented many and varied political and religious views. As well as MPs, trade unionists and church leaders the groups ranged from the Milton Keynes Peace Movement to the Ecology Party and the Latin America Bureau.
>
> (BBC 2, 22:40, 23 May 1982)

But the picture on the main bulletins is rather different, giving lower numbers for the turn-out and stressing the 'revolutionary communist' and 'left-wing' participation:

> several thousand people ... among them revolutionary communists supporting Argentina ... speakers including left-wing Labour MPs Tony Benn and Dame Judith Hart.
>
> (BBC 1, 17:45, 20:55, 23 May 1982)

> 4,000 people were there, including Mr Tony Benn.
>
> (ITN, 18:30, 20:45, 23 May 1982)

Only one interview is shown in the reports – and it is put to Benn rather than to any of the other speakers at the rally (who included a bishop, a Social Democrat, and an Argentine ex-political prisoner). The question is: 'As news of the landing by the Task Force dominated people's thoughts today I asked Mr Benn whether the rally was not inopportune?' (ITN, 18:30, 20:45, 23 May 1982). The marchers were introduced with suspicion – '*it was called* a march for peace' (ITN, 18:30, 20:45) – and as a potential source of trouble. The BBC 1 report opened with film of police vans – 'a substantial police *task force* gave protective cover to the demonstration' (BBC 1, 17:45) – although it did not tell us about the police threat to ban the demonstration altogether (lifted only at the last minute after MPs appealed to the Home Secretary). In this report counter-demonstrators, from the anti-CND pressure group the Coalition For Peace Through Security, were described as 'pro-Falklanders', as if by proposing a ceasefire and negotiations the peace marchers were 'anti-Falklanders'. In fact it is not clear that all the Falkland Islanders believed that the best solution was to send the Task Force. As early as 27 April 1982 a very senior BBC editor is recorded at the confidential NCA meeting as saying that he had received a call from a Falkland Islander 'to the effect that Tony Benn was the first politician to have talked sense about the crisis'.

'Pro-Falklanders' (BBC 1, 19:45, 23 May 1982).

'There'll always be an England' (BBC 1, 21:00, 12 May 1982).

We can compare the above coverage to that of 'pro-war' mobilization. This is the end-of-bulletin item in a main BBC 1 news, accompanied by shots of a small crowd waving Union Jacks:

> And finally, a display of patriotism on Merseyside tonight, where more than 500 people gathered to sing songs as a sign of their support for the British troops out in the South Atlantic. The idea was the brainchild of a Liverpool mother of three, and she advertised it in a local paper. The response was so enthusiastic, she cancelled plans to hold the rally at a local park, and arranged it at the Pier Head, where ships sailed past to join the transatlantic convoys of the last war. The people went on singing for over an hour: (*Singing*) 'There'll always be an England, And England shall be free.'

(BBC 1, 21:00, 12 May 1982)

The 'display of patriotism' organized by a 'mother of three' in support of the Task Force is presented as good news – 'the response was so enthusiastic' – in contrast with the guarded and stereotyped approach to the displays of the peace marchers.

'Things in Their Aircraft Factory Will Never Be Quite the Same Again' (ITN, 13:00, 29 June 1983)

The war in the Falklands ended on 14 June 1982. But the spirit of the Falklands was to live on. The Prime Minister's initial reaction to the Argentine surrender was: 'It's *Great* Britain ... it's been everyone together and that's what matters.' Her speech on 3 July 1982 – 'We have found a new confidence, born of the economic battles at home and tested and found true 8,000 miles away' – and Nigel Lawson's proclamation on 22 June 1982 – 'Nothing could have signalled more clearly that the long years of retreat and self-doubt are over ... it's the rebirth of Britain' – show how the government was determined to carry the carefully fostered spirit of national unity and hard-working values beyond the fighting in the South Atlantic and into the everyday battles of domestic politics and industrial relations.

The link between the military victory and industrial relations was taken up by the media. The BBC's industrial correspondent asked David Howell: 'Is the government going to meet this strike with the same resolve it showed over the Falklands?' (BBC 1, 18:00, 27 June 1982). In fact the link had already been established on the news, with reports on how productivity shot up in the British companies supplying the Task Force:

> The company making the special apparatus has been working seven days a week since the navy placed the order last month. An order had been expected, but five days after the attack on the *Sheffield*, the signal came – send them now. Production leapt from 50 a month to nearly 2,000 a week,

and suppliers cut through red tape to deliver parts in record time.

(BBC 1, 11:40, 11 June 1982)

It was clear that the image of national unity on the home front was not a special case confined to the Falklands War itself and the constraints imposed by the fighting. It is equally useful in peacetime:

> Only now is one of the engineering success stories of the Falklands War becoming apparent.... The speed with which the conversion work was carried out, in days rather than months, is being hailed in Whitehall as a shining example of what can be achieved by British industry when the chips are down.... In the vast British Aerospace assembly plant hangar, a long-forgotten wartime spirit was rekindled. They built forty Lancaster bombers a week here during the nation's darkest hours, and now a job which in peacetime might have taken a year or more was completed in just eighteen days.... The company hope it'll prove to be an important lesson for the future, and that things in their aircraft factory will never be quite the same again.
>
> (ITN, 13:00, 29 June 1982)

PUBLIC OPINION

The issue of public opinion on the war was rarely analysed in television news coverage. In the seven-week sample period we found the BBC and ITN each carrying news items on only three of the numerous opinion polls. Public opinion was not treated as controversial or particularly newsworthy, on the grounds that it was taken to be largely in support of the military campaign. As Patricia Holland writes about the press:

> The popular papers, indeed, construct 'public opinion' as one of the characters in their drama. It becomes a kind of affirmative Greek chorus, a crowd which occasionally troops onto stage to offer patriotic support to 'the nation' and 'our boys'.[8]

Since it was the backbone of the newsrooms' framework for understanding the war, the belief in massive public support was rarely stated explicitly. More often it was revealed indirectly, for example, in the way interviewees' claims were treated. Contrast two interviews on one bulletin. When Tony Benn says: 'We must stop the killing now. That's the way world opinion has been going, that's the way British opinion has been clearly expressed', the interviewer immediately challenges him: 'What evidence do you have for saying that?' (ITN, 13:00, 5 May 1982). (In reply Benn quotes the *Sunday Times* poll, which was not reported on the TV news, in which 60 per cent said the return of the Falklands was not worth a single serviceman's life.) However, when the chairman of the Conservative Defence Committee, Anthony Buck, appears a few minutes later and says: 'I think that the rightness of the British cause and the clear wishes of the Falkland Islanders will cause there to be a vast majority of reasonable and sensible people seeing that our cause is right, and that it as I say does not pay to appease fascist dictators', the same interviewer lets his claim about 'the vast majority' pass unchallenged.

The broadcasters can of course, like Benn, point to public-opinion polls in their defence. The various polls show a consistent majority 'satisfied with the government's handling of the crisis', which can be used to justify the assumption that the public is supporting the war. But this needs to be looked at more carefully. One of the problems with opinion polls is that they are used to reduce complicated issues, about which people may have a range of opinions or none at all, to flat 'yes-or-no', 'for-or-against' results. This packaging of people into camps seriously distorts and misrepresents actual opinion. Take the *Sunday Times* poll that Benn quoted: 60 per cent say the Falklands are not worth a single life, and yet in the same poll 70 per cent say they are satisfied with the government's handling of the crisis, with only 23 per cent dissatisfied. The point is that although the polls went on showing support for the government at around 70 per cent, this cannot be straight-forwardly read as 70 per cent support for the military option (any more than 23 per cent dissatisfaction can be read as 23 per cent anti-war feeling). Many obviously agreed with the sending of the Task Force, wanted to see Britain take some decisive action against the Argentine 'aggression', but did not want a shooting war. The Task Force was, after all, portrayed as a 'back-up' for the diplomatic effort. Their opinion on British policy would depend on what options seemed open. Another of the problems with opinion polls is the assumption that every individual has a fixed attitude to every question at any one time, without allowing for uncertainty or discussion. Since the country did not divide neatly into pro-war and anti-war factions the pollsters' results depend very much on the questions they choose to ask, and therefore need to be interpreted carefully.

ITN's *Weekend World* commissioned a poll for their programme on 9 May 1982. It is a crucial example since it is the only poll in the rather thin coverage of public opinion that was taken up on the news of all three channels. It was presented on all the bulletins as a reaffirmation of high and rising public support for government policy and military escalation. The reports began:

> The latest opinion poll suggests that most people in Britain still back the government's handling of the Falklands crisis.
>
> (BBC 1, 17:50, 21:00; BBC 2, 20:05, 9 May 1982)

> A new opinion poll shows that more people are now prepared to accept British casualties in the Falklands.
>
> (ITN, 18:30, 9 May 1982)

Later on ITN this interpretation was strengthened:

> Public opinion here seems to be hardening in favour of decisive action to

retake the Falklands, even if it means more British casualties.

(ITN, 20:45, 9 May 1982)

After these introductions the newscasters go on to present results from two of the questions in the poll, although, as the illustrations show, they give a confusing variety of questions and percentages.

For instance, BBC 1 at 17:40 shows 55 per cent 'for invasion' (interestingly the BBC graphic for public opinion is two soldiers), while ITN has 70 per cent wanting 'to launch an invasion', and by 20:05 the BBC has 70 per cent 'for invasion if "no other alternative"'. If we go back to the original poll, the question on the possibility of an invasion was:

> If the Argentine government refuses to compromise and the British government decides that a long-term blockade of the island is too risky, what should the British government do?
>
> Should they:
> – launch an invasion of the Islands?   70%
> or
> – abandon their claim to the Islands?   18%
>
> Don't know   11%

The full question – never read out on the news – is a very limiting one. It asks about support for an invasion *after* ruling out the other options, *after* negotiations have failed, and a long-term blockade is ruled out. Any other options, like economic sanctions or UN administration, are excluded: the choice is to invade or abandon Britain's claim. It is a typical case of the way opinion polls on complex subjects often remove all the doubts and reservations that make up people's opinions so that they can reduce the question to a simple statistic. It might be interesting to know that, when 1,000 people are offered this narrow choice, 70 per cent opt for invasion once everything else has been ruled out, while 18 per cent (nearly 1 in 5) are prepared to abandon the British claim altogether if invasion is the only way to pursue it. But since it does not tell us what people think of the *true* situation – in which there was still a possibility of a negotiated settlement and (according to the Defence Secretary, who was interviewed on the same news bulletins) the British were in a position to maintain a long blockade – it does not justify the TV news interpretation, particularly not ITN's claim that public opinion 'seems to be hardening in favour of decisive action to retake the Falklands', or the bald 'launch an invasion ... 70%' on the screen, which implies that 70 per cent want an invasion *now*, without making it clear that the opinion was given in the hypothetical situation that an invasion was the *only* way to defend the Falklands.

The second opinion-poll question that the news chose to tell us about was the one on loss of life. The question was:

ITN, 18:30, 9 May 1982.

BBC 1, 21:30, 9 May 1982.

Do you think that the recovery of the Falkland Islands is worth the loss of more British servicemen's lives if that should prove to be necessary?

Yes   55%
No   38%
Don't know   7%

Once again the wording of the question is by no means neutral; it asks if the loss of British lives is worth it *if* it proves to be 'necessary'. Apart from the documented tendency of people to reply 'yes' to yes-or-no pollsters' questions, the question assumes that loss of life *will* be necessary. Previous polls by the same organization, ORC, had asked a different question: 'How many British soldiers' and sailors' lives would you be prepared to see lost in order to regain the Falkland Islands?' A majority had always replied 'none'. No doubt ORC had to change their question after some British lives were lost; but it is impossible to tell if the new result represented a real 'hardening' of opinion to accept casualties, or reflected only the change of wording to 'necessary' casualties. Television news did not consider these points. The BBC rewrote the question altogether picking out the 55 per cent figure and presenting it as 55 per cent 'for invasion', which is odd since there was another question specifically about invasion. ITN introduced the whole item with the claim that '*more people are now prepared to accept* British casualties ... public opinion seems to be hardening', latching onto the change from previous polls when most people opposed any casualties, but without telling us that the question had been changed, and without giving the full question.

This careless interpretation on the news represents the reporting of the public-opinion poll to fit a newsroom viewpoint. This is clear if we look at the missing results, the questions that were left out of the reports. A striking case is the question on UN administration and negotiations:

Do you support or oppose the idea that the United Nations should administer the Falkland Islands for an interim period during which Britain and Argentina negotiate about the future of the Islands?

Support   76%
Oppose   19%
Don't know   8%

The 76 per cent majority in favour of handing the Falklands over to the UN while the British and Argentine governments hold more talks was a significant rise on the 63 per cent majority when the same question was asked in the previous ORC poll (before there were any British casualties), showing widespread and rising agreement with what was in effect the 'Peace Party' argument for UN administration and more negotiations. Like all poll questions, it avoids the complications (with no mention of Argentine withdrawal for instance, or the brief for negotiations), so it cannot be used as evidence for a straightforward 76 per cent support for UN administration on any terms; but it does help clarify the context of the more hawkish results that the news *did* tell us about. It means that neither the 76 per cent paper majority for the UN and talks, nor the 70 per cent paper majority for invasion represented blind determination for any one course, that there was no unqualified 'pro-war' landslide and that opinion depended, quite sensibly, on the options presented. But the news told us about only one side.

The poll question on support for government policy is also instructive. The BBC reports on the poll introduce it as more evidence that 'most people in Britain still back the government's handling of the Falklands crisis'. This was true; but the reports go on to present support for an *invasion* as if the government policy that most people backed was a policy of invasion. This is misleading on two counts: first, official policy at that time, so far as the public knew, was to keep all options open, including the peace talks, economic sanctions and the military blockade. Second, the question that produced the usual result of majority backing for the government was:

How do you feel about the government's policy of trying to regain the Falkland Islands by *diplomatic means* [our italics] backed by the threat of the use of force?

Strongly support it	59%
Quite strongly support it	17%
Neither support nor oppose/don't know	10%
Quite strongly oppose it	5%
Strongly oppose it	6%

The question can be criticized for ruling out any uncertainty about what government policy was (for instance, any doubts about the British government's good faith in diplomatic negotiations); but as it stands it shows once again that there was support for a 'policy of trying to regain the Falkland Islands by diplomatic means', and that public opinion was not demanding the use of force (invasion, for instance) for its own sake – force was presented as a 'threat' to 'back' peaceful negotiations. The high support for this very specific policy as it is put in the poll question is not the same as a public mandate for *any* government or military policy in the Falklands.

One more result which did not appear on the news was the sex difference in the answers. Women gave noticeably less support than men to military options and the sacrifice of life. This raises questions about what 'public opinion' really is. Quite apart from the way opinion polls can be selected, manipulated and abused, it is not clear exactly what the most scrupulously reported poll is supposed to measure. Polls add together the views of different individuals, as if all opinions were equal; but that does not necessarily mean that they uncover an underlying 'national will' of 'the people'. For one thing, the people are not an undivided mass (thus men's and women's opinions differ). Also, everyone's individual opinions are not held with the same force or passion, so what does it mean to add them together? One of the major influences on opinion is the mass media themselves – especially since opinion about the war was so dependent on the information the public had about what the war meant and what other options were open. We have here a situation in which television selectively informs people's attitudes, then selectively reports on what those attitudes are, and finally, as we have seen, uses this version of public opinion to justify its own approach to reporting.

NOTES

1   H. Tinker, ed., *A Message from the Falklands*, London: Junction Books, 1982, p. 82.
2   Servicemen too know the human costs of the fighting from direct experience; but the conditions of their service prevent them from expressing their views in public.
3   This represents the percentage at a given moment in time but such family arrangements are a stage of life which many people pass through. Consequently at any given moment some people have just left such arrangements and others are about to enter them.
4   There are two possible exceptions: one woman is shown getting married (BBC 1, 22:10, 8 May 1982), but this is obviously before her husband leaves for the South Atlantic; and a group of women are shown talking to their MP (BBC 1, 21:00, 26 May 1982), but they are talking about waiting for information about their husbands.
5   The BBC's Assistant Director-General notices this too. The NCA minutes of discussion about interviewing relatives record: 'Certainly, ADG said, he would seek the sacking of any reporter who asked "How do you feel?"' (NCA, 8 May 1982); 'The return of the *QE2* had been another example of superb coverage by constant repetition of "How did/do you feel?" ADG said enough was enough' (NCA, 15 June 1982).
6   At that week's NCA meeting, the BBC's Director of Public Affairs 'suggested special caution in the weeks ahead, over the question "has it all been worth it?"' (NCA, 15 June 1982).
7   A *Newsnight* feature dwelt on the differences: 'Argentine politics are not Western ones.... Argentine's sense of relentless economic decline.... The Falklands conquest is almost the only symbol of greatness that the country has.... Argentina is a deeply fragmented society with each interest group bent on self-advancement to the detriment of and the exclusion of the others. Decisions are impulsive, not subject to outside checks and balances; miscalculations are easier to make in such a system. And besides, in their personal and national culture, a man never climbs down, never admits he's wrong, and it all makes Argentina a very difficult country to deal with' (BBC 2, 22:40, 23 May 1982). Some of the same criticisms ('economic decline', 'only symbol of greatness', 'deeply fragmented society', 'miscalculations', 'never climbs down') could be applied to Britain, but they are not. Instead Argentina is held up as the country with problems.
8   Latin American Bureau, *Whose Crisis?*, London, 1982, p. 20.

Chapter 7

The British media and the Gulf War*

Greg Philo and Greg McLaughlin

When the Gulf crisis began in August 1990, most people in Britain had no detailed knowledge of the Middle East and there was no desire to go to war with a country such as Iraq. Yet in a short period, a majority of the population was convinced that a war was necessary, that it would be morally justified and that it would very quickly destroy Saddam Hussein.

This change in public belief resulted from a very successful campaign of mass persuasion by politicians, the media and others in favour of military action. Voices against this were drowned by the chorus for war. This chapter reviews some of the main elements of that campaign.

THE PORTRAYAL OF IRAQ AND SADDAM HUSSEIN

Because most people knew so little about Iraq, it was possible for the media and politicians to present the conflict in very simple terms. Saddam Hussein was shown as a monster similar to Adolf Hitler. The war was then presented as an offensive against Hussein rather than against the people of Iraq. Thus, as the war broke out, one of the major tabloid newspapers had as its headline: 'GO GET HIM BOYS' (*Daily Star*, 16 January 1991).

The *Daily Mirror* and the *Sun* are the two largest papers in Britain with a combined readership of around 20 million people. On the day the war broke out the *Daily Mirror* divided its front page into two sections. The first section had a headline saying 'THE HEROES'. This was over pictures of a young British soldier and an RAF pilot. The pilot is quoted as saying: 'IT WOULD BE A HELL OF AN END TO MY CAREER TO KO SADDAM'. The second section has the headline 'THE VILLAIN', which is over a picture of Saddam Hussein.

On 10 January the *Sun* published an editorial calling for war and demanding that Iraq and its leadership be 'destroyed once and for all' but said

*This chapter was originally published in 1993 as a report by the Glasgow University Media Group.

nothing about the effects of the war on the mass of the population who live in that country:

SO LET THERE BE WAR – Today the world teeters on the brink of war. There is only one guilty party – the Iraqi leadership. The time has come for them to be punished. Iraq and Saddam Hussein must be destroyed once and for all.

But, in fact, the Iraqi leadership would be well protected from the effects of bombing. The destruction would mostly be felt by the civilian population of cities and by the conscript army which was located in Kuwait. The British media did not report in this period that most of the population of Iraq was composed of Shi'a Muslim and Kurdish people who were themselves oppressed groups within the country. Consequently, some of the moral issues involved in attacking the Iraqi population could be avoided by focusing attention on the character of Saddam Hussein.

THE 'INEVITABILITY' OF WAR

The propaganda device of equating Saddam Hussein with Hitler was a crucial element in the argument for using military force. It must be said that this propaganda had an element of truth since Saddam Hussein was a truly monstrous figure, but he clearly did not constitute the same threat that Hitler had been in 1939. The purpose of linking Hussein and Hitler was to rule out any policy apart from war. Anything short of military force (for example, using economic sanctions) was seen as 'giving way' to dictatorship. In Britain the word 'appeasement' has special connotations – it is associated with the Munich Agreement of 1938 and the policy of making concessions to Adolf Hitler. Thus, in the context of the Gulf War, economic sanctions were equated in the tabloid press with appeasement. The *Sun* referred to 'spineless appeasers' who believe 'a combination of sanctions and sweet reason will be enough' (16 January 1991). The *Daily Express* referred to 'the appeasers and the give-sanctions-a-chance-brigade' (16 January 1991). *The Times* describes 'the notorious appeaser's remedy of "giving sanctions longer to work"' (15 January 1991). This is an odd combination of ideas. The destruction of a national economy does not imply 'appeasing' its leader. The appeasement policy in relation to Hitler had nothing to do with any attempt to destroy the German economy. But the equation of Saddam Hussein with Hitler, and the disparaging of any alternatives other than fighting, were important elements in the arguments for using military force.

In the national British press only the *Guardian* argued against using force. Its editorial on 15 January quoted a CIA report that sanctions had stopped 97 per cent of Iraqi exports. BBC news also ran a brief item two days before the outbreak of war that pointed to the success of sanctions. An American economist was interviewed and stated that they were having: 'More than ten times the impact [than on] economies in past episodes, where sanctions have *succeeded* in achieving their goal' (BBC 1, 21:00, 14 January 1991). These, though, were exceptions. The general flow of media coverage overwhelmingly suggested that war was inevitable if 'negotiations' failed. We can see this clearly in this front page from the *Sun*: 'IT LOOKS LIKE WAR – *Battle stations as Gulf talks collapse*. War in the Gulf looked inevitable last night after last ditch peace talks failed' (10 January 1991, emphasis added). We can see the same themes on television news. Thus, after the collapse of President Mitterand's last-minute attempts at negotiation, we hear that: 'All efforts to find a peaceful solution to the Gulf crisis seemed to have ended in failure tonight' (BBC 1, 21:00, 15 January 1991). And on ITN: 'War in the Gulf looks unavoidable. Iraq said tonight that it was ready for it. It rejected any final peace initiatives' (22:00, 15 January 1991). There are no headlines suggesting that if 'negotiations' fail then the west could develop its successful policy of economic sanctions. The juxtaposition of 'negotiations' and 'war' is therefore crucial. They were the two alternatives presented to the public. If one 'failed' then the other was 'necessary'.

Once the war had begun, there was some discontent amongst British journalists about manipulation of the media by politicians and military authorities. In one brief moment (in an early-morning programme) a BBC journalist comments on how 'negotiations' had been used by politicians to prepare the public for war. He is the BBC correspondent in Paris and he is asked by another journalist about changes in French public opinion:

> We have the last-minute peace initiative which, I am told, President Mitterand knew perfectly well didn't stand a chance. But he did it for internal opinion, to persuade the French public that he really had done everything and there was no alternative. And he's coaxed them slowly in press conference after press conference into believing that war was the only option and I think he has been remarkably successful.
>
> (BBC 1, 10:00, 23 January 1991)

The tabloid press in Britain greeted the outbreak of war with the same patriotic fervour they had shown in the Falklands War of 1982. The *Sun* printed a Union Jack across the whole of its front page and invited its readers to cut it out and display it in the windows of their houses (16 January 1991). *Today* had its whole front page devoted to a picture of a young sailor with the headline: 'YOUR COUNTRY NEEDS HIM' (16 January 1991). Later, when there were British casualties and captured pilots were shown on Iraqi television, the *Sun* screamed for vengeance with the headline: 'BASTARDS OF BAGHDAD' (22 January 1991). Television was more discreet. In fact, with echoes from the Falklands War, the BBC was attacked in the popular press for referring to 'the British troops', rather than saying 'our troops' or 'our boys' (*Sun*, 16 January 1991).[1]

There was another argument that was used successfully in Britain to press for war. This was that a new type of conflict was now possible – a war that could be fought almost without casualties.

THE CLEAN AND EASY WAR

By presenting the war as a fight against Saddam Hussein, the issue of what would happen to the mass of the Iraqi population was temporarily avoided. But as the war developed, there was a growing concern about the effects of bombing on civilians. The western military countered this by emphasizing the 'precision' and 'surgical' nature of the bombing. After the war it was revealed that in fact only 7 per cent of the bombs dropped were 'precision' or laser-guided weapons. But as the war began, both press and television in Britain became obsessed with the sophistication and power of western weaponry. Newspapers featured extensive maps and diagrams showing different types of weapons and their capacity for destruction. The *Daily Express*, for example, had such a map next to an editorial supporting the decision to go to war. Beneath the map were the words: 'THE ARSENAL OF DEMOCRACY – How the massive fire power of the allied forces in the Gulf lines up against Iraq's army' (16 January 1991). Television news showed pictures of the Prime Minister in a Challenger tank giving the thumbs-up sign. Both news and current-affairs programmes featured an extraordinary number of interviews with military personnel.[2] Television coverage at this time was criticized for its fascination with the military and for its naive approach to the view that killing and destruction could be 'managed' and 'controlled'. The television critic of the *Observer* newspaper commented that 'when this is all over, a lot of hacks are going to be ashamed of themselves' – because they 'did not hoot incredulously when an apparently sane Colonel talks of a "hands-off" war' (13 January 1991).

The excitement in the media about military technology was given an additional boost when the Americans began to show video pictures of successful bombing raids. The conflict had now become a *Star Wars* video game.[3] The *Daily Mirror* captures the atmosphere:

The world watched in awe yesterday as Stormin' Norman played his 'home video' – revealing how allied planes are using *Star Wars* technology to destroy vital Iraqi targets.

Just like Luke Skywalker manoeuvring his fighter into the heart of Darth Vader's space complex, the US pilots zeroed into the very centre of Saddam Hussein's Baghdad.

(19 January 1991)

On BBC 1, David Dimbleby, who was their anchor man for news about the war, spoke of 'the most vivid description anybody can ever have seen of the precision bombing that has been carried out by the US forces' (10:00, 18 January 1991). When interviewing the US Ambassador, he says the bombing, suggests that America's ability to react militarily has really become quite extraordinary, despite all critics beforehand who said it will never work out like that. You are now able to claim that you can act precisely and, therefore – to use that hideous word about warfare – 'surgically'.

(10:00, 18 January 1991)

The Pentagon videos seemed to transfix journalists. At the briefing in Riyadh, in a whole room filled with reporters, not one asks: 'If the Americans have videos of bombs landing on target, do they not also have videos showing where they have missed?' In some instances, journalists' fascination with hi-tech weaponry sat uneasily with the humanitarian ethos of broadcasting. The assumption that 'surgical precision' ensured low civilian casualties helped to resolve their dilemma. This was exemplified live on BBC when two journalists analysed replays of the Pentagon videos. Like two sports commentators, David Dimbleby and defence correspondent, David Shukman, were almost rapt with enthusiasm. They called for freeze-frames and replays and they highlighted 'the action' on screen with computer 'light-pens':

SHUKMAN: This is the promised hi-tech war. Defence contractors for some time have been trying to convince everybody that hi-tech weapons can work.... [It's] certainly always been the case that a number of us have been very cynical about the claims of these manufacturers [*describes bombing of Iraqi Air Command HQ, Baghdad*]. The allied strategy had always been to endeavour to avoid civilian casualties. Now, by isolating that ... building [*draws circle around subject*], pinpointing ... the most vulnerable part of it, they are able to destroy [it]; no doubt kill all the occupants of it but ... without causing casualties amongst the civilian population around.

Only at this point does Dimbleby rationalize the moral implications of the 'hi-tech war':

DIMBLEBY: Let's just see the final stages of that attack again! [*VTR replay*]. It does strike one that there is something appalling about watching the destruction of human life which is conducted in such a surgical style as this. I know it's irrational – a bomb in the Second World War falling at random from the sky is just as horrific – but one knows that in that building there is the staff of the Iraqi air-defence forces who are about to be bombed out of this world by the most astonishing technology.

(BBC 1, 18 January 1991)

What is interesting here is an apparent acceptance that bombs 'falling at random from the sky' are an obsolete technology and that the entire allied bombing campaign was being conducted using 'smart' weapons. This is hardly surprising in the first few days of the war since information was being filtered through official channels. In that period, the only available evidence of the results of the bombing was shown in the very same, selective Pentagon videos. So, with little or no information about the bombing of cities such as Basra, and with no enquiry into the possible inaccuracy of hi-tech weaponry, the allies were able to present a story of a hi-tech operation to destroy military targets in and around Baghdad.

Some newspapers such as the *Sun* showed an open delight in the destructive power of the allied forces. In one edition, it ran a full-page feature on the weaponry of the B-52 bomber under the heading: 'DEATH CARGO OF THE JOLLY GREEN GIANT' (24 January 1991). This report ended by quoting former defence chief Alexander Haig: 'I ordered B-52 carpet combing raids in Vietnam and I have seen them reduce men and material to jelly. They will turn Iraq into a talcum powder bowl' (24 January 1991). In the *Daily Mirror* a complete front page was given over to the headline: 'WE'LL BOMB THEM TILL THEY'RE NOT THERE ANY MORE' (19 January 1991).

The effects of the bombing on civilians became dreadfully apparent with the destruction of the Al-Amiriya bunker on 13 February. The *Sun* claimed that the event was a fabrication – that it had been made up for Iraqi propaganda purposes. Its front-page headline was: '10 FACTS TO DAMN SADDAM' (14 February 1991). The lead story beneath this headline suggested that the bodies found in the burnt-out bunker could have been brought there from elsewhere:

> Saddam Hussein tried to trick the world yesterday by saying hundreds of women and children died in a bomb attack on an 'air raid shelter'. He cunningly arranged TV scenes designed to shock and appal.... The charred bodies covered with multi-coloured blankets could have belonged to anyone.... The hidden 'civilian' casualties may have been Iraqi military casualties.

> (ibid.)

The television news showed more concern for the suffering of the Iraqi population, but even so, both BBC and ITN were very nervous about carrying material on civilian casualties.[4] When ITN reported the bunker bombing, it announced that it had cut material sent by its own reporter in Baghdad, because it was 'too distressing':

> NEWSCASTER: The Iraqis didn't censor any part of Brent Sadler's report, but we at ITN did edit out some scenes because we regarded them as too distressing to broadcast.

> (ITN, 13 February 1991)

The Americans defended their action by stating that the bunker was a military installation. The BBC took up this theme and their reporter in Baghdad was questioned intensively on the issue by the newscaster:

> NEWSCASTER: A few moments ago, I spoke with Jeremy Bowen in

Baghdad and asked him whether he could be *absolutely sure* that there was no military communications equipment in the shelter, which the allies believe was there.

BOWEN: Well, Peter, we looked very hard for it ... I'm pretty confident, as confident as I can be that I've seen all the main rooms....

NEWSCASTER: Is it conceivable it could have been in military use and was converted recently to civilian use?

BOWEN: Well, it would seem a strange sort of thing to do....

NEWSCASTER: Let me put it another way Jeremy, is it possible to say with *certainty* that it was never a military facility?

The newscaster closed his interview with a final qualifier to camera: 'Jeremy Bowen speaking a few minutes ago – subject, of course, to Iraq's reporting restrictions' (BBC 1, 18:00, 14 February, 1991, newscaster's emphases).

But after the war an ITN journalist, Nick Gowing, revealed that US intelligence had been at fault:

> With world attention focused elsewhere, sources have [now] told ITN that in the White House, on 27 February, the US National Security Advisor, Brent Snowcroft, told the [British] Foreign Secretary, Douglas Hurd, that US intelligence had been at fault. In other words: the bunker bombing was a military mistake.[5]

The issue of civilian casualties was politically very sensitive. In the period of the war both BBC and ITN were afraid of being accused by British politicians of showing 'Iraqi propaganda'. Such propaganda might include anything that gained sympathy for the Iraqi population. Consequently, in the early days of the war, pictures of civilian casualties provided by the Iraqis were accompanied by heavy qualifications that suggested they might not be authentic. These qualifications reduced the emotional impact of the pictures and protected the broadcasters against future criticism. The examples that follow are all from a *single* ITN item. The newscaster introduced it by stressing that most of it was filmed by a Jordanian cameraman using an ITN camera:

> The latest pictures to come out of Iraq show extensive damage caused, the *Iraqis say*, by allied bombers.... This is an image of life in Iraq that Saddam Hussein is *anxious for the world to see and believe*.... The pictures were *supplied by the Ministry of Information.... As propaganda* it graphically illustrates the suffering ... [the pictures are] *being used as a weapon.... As a means to influence world opinion....*
>
> Iraqi-supplied material draws *natural suspicions about its authenticity* ... these people *are claimed by Iraq* to be recent victims of the bombing but *they have not been independently verified* as such.
>
> (ITN, 21:45, 26 January 1991)

By 1 February, ITN had its own personnel in Baghdad and showed dramatic pictures of the effects of cruise missile strikes in civilian areas. In one telling sequence, the reporter, Brent Sadler, debunks the myth of the 'hi-tech', 'clean and easy war':

> [*holds up debris of Cruise missile*] Simple gun-fire brought down this hi-tech weaponry, a computer-guided system for which this Iraqi woman articulated her hate.
> WOMAN: This is not a game! Those are human lives!
> (ITN, 22:00, 1 February 1991)

But it was only after the war had ended that its full human costs were made more apparent.

AFTER THE WAR

The contradictions involved in using military force were shown clearly at the end of the war when the Iraqi army, which was fleeing from Kuwait, was destroyed at the Mutla Gap. The horror of this destruction influenced public opinion, but there was an additional contradiction revealed by the British journalist, Kate Adie, who reported from the scene. She noted that many of the Iraqi soldiers were in fact Kurds, who were themselves an oppressed group within Iraq. Those who died there 'turned out to be from the north of the country, from minority communities, persecuted by Saddam Hussein – the Kurds and the Turks' (BBC 1, 21:00, 1 March 1991). The bulk of the army in Kuwait had in fact been Shi'a Muslims. This was revealed by ITN: 'The Shi'as have a powerful incentive for opposing Saddam Hussein. Most of the thousands of conscripts who died in the trenches of Kuwait were Shi'as' (ITN, 22:00, 4 March 1991).

As the war ended, it emerged that the western military had actually destroyed an Iraqi army composed mainly of these oppressed groups while leaving the troops who were most loyal to Saddam Hussein (the Republican Guards) intact as a military force. Hussein then used the Guards to violently suppress revolts by the Kurds in the north of Iraq and the Shi'a Muslims in the south. When this happened there was a substantial change in the attitudes of some of the British media. The political consensus was split and the leaders of both Britain and the USA were attacked in the press and on television for ignoring the plight of the Kurds. This new campaign was led primarily by the *Guardian*, the *Daily Mirror* and by television news, which consistently criticized these politicians with the charge that they had invited the people of Iraq to revolt against Saddam Hussein. The politicians were being challenged to show that their statements about a 'war for democracy' were more than cynical rhetoric. Perhaps one reason for the strength of the media response was that much of the British media had themselves endorsed this rhetoric. There were now many doubts being expressed about the morality of the war and there was a growing feeling amongst journalists that the media had been manipulated for crude political purposes.

Certainly, one result of the war was that journalists became more aware and concerned about the processes by which public consciousness is shaped. There were occasional discussions between journalists about this that were broadcast during the war and which were unlike anything seen before on public television. The following example from the BBC was broadcast live to a small morning-time audience but it is still extraordinary since it is between two senior journalists, David Dimbleby and Mark Mardell. They had an open discussion in which they criticized the 'news managers' for manipulating public opinion:

DIMBLEBY: I'm getting a bit uneasy about the way that this war seems to be being presented politically. There seems to be, creeping in, a feeling that Washington and Number 10 ought to be able to raise and lower expectations at will about this war.

They start off with everybody terrified there will be casualties, and so they say it's been a very successful first day. They then see newspaper headlines and public opinion thinking, or they think it thinks, that the war is going to be over very quickly, so they then induce a mood of pessimism.

Now you are reporting this morning that Number 10 is very keen to make sure that people don't feel pessimistic. I'm not sure that I like the idea of my opinion and yours and the public as a whole being subjected to this kind of psychological pressure about the war. . . . Don't you get the feeling that there is slightly too much pulling of the levers of public psychology on this?

(BBC 1, 10:00, 23 January 1991)

Mark Mardell replied: 'I always get that feeling to be perfectly honest' (ibid.). He also referred to 'fear of the Vietnam factor' as one explanation of the official approach to 'mood management'. Releasing too much information about the progress of the war, it was thought, might sway public opinion against seeing it through to the end. Philip Knightley suggests that these fears had been acted on long before the Gulf crisis. The system of strict accreditation of journalists to 'media pools' was devised by the Ministry of Defence and implemented during the Falklands War in response to the debate in the USA about the media's role during the Vietnam War.[6] The degree to which British journalists accepted the MoD's restrictions was heavily criticized at the time, not least by American reporters. The ABC's London correspondent, Walter Rogers, thought that a more defiant approach would have changed the situation entirely: 'If the British press had stood up to the [MoD] and said, "Ain't no way we're going down there and playing by your ground rules!", the [MoD] would've had to have backed down.'[7] Asked why he thought British journalists played along, Rogers put it down to cultural specifics: 'Because you're tradition-bound and it is the tradition here [in

Britain] that if a journalist wants to get along, he's got to go along with the government.' Yet, the British way of doing things made a considerable impact in America. The pool system was adopted by the US in advance of its invasion of Grenada in 1983 and perfected by the time it invaded Panama in 1989.[8] Few American journalists refused to compromise.

At its annual conference in Japan, 24 April 1991, the International Press Institute issued a condemnation of reporting restrictions during the war; these, it said, had 'prevented a balanced picture of events, including the full extent of human suffering'.[9] Even in the aftermath of the war, when strict media management was no longer in effect, current-affairs and documentary output on British television tended to focus on what was happening outside Iraq. A picture of 'the full extent of human suffering' was still missing.

In May 1991, John Simpson introduced a special BBC documentary series on the effects of the war on the people of the Middle East and referred to a most noticeable gap in television's saturation coverage of the war: '*As for the human casualties, tens of thousands of them, or the brutal effect the war had on millions of others ... we didn't see so much of that.*'[10] We cannot explain such absences by government restrictions alone and it is not correct to see the British media as being simply forced along by politicians in the early stages of the war. Many of them, especially the popular press, were willing participants in a mood of patriotism and near euphoria. They could not resist such a 'good story' and the chance to present a real war as a kind of Hollywood movie in which 'our side' were the 'good guys'.[11] Only later did some of them contemplate the human cost.

NOTES

1 See Glasgow University Media Group, *War and Peace News*, London: Routledge, 1985.

2 David Morrison, *Television and the Gulf War*, London: John Libbey, 1992, p. 70. In a sample of 5,388 appearances by interviewees, 23 per cent (1,188) had direct links to the military, with another 95 appearances by 'military academics', and 148 by Defence Secretary, Tom King. However, there is no indication as to the number of appearances by alternative or oppositional voices in this sample. Instead, Morrison fixes an 'Others' category which, at 40 per cent (2,156), is by far the largest.

    The American media monitoring group, Fairness and Accuracy in Reporting (FAIR), showed that in a sample of 2,855 minutes of US TV news coverage of the five-month build-up to the Gulf War, only 29 minutes dealt with opposition to war. At a special conference on US news coverage of the war in New York, December 1991, the denial of access to oppositional voices was a central issue. Some criticisms of this came from unexpected quarters, including Daniel Gergin, Director of Communications for the Reagan administration, 1981–4 (*Guardian*, 4 January 1991).

3 Morrison, *Television and the Gulf War*, pp. 41–62. In a survey of 212 children, 146 responded to the question 'What sticks in your mind?' about television coverage of the war; 17 (12 per cent) referred to the Pentagon videos. Out of 150

children who said they talked about the war with their peers, 45 (30 per cent) said they discussed weapons and equipment. Asked if their parents made a point of talking to them about the Gulf War, 13 per cent of a smaller sample of 76 children referred to discussions about weapons and equipment.

4   *Ibid.* pp. 71–3. Morrison observed 8,028 images in his sample of coverage. Only 1 per cent were of death and injury, compared with 7 per cent from military press conferences and 5 per cent showing military equipment and manoeuvres.

5   N. Gowing, *Spectrum*, ITC, summer 1991.

6   P. Knightley, 'Here is the patriotically censored news', *Index on Censorship*, April–May 1991, pp. 4–5.

7   Channel 4, *Diverse Reports*, 7 January 1983.

8   P. Schmeisser, 'The pool and the Pentagon', *Index on Censorship*, April–May 1991, pp. 32–4, and R. O'Mara, 'In a gulf of darkness', ibid., pp. 30–1. The full potential of the pool system seems to have been underestimated in some circles, even by critics. For example, in its Gulf War bulletin, Article 19 pointed out that the system was not 'activated' until the latter half of the invasion of Panama, since the media were kept isolated at US bases, well away from the action (*Stop Press: The Gulf War and Censorship* 1, 15 February 1991, p. 6). After Panama, the US Department of Defence commissioned a review of its relationship with the media. The end result, the Hoffman Report, criticized the Department for excessive secrecy and noted that the pictures and reports sent back from Panama by the news pool were of 'secondary value' (N. Levinson, 'Snazzy visuals, hard facts and obscured issues', *Index on Censorship*, April–May 1991, p. 27). In view of the fact that the most critical phase of the invasion was carried out without public knowledge, it could be argued that the pool system was very successfully activated from the outset.

9   *Guardian*, 25 April 1991.

10 BBC 2, *Our War*, 25 May 1991; a four-part documentary series on the effects of the Gulf War on Kuwait, Israel, Egypt, Jordan and on the Palestinian people.

11 The gung-ho tone of reporting was much in evidence in the coverage of further bomb attacks on Iraq in January 1993; see G. Philo and G. McLaughlin, 'ITN passes the Tebbit test', *New Statesman & Society*, 29 January 1993, p. 17.

Part III

Politics and media

Chapter 8

Political news

Labour politics on television*

Greg Philo, Peter Beharrell and John Hewitt

He described a conversation he had had with Tony Benn, MP, in the course of which Mr Benn had re-stated his well-known criticism of the BBC's coverage of politics, claiming it concentrated on personalities rather than politics; that the BBC traditionally inhabited the old centre ground of the man of good will and intent; and that it portrayed this centre ground as being held by people like Jim Prior, Ted Heath and Shirley Williams who were the good guys and girls with whom most of those who worked for the BBC sympathised on a personal level. In doing so, Tony Benn claimed that the BBC was taking sides in a battle going on within the two main parties themselves. [Our correspondent] said he had countered these suggestions vigorously but he had wondered whether there was not a grain of truth in some of them somewhere.

(BBC News and Current Affairs minutes, 13 January 1981)

For this study of how politics is treated on television news we have taken a number of samples. The first comes from the period when the Labour Party was in power and relates closely to our material on economic coverage. It demonstrates how left-wing policies such as Labour's industry bill fared on the news. The second sample comes from the period after 1979 when Labour is in opposition. The political debate here is not only over policies but also about the nature of the Labour Party itself. This study involved a detailed analysis of interview questions, statements made by journalists, and information and comments they have chosen to report. We recorded all television news programmes each night for three weeks in the period following the Labour and Conservative Party conferences (20 October–10 November 1980). The main story in this period was the struggle for the Labour leadership following the resignation of Jim Callaghan. In addition, we

---

*This chapter is abstracted from *Really Bad News*, published in 1982 (London: Writers & Readers Co-operative).

analysed a number of other news and current affairs programmes on later issues such as the deputy leadership campaign, to see whether the tendencies and patterns we had found were constant over a long period.

REALISM AND SOCIALISM

The news has treated the political views and policies of the Right quite differently from those of the Left. Healey's budget in 1975 was presented as a necessary and realistic response to 'high' wage awards. Healey's views and warnings were constantly 'rubbed in' by reference to 'official' information and authoritative sources. Rationality and hard 'realism' are presented as the prerogative of only one view – his. What is apparently the pragmatism of the 'actual' world is set against the 'political' demands of the Left. This view is summarized in this BBC commentary on the budget: 'One of our Westminster staff said criticisms and praise were evenly matched. Right-wingers said the budget was realistic, left-wingers said that it wasn't socialist' (BBC 1, 21:00, 16 April 1975).

The possible rationality of left-wing policies is not explored in the same way. The core of the Left case on inflation and economic decline was that these resulted from the decline in private investment, sometimes referred to (though not on the news) as 'a strike of capital'. There were a small number of references to the problem of investment, but these were greatly outweighed by references to wages and wage inflation. The reasons for the decline in investment (for example, that capital was moved abroad) remained unexplored. In general the decline in investment, where it was mentioned, was treated rather as a natural and unavoidable disaster. The Left's case, that investment is critical to an understanding of both inflation and economic decline, appeared only in brief and fragmented references. There were only three of these in the whole four-month period of our study and all were reports on the views of Tony Benn. He was quoted as follows:

> The Industry Secretary, Mr Benn, today gave his explanation for the country's industrial failure, for which he said working people had become the most popular scapegoats. The real cause was lack of investment, and he said inflation was the result of overpriced goods produced with outdated equipment by underpaid workers.
>
> (BBC 1, 21:00, 25 January 1975)

One solution proposed by Tony Benn was the industry bill of 1975, which was intended to reverse the decline in private investment. Ten days before it was introduced in the Commons, the Department of Trade and Industry produced figures predicting a disastrous fall in industrial spending on plant and equipment. These crucial figures were reported on the television news in January, but significantly were never used to explain or justify the industry bill, which was reported quite separately. On the news, only some warnings are 'rubbed in'. Because the rationality and logic of the Left's case are absent, the news may present it as mere utopian dreaming.

In television coverage of the 1979 Labour conference, the simple assumption that the right wing has a monopoly of 'realism' is again evident. On BBC 2, for example, a journalist commented: 'Two conflicting themes have dominated this conference – the call of principle, the demands of reality' (BBC 2, 23:00, 3 October 1979). This coverage starkly illustrates central features which recur over the following two years. The desire for change towards 'democracy' in the party is shown as the prerogative only of the Left and is represented merely as an attempt at crude control. Through all this runs the media's obsession with Tony Benn.

At the conference a call was made for change in the party's organization: essentially for a shift in power from the parliamentary Labour Party to the national conference and to constituency parties. Inside the Labour Party, there were three sets of opinions on the proposed changes. The right wing opposed them and attempted to dismiss the debates as foolish internal squabbling, fomented by the Left to further their own ends. They demanded party unity, based broadly on the existing party structure and their position within it. The Left case was that internal democracy (and party reform) was necessary to reflect grassroots opinion and to establish an alternative socialist strategy – such a platform had to be worked out before seeking re-election. A third group supported the constitutional changes on their own merit and did not identify themselves with the 'left wing'.

The BBC's coverage pursued the views of the first group – that it was all down to the machinations of the Left. This was, of course, hotly disputed by many in the party. Thus a journalist interviewed Frank Allaun:

BBC JOURNALIST: Can you deny that the object of these reforms is to ensure greater left-wing control of the party, Mr Allaun?
ALLAUN: I certainly do. I say the object of these reforms is to make the party more democratic, so that the parliamentary leaders respond to the decisions of the rank and file.

(BBC 2, 13:00, 1 October 1979)

And a later interview with Eric Heffer:

JOURNALIST: How do you feel that the Left has fared . . .?
HEFFER: Well, I'm not sure you can actually say it's just the Left who want reselection.

(BBC 2, 23:00, 2 October 1979)

There is a notable absence of such questions as: 'Mr Healey, can you deny that your calls for unity are no more than an attempt to avoid criticism of the last government?' A central theme for the BBC was that the constitutional changes were intended to ensure greater left-wing control of the party. The proposals for democracy and accountability appeared merely as a facade behind which the Left could work. One of the key proposals was that the National Executive should have ultimate control over the content of the party's manifesto. Of 17 references made by the BBC to the decision on this, 13 were introduced as either 'another victory for the left wing' (BBC 1, 19:30, 31 October 1979), 'strongly supported by Mr Benn' (BBC 1, 17:40, 31 October 1979) or 'a serious defeat for Mr Callaghan' (BBC 1, 12:45, 31 October 1979). Only two references described the changes as having anything to do with 'democracy' and 'accountability'.

Such coverage has the function of isolating the Left and of downgrading their case. More seriously, it involves a major distortion of the range of views inside the Labour Party. The beliefs of those who favoured reform but who were not on the Left were substantially ignored. This was commented on in *Labour Weekly* by R. Websdale, a delegate who had moved one of the motions for reform: 'I am astonished that the commitment to democratize is viewed as the prerogative of solely the left wing' (5 October 1979).

The amount of attention given to Tony Benn is extraordinary. A range of policies are presented as though they 'belonged' to one individual, rather than having any broad support within the party. On Wednesday 3 October the BBC covered the conference's vote on the Party's manifesto and a speech by Benn (ITN was on strike at the time).

NEWSCASTER: Mr Benn's day at the Labour Party Conference. . . .
REPORTER: Very much Mr Benn's conference, then. . . .

(BBC 1, 12:45)

NEWSCASTER: An ovation for Tony Benn, as the Labour Party conference at Brighton gives the National Executive control over the party's manifesto. The change, strongly supported by Mr Benn, was carried. . . .
REPORTER: So Mr Benn won the two most significant of the three votes he needed to change the balance of power within the Party.

(BBC 1, 17:40)

NEWSCASTER: An ovation for Tony Benn. . . . The change on procedure, strongly supported by Mr Benn. . . .

(BBC 2, 19:30)

While BBC 1's *Nine O'Clock News* bulletin referred only to Labour's 'left wing', the visual display showed Tony Benn on the platform, and the conference delegates applauding. The 'left wing' becomes synonymous with Benn. Even his absence is noteworthy. Interviewing Eric Heffer on BBC 2, a journalist persistently inquired why he, Heffer, rather than Benn was speaking for the Party's Executive:

JOURNALIST: Where is Tony, why is he not speaking in these debates? . . . Are you not surprised to be replying to all these debates, not having Tony or anybody else?

HEFFER: I think the media really has gone out of its way to build up this picture that we're all creatures of Tony.

(23:00, 2 October 1979)

Benn is not given status in the same way as other political figures. On the following day, Healey appeared and was described on BBC 2's 7:30 *News* as 'Shadow Chancellor' while on BBC 1's *Nine O'Clock News*, Benn was referred to simply as 'Labour's leading left-winger'.

THE LEADERSHIP ELECTION, 1980

We began by looking at the range of opinions that existed at that time in the Labour Party, primarily over the issue of internal democracy. There were other issues dividing the Right and Left which were raised briefly, such as campaigns over nuclear disarmament or membership of NATO. But these did not form the basis of major rows in the party at that time.

The second phase of our analysis was to examine which themes were taken up by television news and used to underpin and direct the coverage. The leadership struggle raised key issues, not just over who would win, but over how the leader should be elected. The right to select the leader was one part of the intensive debate which now raged over internal democracy. The 1980 conference had thrust to the fore all the different questions over how each section of the party was to relate to the others. Who was to decide policy? What were the relations to be between the National Executive and the parliamentary Party, between MPs and their constituency parties, between these and the rest of Labour voters, and what was to be the role of unions in the Party as a whole?

To the extent that television news covered these themes it did so almost exclusively from the point of view of the right wing of the Labour Party. We found here, that the news operated against not only left-wing policies, but the presence of the Left in the party as such. They are presented as a persistent source of trouble and problems. What the Left see as demands for democracy and for MPs to be accountable was presented on the news as merely a series of 'threats' and 'undue pressures'. The effect of this was to produce a crude caricature of the Left position and to miss out a whole range of other opinions at the Centre of the party.

The immediate context for this construction was the 1980 conference and the attacks made by right-wingers such as Shirley Williams on alleged 'Left fascism'. The vision of the Left as an insurgent force, variously engaging in 'bullying', 'intimidation', 'blackmail','undue pressure' and 'dictatorship', was a key organizing principle for subsequent news coverage. Broadcasters did much more than merely report the views of the Right. They effectively adopted these as their own, and channelled the flow of information to fit in with them. Such coverage can in no sense be regarded as 'balanced'. On the same evening as Shirley Williams made her statements, other fringe-meeting speakers were underlining what right-wing domination of the National Executive had meant in the past. One speaker recalled how his local party had been disciplined – their crime was that their banner had been taken on a CND march to Aldermaston. There were accounts of blacklists that had operated against left-wingers who wished to stand for election to parliament. The news cameras were present at this meeting: such material could have been used; but autocracy was constructed in the media largely as a prerogative of the Left.

In the whole period of this study there are fourteen occasions when any person or group on the Right was referred to as either 'bullying' or as engaged in 'illicit' or otherwise undemocratic behaviour. By comparison, there are fifty-two occasions when those on the Left are reported as 'bullying', 'intimidating', 'bordering on dictatorship' or in other ways acting undemocratically. There are also a small number of reports carried of the Right and Left denying these accusations.

The Labour Party is in its nature a highly diverse body, in which people and groups with widely differing ideologies are present. But the organizing principle on which media coverage was based presumed that 'entryism' came almost exclusively from the Left. Little or no attention was paid to the activities of right-wing groups which did not accept the party's constitution – except when they are portrayed as the victims of 'intimidation'. There are no searches for 'blue moles'.

Once this general framework is established, then political questions are reducible simply to: is the Left blackmailing and dictating or not? The coverage is then structured to answer this with a very firm yes! What the Left see as requests for information or consultation are constantly presented by TV journalists as forms of intimidation. Interview questions (on both channels) frequently repeat this theme. For example, one major story at this time was concerned with the letter sent by the Labour Co-ordinating Committee to local constituency parties. The letter recommended that MPs fill in their ballot papers for the Labour leadership at the General Management Committees of their local parties after a vote had been taken by Party members. The people who sent the letter argued that members had the right to know how their MP was going to vote, and that s/he should know their views. They denied that this constituted an attempt to 'order' MPs how to vote. Michael Meacher, one of the letter's authors, pointed out that the word 'mandate' had deliberately not been used (BBC 2, *Newsnight*, 20 October 1980). Even if it had, it is not clear why to 'mandate' somebody should be regarded as undemocratic. Still in this case, the Left argument was that they had not wished to go even this far, and that the letter insisted only that there be consultation and open voting. As Tony Banks summarized it in the *Guardian*, 'representatives should not need secret ballots' (22 October 1980). The right-wing opinion of the letter was that it did constitute an attempt to order MPs how to vote, and that this should be regarded as a form of blackmail. If MPs did not represent the views of their local parties, then they might not be reselected. Denis Healey termed this 'a naked appeal to blackmail and fear'.

The view of the right wing was overwhelmingly pursued by the television news on both channels. On only one occasion was the meaning of the letter interpreted by media personnel according to the view of the people who had sent it. On BBC 2 on the 20th it was reported as: 'A letter recommending local constituency parties to summon their MPs to explain how they intend to vote' (*Newsnight*, 20 October 1980). The actual text of the letter was quoted three times. There were ten occasions on both channels when it was interpreted by journalists according to the view of the *Right*. For example on ITN it was referred to as: 'saying in effect that MPs should be made to vote as they are told' (ITN, 22:00, 20 October 1980) and on the BBC as urging: 'the constituency parties to order MPs how to vote in Labour's leadership election' (BBC 1, 17:40, 21 October 1980). Whatever the 'real' meaning of the letter, the view of the right wing was that it should be regarded as blackmail and intimidation. This view is again overwhelmingly represented in the news in reported statements.

There are *three* occasions when the Left was reported as defending the letter, as in this example from ITN: 'The Labour Co-ordinating Committee have defended the letter saying it was only asking for honesty from MPs, not mandating, dragooning or instructing' (ITN, 22:00, 21 October 1980). The Right is reported *thirteen* times, referring to the letter in terms such as 'bullying tactics' (BBC 1, 21:00, 20 October 1980), 'naked blackmail by Mr Benn's supporters' (ITN, 17:45, 21 October 1980) and in headlines such as 'Labour's Right says Left is sending threatening letters' (ITN, 22:00, 20 October 1980). On many news programmes, only the right-wing version is reported. When references to the Left case do appear, they have the status of mere tokens since the news is organized around the Right view in terms of headlines, correspondents' definitions, interview questions and summaries. For example, in this BBC programme the juxtaposition of the two views is preceded by the newscaster defining the letter in terms of MPs being 'told' how to vote:

> Tonight, Michael Meacher MP and other members of the left-wing committee on which Mr Benn sits have replied to a new attack about a letter they have sent to the constituencies. It urges all local party members to tell their MPs how to vote next month. The committee's view: 'We're asking for honesty not secrecy.' Mr Healey's view: 'It's a naked attempt at blackmail.'
>
> (BBC 1, 21:00, 21 October 1980)

It might be noted in passing that Mr Benn does not sit on this committee and has stated that he did not know the contents of the letter until after it had been sent.

News programmes offer only an illusion of balance whereby alternative views are presented as a kind of Aunt Sally to be knocked over in the dominant flow. ITN, on the same evening, has this headline: 'Healey says Left letter was blackmail.' The report runs as follows:

> NEWSCASTER: Mr Denis Healey has launched a fierce attack on the left-wing Labour Co-ordinating Committee who are supporters of Mr Tony Benn. In an interview with ITN he denounced a letter in which they urged constituency activists to tell their MPs how to vote in the leadership ballot as 'a naked appeal to blackmail and fear'.
>
> (ITN, 22:00, 21 October 1980)

This leads to an interview with Healey in which the journalist again pursues the same theme:

> NEWSCASTER: This is what he told [our journalist] earlier today:
> HEALEY: I found that absolutely disgraceful. It was a naked appeal to blackmail and fear....
> JOURNALIST: But it is a real threat isn't it – that reselection – saying that you won't get your job back as an MP – it could swing the balance against you?
> HEALEY: Well, I don't think so. I think many people will be stiffened in their resolve by this naked attempt to blackmail them.
>
> (ibid.)

The interview with Healey is long, but at no point does the journalist take up the Left theme that the whole argument is being used as a smokescreen by right-wing MPs who wish to avoid any form of consultation. After further questions on the new electoral system and why Denis Healey wished to be leader, the final question from the journalist on this news is: 'Do you think Mr Benn is out of touch with the average Labour voter?' After Mr Healey's firm agreement on this, the newscaster returns and finally there is the brief reference to the Left position:

> The Labour Co-ordinating Committee have defended their letter saying it was only asking for honesty from MPs, not mandating, dragooning or instructing. And Mr Tony Benn has said he will only stand for the leadership after the new selection procedures are introduced. Mr Benn told a Labour meeting in London, 'What's happening now isn't a real election. When there is a real election I will be a candidate'.
>
> (ibid.)

In the summary at the close the dominant themes of this news are referred to again. Such summaries and headlines are important, because in them journalists compress what they take to be central in the news. While a number of accounts and comments may be present in the whole programme, only some survive for reiteration. The concluding summary for this news is:

Mr Denis Healey has strongly attacked the left-wing Labour Co-ordinating Committee, who are urging local constituency workers to tell their MPs how to vote in the leadership battle. Tonight an ITN poll shows Mr Healey just ahead of Mr Foot.

(ibid.)

That the news pursues the logic of one set of political beliefs is shown very clearly in the structuring of interviews. Journalists sometimes claim that they deliberately play the part of devil's advocate and ask 'oppositional' questions to whoever is being interviewed. This is supposed to provide lively television and vigorous probing of issues. But in the case of this story, it did not happen. The same assumptions were overwhelmingly pursued whether a right-winger was being interviewed or a left-winger such as Michael Meacher. He had appeared on the BBC 2 *Newsnight* programme the previous day. This item is introduced as follows:

And Labour's far Left gave another stir to the Party's troubled waters tonight. They were calling on constituency parties to insist on ordering their MPs to write in their choice of Labour Leader on his ballot paper. I will be talking in a moment to the left spokesman, Mr Meacher, and to an MP on the right of the party, Mr Mike Thomas.

(BBC 2, *Newsnight*, 20 October 1980)

The interview is introduced with a quote from the letter and a reported statement from David Owen:

INTERVIEWER: Dr David Owen has tonight attacked the letter. The former cabinet minister and leader of the right-wing Campaign for Labour Victory called on all candidates to condemn it. It was not the time, he said, for weasel words. He said: 'The letter fulfills all our worst fears about the tenuous nature of some people's commitment in the Labour Party to representative democracy.'

Well now, Michael Meacher, can you tell us, some MPs might accept, quite a lot of them, that they are accountable to their constituency parties. Are you now saying that they must quite simply take orders from you?

MICHAEL MEACHER: We are not saying that at all. There is no question of a mandate, the word mandate isn't used and we are not recommending there should be a mandate on MPs.

(ibid.)

All the questions put to Meacher follow the same assumptions. The two which follow are:

But in the discussion here it says he must present his ballot paper to the GMC to be filled in after a vote has been taken. After the vote has been taken, must he fill it in with the name of the candidate being voted?

And later:

> When you say the CLP activists will of course be fully aware that the conference endorsement of reselection will herald a new era of cooperation – does that mean that you think that the constituency should somehow threaten the MP? If he doesn't vote the way they want him to, they should sack him?

When the interviewer turns to the right-wing MP, his question is: 'Now Mr Thomas, are you going to take your ballot paper to your constituency management committee and ask them how you should vote?'

Mike Thomas replies that he will not and that when he casts his vote it will be as a representative of 18,000 Labour voters in his constituency. The only time that a 'left-wing' question is asked here is when, after this, Michael Meacher intervenes and takes on to himself the role of interviewer.

> Can I ask Mike Thomas how he proposes to take the view of 18,000 members in his constituency. I mean is that not really a complete fiction and doesn't it really mean that the right wing of the party wishes there to be no discussion really with their constituency party or even if there is discussion to go away secretly afterwards and do exactly what they think themselves?
>
> (ibid.)

There follows a heated discussion between Meacher and Thomas, with each accusing the other side of being undemocratic. Into the fray steps the interviewer and once more channels the discussion into a 'right' framework, in a further question to Meacher:

> INTERVIEWER: To take up on Mr Thomas's earlier point, you talk about a wider franchise. Why are you going back to your constituency now to ask them how you should vote for the leader – on talking to only 20 or 30 members of your local Labour Party. Why not to the thousands of them . . .?
>
> MEACHER: I would very much hope we have a meeting when thousands of people will come, but let me say this about the GMC, so far from being – I don't know what it is in Newcastle East, it isn't a smoke-filled room in Oldham – it is a representative group.
>
> (ibid.)

Such coverage establishes a very specific image of the Left. It comes to be associated with 'trouble' as naturally as Leyland comes to be associated with 'strikes'. The first sentence of the above report establishes the theme: 'And Labour's far Left gave another stir to the Party's troubled waters tonight'. The powers of darkness are assembling and we are being warned. From the same bulletin we have: 'Within the lower reaches of the Party tonight . . . there is a darker mood.'

In this coverage the alleged influence of Tony Benn is a pervasive theme. The politics of the Labour Co-ordinating Committee – on which he does not sit – are denoted by a series of references to him.

He was angry about a letter from the left-wing Labour Co-ordinating Committee *in which Mr Tony Benn is involved.*

(BBC 1, 21:00, 20 October 1980)

The Labour Co-ordinating Committee, *a group close to Mr Benn*, have sent a letter. . . .

(BBC 2, *Newsnight*, 20 October 1980)

A committee *closely associated with Mr Tony Benn urges the constituency* parties to order MPs how to vote.

(BBC 1, 17:40, 21 October 1980)

Tonight Mr Michael Meacher and other members of the left-wing committee *on which Mr Benn sits* have replied to a new attack.

(BBC 1, 21:00, 21 October 1980)

The letter sent by *Mr Benn's friends* in the Labour Co-ordinating Committee. . . .

(ITN, 17:45, 21 October 1980)

The left-wing Labour Co-ordinating Committee *who are supporters of Mr Benn.* . . .

(ITN, 22:00, 21 October 1980)

'And to ensure a balanced and impartial discussion of the latest government measures, I have with me a government spokesman and a wild-eyed Trot from the lunatic fringe.'

In chapters 1 and 2 we showed that in industrial and economic coverage the pattern of how to understand 'strikes' and 'wage claims' is laid down very thoroughly in some parts of the news. Later the constant monitoring of these makes sense without having to be actually told all the time that wages = inflation. If a newscaster says, 'and now another wage claim' we can be expected to know what is implied. The references to who is involved with Tony Benn operate in a similar fashion. Television takes its cue from the press and performs the major function of pointing out what Benn is involved in and who knows him. Of course there is nothing wrong in reporting what Benn or any other politician is doing, but in these cases the labels and the commentary are used as a substitute for debate. There is no real analysis of what is going on in the party or who is arguing for which policies. Instead we have simply the latest 'trouble' from the Left and Benn. The story is not initiated as an account of the Labour Co-ordinating Committee or its intentions, but is rather the latest set of complaints about them.

THE LANGUAGE OF STRUGGLE

The television news acts as a compère when describing conflicts within the Party, but is clearly standing on one side of the ring. If the Left win then the language may be of trouble and turmoil. For example, the events of the 1980 Party conference were described on BBC 1 as: 'The Labour Conference has been plunged into turmoil tonight over the dramatic result in the way Labour's leader is elected' (BBC 1, 21:00, 1 October 1980). But if the Right hold off the 'trouble', 'turmoil' and 'stirs' of the Left, then the story may be told quite differently. In the period of our study, there are a number of arguments between Labour's National Executive Committee, which had a left-wing majority, and the parliamentary Party, which was more to the Right. In one such conflict, the Left argued that the leadership election should be delayed until after the new electoral college was set up. The outcome of this struggle is referred to quite differently: The 'moves' of the left wing are now being 'thrown out'.

> Well, it's almost certain that the party's MPs will throw out the NEC call for a delay.
>
> (BBC 2, *Newsnight*, 22 October 1980)

> It is almost certain that when Labour MPs meet next Tuesday, they will throw out the NEC's proposal.
>
> (BBC 1, 14:00, 22 October 1980)

> Labour MPs have thrown out moves by the left wing to postpone the Party's leadership election.
>
> (BBC 1, *Late News*, 28 October 1980)

The words 'move' and 'bid' are much more frequently used to describe the actions of the Left than of the Right. In isolation these words cannot be taken to prove anything. But their use in the overall context of the coverage is part of a pattern in which the Left is presented as an insurgent force, against which others 'firmly assert' their rights:

> NEWSCASTER: A *left-wing move* to make public the way MPs vote was also defeated. Here is our political correspondent. . . .
>
> JOURNALIST: By defeating *left-wing moves* to postpone the election Labour MPs have *asserted firmly their right* to choose their own leader whatever the rest of the party does.
>
> (ITN, 22:00, 28 October 1980)

The NEC is not referred to as 'firmly asserting its rights'. It simply 'wants to put off the leadership election' (BBC 1, 19:00, 22 October 1980). In such coverage, 'left-wing moves', 'trouble' and 'domination' go together quite effortlessly. The following day, the National Executive is again reported as arguing with the parliamentary Party.

> The *left-wing dominated National Executive* had rejected pleas by . . . Mr Denis Healey and Mr Michael Foot that Labour MPs should be given more time to express their views on how the Party leader should be chosen in future.
>
> (BBC 1, 21:00, 29 October 1980)

The word 'domination' takes on a very specific meaning in such a context. It is not used to mean anything so simple as having a 'majority'. In the whole of the period analysed, *only* groups identified as left-wing are referred to as 'dominating'. Thus we have the 'left-wing-dominated National Executive', 'the left-wing-dominated constituency parties' (BBC 1, *Nationwide*, 20 October 1980) but 'heckling from the right-wing majority' (ITN, 28 October 1980).

One reason why the words 'domination' and 'left-wing' go together with such ease in this coverage is that the views of the right wing on 'intimidation', etc., are featured much more often and more prominently than the views of the Left in headlines, summaries and especially interview questions. After the meeting on 29 October when the Left on the NEC had 'rejected' the 'pleas' of Healey and Foot, there is a statement to camera by the right-winger David Owen. He argues on BBC 1 that the National Executive is 'bouncing' the conference and is thus acting undemocratically:

> The parliamentary Party have no view other than the decision they took before conference against an electoral college and the general feeling is that we are being bounced, into a situation in which the NEC comes forward with model resolutions much too soon without genuine consultation with the parliamentary Party.
>
> (BBC 1, 21:00, 29 October 1980)

The view of the Left is, as we have seen, that it is the parliamentary Party who wish to avoid consultation. David Owen is not questioned on this by the interviewer, but rather his version is taken up and used as the basis for questioning others leaving the meeting.

> INTERVIEWER: Some of the shadow cabinet think they are being bounced.
> NEIL KINNOCK: I think one or two of them always say that. They seem to be extraordinarily bounceable. I don't think anybody was bounced on either side or in any respect whatsoever this morning, and it would be fiction for anybody to say that they were being bounced.
> INTERVIEWER: [*to Michael Foot*] Some members of the shadow cabinet feel they have been bounced this morning.
> MICHAEL FOOT: Well, I don't know. I don't answer such questions as that because you are putting words in their mouths and you are not putting any in mine.
> INTERVIEWER: You don't feel bounced?
> FOOT: No, I don't feel bounced.
>
> (BBC 1, 21:00, 29 October 1980)

The ITN main news that night concluded its section on the meeting with the statement from David Owen. It follows the latest odds on the leadership candidates and a brief interview with Michael Foot.

> NEWSCASTER: . . . Mr Healey did everything he could to look the confident favourite today as he went to the joint NEC shadow cabinet meeting. Mr Peter Shore was unruffled though the smart money says he could be the first to go, or if not him, Mr John Silkin, but Mr Foot seemed happy.
> FOOT: I am always optimistic. Nothing could ever make me anything other than optimistic.
> INTERVIEWER: One commentator put you this morning as favourite.
> NEWSCASTER: The shadow cabinet were unhappy. Dr Owen said he felt MPs were being bounced.
>
> (ITN, 22:00, 29 October 1980)

The statements by Michael Foot and Neil Kinnock, which contradict this view, are not included here.

The following night ITN again highlights the theme of Left 'intimidation'. The trailer at the end of the first half of *News at Ten* states: 'Mr Michael Foot, standing for the leadership of the Labour Party, says MPs should not be intimidated by their constituency parties. He talks to us in Part Two' (ITN, 22:00, 30 October 1980). What has happened is that both the main contenders to the leadership are being pressed by journalists into commenting on the alleged 'activities' of the Left. In an interview shown on this ITN news, Michael Foot replies by specifying the rights of each section of the Party. His exact words are as follows:

Members of Parliament have got the right to exercise their judgements – that's what they are there for. They have got the right to exercise their judgements in their choice and selection of their leader and their deputy leader and their Parliamentary Committee and they know how to do that and I'm against any form of intimidation against them doing their job. Of course they can consult with their General Management Committees and most of them do, and their General Management Committees have got a right to say to them 'We want you to consult us', but the Member of Parliament must exercise his own rights and I'm sure Labour members are going to do it.

(ibid.)

It is this reply that has been represented as his saying, 'MPs should not be intimidated by their constituency parties on how they vote'. The selection of his words tends in the direction which the news is systematically pursuing. From the same text he could just as easily have been reported as saying, 'Michael Foot has reasserted the rights of constituency parties on consultation with MPs'. But ITN has chosen to highlight criticisms of the Left, just as on the previous day it concluded the NEC report with the comments of David Owen.

The chosen theme in discussing the constitutional issue is this 'unreasonable pressure'. The interview questions put to Michael Foot on this were as follows:

[1] INTERVIEWER: [Are you] a bridge builder, a peacemaker inside the party?
FOOT: Well, yes, but not a caretaker. . . .
[2] INTERVIEWER: Are you the sort of man who can be *pushed about by the Left* inside the party if they pushed you into standing against your will?
FOOT: They didn't push me into standing against my will. . . .
[3] INTERVIEWER: If you are a bridge builder in the Party, is there not a real struggle going on to control Labour MPs, by the Party outside, and can you avoid taking sides on this?
FOOT: Members of Parliament have got the right. . . .
[4] INTERVIEWER: More specifically they have an absolute right to vote for whom they like in this election.
FOOT: Of course they have that right. . . .
[5] INTERVIEWER: There was a recent letter that suggested that local parties might reselect or sack an MP who went against their wishes.
FOOT: No, I'm against such a proposition and this is a distraction.
[6] INTERVIEWER: [Is it] unreasonable pressure?
FOOT: Yes of course. This is a complete distraction. . . .

(ITN, 22:00, 30 October 1980)

'Are you the sort of man who can be pushed about by the Left . . .?'

Not all of these are in fact questions. The fourth is a statement about the rights of MPs and the second simply assumes the behaviour about which questions are apparently being asked. The BBC also pursues the same theme in an interview a few days later. In all this, Michael Foot is in an invidious position, since the clear implication of some questions is that he is in receipt of 'dirty votes'. These supposedly come from illicit behaviour and 'intimidation' – the existence of which the media has done so much to establish.

> INTERVIEWER: Many MPs have been asked very openly by their con-
> stituencies how they will vote in the election. A lot of that pressure has
> been in your favour. *Do you accept that a significant number of your votes
> may have come from this pressure, and if so are you happy with that fact?*
> FOOT: No, I'm against any form of intimidation. . . .
> INTERVIEWER: What do you say to any MP who is under *this sort of
> pressure*? What should he say?
> FOOT: An MP in my opinion should consult with his local party . . . but he's
> not there to be dictated to by his local party. He must use his own
> judgement. . . .
> INTERVIEWER: He should use his own judgement even if he runs the risk of
> reselection and losing that afterwards?
>
> (BBC 2, *Newsnight*, 4 November 1980)

By such processes of highlighting, selection and endorsement, the news gives credibility to one account over others. There is an almost total absence on the news of the point of view that 'this sort of pressure' might be quite reasonable or democratic. Whatever the parliamentary Party thought, there is no doubt that many people in the constituency parties believed that MPs should be subject to a democratic mandate. The senders of the LCC letter maintained that all they were asking for was an open discussion. But even if they had suggested a mandate it would not be acceptable for 'neutral' media to promote the view that this was 'undue pressure' and 'threats'. One news programme did film, without comment, a local party meeting (BBC 2, *Newsnight*, 30 October 1980). It showed quite clearly the stark difference between the normal media view and that of many local members who argued simply that Labour MPs should represent the views of the Party. It showed also an intense and rich debate on the nature of the Party, its history and what it was to become. It raised many questions and issues on the Right and Left which were absent from the rest of the news: Was Healey a monetarist? Could any of the candidates be trusted in the face of patronage and secrecy in parliament? The range and depth of the arguments put into sharp relief the shallowness of the rest of the coverage. Nearly half of this in our sample was taken up with predictions and questions on who was going to win and the latest odds from Joe Coral, rather than the issues that the election was about. This one programme was so startling because it violated a pattern in which, when issues *are* discussed, journalists see them through the eyes of the right wing of the parliamentary Party, and peer downwards with curiosity and some alarm at the 'pressure' from below. The news is effectively being orchestrated around this view, which is tacitly and sometimes explicitly endorsed. There is a great difference between asking someone their opinion and simply *assuming* that people 'threaten' or 'push others about'.

Chapter 9

The media in a class society*

Greg Philo

INTRODUCTION

The work from which this chapter comes was originally written in 1981. In it we examined some of the key factors which shaped the development of media in our society. We suggested that the historical division between capital and labour was important in understanding the ideological struggles which informed media content. This division was also important in explaining the growth of particular types of media such as the early radical press. Other divisions such as that between competing sections of capital were also significant. This competition had produced the search for new markets, sources of labour and raw materials. The establishment press had developed largely to provide 'news' about these. Such foreign news was especially important for information such as the price of commodities or the dates of shipments. There are other crucial social divisions such as those of gender and ethnicity. The inequalities in these areas had radical effects, both on the staffing of media institutions and on the relative access of different groups to the media.

IDEAS AND INTERESTS

The mass media have had a critical role in the battle of ideas over how our society is to be explained and how the key relationships within it are justified. The defence of relations of private interest has sometimes rested on the assertion that the normal workings of the market economy will somehow benefit everyone within it. This is the ideology of 'consensus'. The problem with such a view is that the normal logic of the system does not promote equilibrium but produces crisis and conflict on a large scale. Of course, when this occurs it has to be explained. But the economic mechanisms which regularly produce basic conflicts and decline are not routinely discussed as an

*I would like to acknowledge the help and comments of John Hewitt and Howard Davis in preparing the original drafts of this chapter.

explanation of problems such as unemployment and inflation.

There is a clear example of this in our analysis of the coverage of the 'troubles' of British Leyland. The distribution of profit as dividends did not merit a headline, even though 95 per cent of the profits over a four-year period were distributed in this way. Lost production and economic decline were attributed to the workforce. There were no headlines saying: A MILLION JOBS THREATENED BY HUGE DIVIDEND PAYOUT. And there was no routine referencing of the movement of capital away from productive industry. The consequences of such a movement and price increases were again laid at the door of working people. Figures on inflation were prefixed by figures on wage claims, but the amounts that insurance companies, pension funds and merchant banks have moved away from productive industry were practically ignored (in 1980, pension funds alone moved over £1,000 million into the buying of property). Recession, inflation and unemployment, if they are not being blamed on wage claims, were in the period of our study most likely to be treated as natural disasters. The world economy is presented as a kind of omnipresent force, and movements in it (balance of payments, exchange rates, cheap imports, etc.) are the problem, but these movements are rarely explained for what they actually are – simply people making money in the most effective way they can. A multi-national firm may be reported as regrettably being forced to close a factory in the north of England because it is uneconomic, but will not usually be spoken of as having made a *decision* to move its capital somewhere else because it can make more money there. The leaders of business and government appealed to the collective interests of the 'nation' below and struggle constantly to create consensus.

This ideology permeates not just the privately owned media, but became the accepted wisdom in all the major social institutions, for example, in the education system as well as in public broadcasting. The BBC developed in close relationship with the state and under Lord Reith it came to embody in its language and programme content a form of liberal capitalist ideology. In practice this was the belief that the class system was basically sound and that as long as working people 'knew their place' they were capable of improvement by gradual exposure to 'high culture'. The benign aspect of this ideology was revealed as a veneer in the General Strike of 1926. Statements by Lord Reith, who was Director-General at the time, are very revealing about the role of broadcasting when class relations and class antagonisms become overt. A critical issue in the strike was whether the state should commandeer the BBC and run it as a propaganda agency in defence of the 'public' interest. Lord Reith opposed this and sought formal autonomy on the grounds that the BBC could fulfil the required function more effectively as a politically independent body. In the end, the state and broadcasting reached a mutually acceptable compromise which exists to this day. Reith commented in his diaries: 'The cabinet decision is really a negative one. They want to be able to say that they did not commandeer us, but they know that they can trust us not to be really impartial' (Reith, 1975: 96).

At this time, and throughout the early years of the BBC, journalists were disciplined and socialized into a distinctive style and ethos. Professor Tom Burns writes in his history of the organization:

> Throughout the 1930s the BBC was ridden with a tight rein. Mild as the incursions by commentators into foreign politics and genteel as discussions between political figures were, there were frequent occasions on which objections were raised in the House and in the press to what were labelled errors in editorial judgement or lapses in taste. Such occasions reinforced the propensity of the chief officials of the BBC to prove themselves even more 'reliable'; and, as ever, self-censorship proved to be the most effective form of censorship.
>
> (Burns 1977: 17)

One of the lapses in taste which Burns cites concerned a BBC producer who was disciplined by the Director-General. He was warned never again to commit so serious an error of judgement as to allow hunger marchers to speak on the radio and say what they thought of the government. The Talks Department, which carried programmes on the condition of the unemployed in the 1930s, allowed people to speak for themselves. This brought down a torrent of criticism from the government and what had been a genuine attempt at social investigation on radio gave way to less contentious programmes.

The BBC came to embody a view of the world from the perspective of the powerful. The extent to which the population at large is likely to acknowledge the correctness and legitimacy of this view will vary according to the period, the state of the economy and the level of class antagonism which exists. At the start of the General Strike, for instance, the TUC warned its members against believing the BBC. In the periods of most intense social conflict there have appeared radical alternative media with substantial audiences. It is important to examine their origins and struggle for survival in the face of commercial competition.

RADICALISM AND CONSERVATISM

The radical press in the 1830s formed around trade-union struggles and programmes for political change. Although it was illegal and subject to intensive persecution by the state it had a much wider readership than the establishment press of the time. One paper, *The Destructive*, carried this editorial which stated the aims of the new press:

> Some simpletons talk of knowledge as rendering the working classes more obedient, more dutiful.... But such knowledge is trash; the only knowledge which is of any service to working people is that which makes them

more dissatisfied and makes them worse slaves. This is the knowledge we shall give them.

(Harrison 1974: 103)

The radical press has grown and declined more or less in relation to the periods of radical agitation in our society. The *Daily Herald*, a labour paper, had in the 1930s one of the biggest daily circulations in the world. The demise of the *Daily Herald* shows very clearly the problems of sustaining a radical press in the face of commercial competition. It was constantly drained by the fact that a mass-circulation paper depends substantially on advertising. For the quality press has not received anything like this kind of subsidy, partly for political reasons and partly because its readership has been too poor to be of much interest to advertisers. There have been many direct political interventions by such interests. The *Daily Herald* suffered constantly from lack of advertising and collapsed even though it had a readership of 4.7 million. It is clearly easier to sustain a radical press in periods of intense political and social agitation because working people are prepared to pay more for it and go to greater lengths to obtain it. The mass-produced establishment press is always likely to be cheaper. It is backed by large capital and even if it makes a loss can be subsidized by large corporations for their own interests. It is in periods of political and social calm, either after major defeats or in periods of economic boom, that the radical press has had the most difficulty. At such times the existing order is likely to be regarded by most people as legitimate, or at least unavoidable.

In any case, some subordinate groups are likely to see themselves as having a vested interest in the existing order. People who work for finance capital in the traditionally more secure occupations, in banking or insurance, have not been as severely hit by the recessions which have affected industrial manufacturing. Even among productive workers there are divisions between 'skilled' and 'unskilled' which are reflected in different attitudes at work and to employers. The 'unskilled' unions when they first developed were very radical, while those of the 'skilled' workers tended to defend the privileges that they had won without seeking a major change. Other groups have also come into being whose whole existence depends on the maintenance of the *status quo*, for example, the forces of the army and the police and large sections of the civil service. These sections of the population are more likely to concede the legitimacy of the existing order, but nevertheless their consent cannot be taken for granted – it has to be worked for.

Political conflict and agitation is always in a 'more or less' state. One effect of consensual ideology has been to make it less rather than more. But this ideology is not something handed down by a 'ruling class' to quiescent and gullible working people. To make sense to the mass audience, even to its more conservative sections, it has to connect with the things that people have struggled for – with their real beliefs and aspirations. Consensual ideology has therefore been closely connected with the major concession of the welfare state and the notion that economic and social management can gradually modify the worst excesses of market capitalism. This idea, that all social and economic problems have a solution, reached a height under the Conservative administrations in the boom and affluence of the 1950s. It appeared to many that living standards for all social classes would gradually improve and that consumerism would replace radicalism. In this period the state had become responsible for the orchestration of this new relation between labour and capital. There was to be no 'them and us' anymore, and each worker might expect a house and a car and, if all went well, eventually a cocktail cabinet that lighted up. From this period all parties were committed to growth and full employment – a commitment which is now having to be abandoned as the economy has moved once more into recession. However, until recently, the provisional and temporary nature of this accommodation of interests was rarely recognized, and its normal underlying strains and stresses were ignored: they were no longer supposed to exist.

CONSENSUS IN TROUBLE

This is the contradiction that faced public broadcasting in the early 1980s. It was committed to an ideological perspective which founded on the view of consensus, 'one nation' and 'the community', while having to report phenomena which could not be fitted easily into this framework of understanding. The broadcasters attempt to relay ideas which are already more or less present and interpret them for what they see as a 'mass' audience. But to secure this consensus they had to make sense of new and difficult social and economic trends like unemployment, investment collapse and inflation. This involves giving meaning to events, facts and figures by providing explanations, stating causes and by editorial comment.

The change in government to the Conservatives in 1979 is a good illustration of the problem the media face in maintaining a coherent, consensual view. This was difficult enough with the economics of Healey and the Treasury, but at least the social contract had a semblance of being an 'agreement' with something in it for everyone. But the BBC was distinctly unhappy with the politics of the New Right and the rise of Thatcherism. It is difficult to say 'we are pulling together' in the face of unemployment, poverty and recession.

KEEPING IN LINE

The development and fine-tuning of consensual ideology can be related in part to conscious policy decisions by senior broadcasters. The state of news broadcasting is monitored from above. Its direction and content are sometimes subject to quite direct interventions, and this is shown by the minutes of senior committee meetings at the BBC. A complete set of these was leaked and reprinted in *The Leveller* magazine. In these, the top management discuss, for example, how a new phase of economic crisis might mean new restrictions on news output:

> The Editor of News and Current Affairs said that at the present juncture stories about this country's currency needed careful handling ... he was inclined, for the first time in his career to suggest that they should always be checked first with the Treasury.... It would be wrong in the present circumstances to put out a major news story of which the Government had no warning.
>
> (*The Leveller*, January 1978: 15)

Such direct and overt interventions are comparatively rare in most areas of reporting. The official line is likely to emerge and be changed through much more informal processes, such as the routine contacts between journalists and civil servants. Journalists are highly dependent on Whitehall as a major source of information, especially on the economy, industry and foreign affairs. Press briefings in this context are likely to be manipulative and journalists who do not toe the line are subject to the ultimate sanction of not being given information. More importantly, the routine working practices of journalists are informed by the class assumptions of the society in which they live, that some people are more important than others and have a greater right to speak. In an article in the *New Statesman* the Glasgow Media Group expressed this as follows: 'When television journalists want to know something important about the economy or industry, it seems natural to them to ask an "important person": a senior civil servant would fit the bill, or a government minister' (*New Statesman*, 6 April 1979). Two weeks later, Richard Francis, the director of news and current affairs at the BBC, replied to our article and simply reaffirmed what we were saying. He wrote: 'the BBC's journalists do indeed find it natural to ask "an important person" – a senior civil servant or government minister, for instance – for they are the people whose decisions largely determine how things will be run in our democracy' (*New Statesman*, 20 April 1979).

The fact that most of the sources that journalists consult in the Treasury, Whitehall, the Department of Employment, the Foreign Office, etc., are all *unelected*, but still wield great power in their own right, had apparently passed him by. Even if they were elected, their views on policies would still only be political *opinions* and should not be treated by journalists in the manner that Moses received the tablets at Mount Sinai. This assumption about who has the right to speak and what is an important information source means that quite contentious information, about how the economy is working and what might be done about it, can be packaged and presented as merely factual. As we show in the case study of economic reporting the latest statistical information on the 'causes' of inflation was presented routinely alongside the latest *political* view by a cabinet minister or a chairman of the Price Commission (see chapter 2).

ECONOMIC INTERESTS

Alongside such specific pressures on the content of the media there are clearly some which emerge from material interests. The pressure for programmes which make money is seen at its purest in the history of US television. In the 1950s companies that were sponsoring programmes actually complained about television drama which showed people living fulfilled lives in spite of being poor. To be happy without commodities was regarded as fundamentally un-American. In addition the demand for high audience ratings at the cheapest cost has led to 'formulae' for producing long-running series with the same basic characters and plots. If one was a 'success' in the ratings then others like it would follow. Single plays were taboo, since anything which 'ended' meant that viewers would change channel and perhaps not come back. Thus we have *Dallas* and *Crossroads* which go on for months or years, with each show having a dramatic 'hook' at the end, so that viewers will turn on next week.

The tedium and repetition of formula westerns, detective stories and comedy shows comes because they have in the end to be basically the same. This is so that people can pick up the plot when they switch from channel to channel as the adverts come on. Central characters frequently repeat what has happened so far, since in the US there are very frequent advertisements. The idea is to 'catch' people as they move channel. Hence on *Star Trek*: 'Captain's log, star date 10/5, we have landed,' etc. Such pressures affect British programming, since commercial companies here are also searching for ratings, and more significantly are making major series with the intention of exporting them to the US market. The style and content of programmes is affected when television is run simply as one part of a business conglomerate.

Although economic interests are important the institutions of the media and certainly of public broadcasting cannot be seen as merely relaying ideology from the state or private capital. The media institutions and the journalists they employ do have some autonomy. They usually wish to claim that their reportage is accurate and trustworthy, although as we show in the case studies of our original work the unconscious political assumptions which they hold produce selection and distortion which often invalidate these claims. Still, the journalists certainly do not see themselves as being passive mouthpieces, and at times actively dissociate themselves from establishment figures. But such arguments are likely to be conducted on an individual level: the media may challenge politicians but not the political or economic system. In the same way it may look at 'isolated' abuses in the economy – it may investigate 'pockets of poverty' or the effects of unemployment in a single area but not usually the nature of the economy which produces these.

CONCLUSION

In our 1981 study we made three specific criticisms of contemporary broadcasting. First, it did not reflect the existing range of views in a balanced fashion. It neglected whole areas of opinion – upgraded some and down-graded others, even within the range of 'sanctioned' debate. Second, broadcasting was undemocratic in its choice of who was allowed to speak and who was defined as important. Unelected officials such as senior civil servants were routinely consulted. This was not a 'balanced' reflection of a democratic consensus. Broadcasters operated hierarchies of status and importance which were informed by class assumptions. Low-status individuals were filmed differently and their opinions were often sought simply as a back-up to the dominant view or as brief unsubstantiated comments in relation to it. Women were rarely interviewed in 'serious' news programmes. A high proportion of news coverage of women was likely to be about either the Queen or Margaret Thatcher. These assumptions on who had the 'normal' right to be consulted meant that the broadcasters had difficulty in dealing with grassroots movements.

Finally, by seeking to process information within what they took to be the consensual view, broadcasters violated their own cannons of accuracy and impartiality. There is a range of arguments about how the economy and society work, which cannot be resolved merely by an appeal to what most people think. Their resolution clearly depends on empirical evidence: for example, on whether wages really are ahead of prices, and if they are, does this mean they are causing inflation? The selection and editing of information to fit a dominant view cannot be justified by saying that this view is held by a number of 'important' people.

REFERENCES

Burns, T. (1977) *The BBC: Public Institution, Private World*, London: Macmillan.
Harrison, S. (1974) *Poor Men's Guardians*, London: Lawrence & Wishart.
Reith, J. (1975) *The Reith Diaries*, ed. E.C. Stuart, London: Collins.

Chapter 10

Political advertising and popular belief*

Greg Philo

In understanding public beliefs about politics we must analyse how political parties have used the media. The crucial issue is how successful they have been in establishing strands of political belief which make sense and 'work' with voters. Of course, the media can distort political ideas and report stories in a way which is partial or simply untrue. But I want to suggest that the dominance of the New Right in the 1980s and Labour's electoral failures cannot be adequately explained in such terms. Rather, Labour was much less efficient than the Conservatives in developing coherent political ideas and making them into a form of popular consciousness. If we think back over this period, it is not hard to make up a list of popular political phrases which explained Conservative political thinking: 'there is no alternative', 'a shareowning/homeowning democracy', 'popular capitalism', 'enterprise culture', 'the miracle economy', 'one-sided disarmament'.

But if we try to make a list of political phrases associated with the Labour opposition, it becomes clear very quickly that it cannot be done. There are certainly general areas where the Labour Party 'scores' better in popular judgement than the Conservatives, such as on health or welfare benefits. But this is because of Labour's traditional policies towards these issues. There are no 'Labour phrases' from popular political debate which are comparable in the sense that they explain immediately what the Conservatives are doing wrong and what Labour would do about it.[1] This is much more than saying that the Conservatives had the best sound-bites. The importance of such phrases is that they can act as key elements of political consciousness. They can form a sort of template through which people interpret their own experiences and desires (see Philo [1990] for a study of the interaction between media messages and audiences). They can also affect how people interpret new information from the media (e.g. reports of trade-union influence in the Labour Party or those suggesting rapid economic decline if Labour is elected).

*This chapter was originally published in *Media Culture and Society*, vol. 15 (1993), pp. 407–18.

The purpose of this chapter is to explain this absence of 'Labour phrases' and to show its consequences – both in electoral failure and in the much broader problem of Labour's inability to develop an alternative public consciousness.

THE CONTEXT

There were four elements in the history of the monetarist experiment of the 1980s which were crucial here. The first was the use of revenues from the oil industry. In the 1970s, when oil was discovered in the North Sea, there had been great popular expectations about the use of the revenue for the regeneration of industry and the rebuilding of the social and economic infrastructure. That this was not done was perhaps the greatest failure of the 1980s. The equation of wasted oil money and unemployment is not accurate or perfect as economic analysis but as a tool for shaping political understanding of the economy it works very well. The second element, linked to this, was the destruction of approximately 20 per cent of manufacturing industry between 1979 and 1981. This could have been imprinted into collective historical memory with every bit of the force of other events such as the 'Winter of Discontent'. As it was, the Labour Party was so preoccupied with its own internal dissension and the breakaway of the Social Democratic Party in 1981 that it was unable to form a coherent and lasting response. But though the impact of the economic destruction on political views was tremendous at the time, it was then allowed to pass from our political memories. It was not made into a persistent focal point of Labour's political advertising and broadcasting.

The third element follows from the weakness of manufacturing and the consequent inability of Britain to compete in international markets. In 1983, for the first time in its industrial history, Britain imported more manufactured goods than it was able to export. This unhappy 'record' for New Right policies should also have been fixed in the political equivalent of neon lights. There was then the outstanding difficulty that, when any economic upturn did occur in Britain, many of the necessary machine tools and high-quality engineering products would now need to be imported. But because elements of economic understanding were missing from routine public knowledge, the Conservatives were able to make the crucial conceptual jump of presenting unemployment as a sign that the economy was getting *better* rather than as a sign of its structural weakness.

The fourth element is the period of economic expansion before and after the 1987 election. The crucial moment occurred when manufacturing output finally returned to its 1979 level. It was a high point of the 'bubble economy' produced by the increase in personal credit, financial deregulation and the pumping of money into the economy through increased state spending, cheap shares and tax cuts. Here, the absence of a critical, interpretive framework for understanding the economy had a crucial impact on the Labour Party's ability to win popular support. This was most obvious in the elections of 1987 and 1992. Research at Glasgow University by Professor Bill Miller has now shown that in the 1987 campaign over half the population believed that the Conservatives were 'best on economic matters for themselves and their family' (Miller *et al.* 1990). They had in fact a 25 per cent lead in this over the Labour Party. Why was the Labour Party so unable to contest this area?

LABOUR'S IMAGE PROBLEM

There were several reasons in the early 1980s why the Labour Party's ideological message was diffuse and confused. After the electoral defeat in 1979, there was an intense and acrimonious debate between the right and left wing in the Party, and in 1981 a right-wing faction split from it to form the Social Democratic Party. The Labour Party did not have a well-developed communication strategy in this period and this, combined with the trauma of the splits and divisions, affected its ability to offer clear messages. It was apparent at the time that many professionals within the Party actually preferred the messages of Party broadcasts to be bland rather than to risk upsetting one or other of the factions. By the 1983 election, the Labour Party was still in confusion. The political opposition to the Conservatives was divided with the emergence of the Social Democratic Party who were now in alliance with the Liberals. Conservative support had meanwhile been solidified by the Falklands War and Mrs Thatcher was re-elected, but with 600,000 fewer votes than in 1979. Labour's electoral defeat produced a new leadership in the Labour Party and a decisive change was made in its communications strategy. Labour chose the 'dream ticket' of Neil Kinnock as leader and Roy Hattersley as deputy on the assumption that they would unite the Party and be electorally acceptable to the 'middle ground' of voters. Labour had watched the grooming of Margaret Thatcher's television image by Gordon Reece, her media adviser, and the hiring of Saatchi and Saatchi by him to advertise their message. The Conservatives had also set up a sophisticated communications machine run by Cecil Parkinson for the 1983 election (which could, for example, co-ordinate all major Conservative speakers to focus on a specific issue for a single day). In response, the Labour Party brought in Peter Mandelson, an ex-television producer, as their director of communications. They believed it was time to promote and control the images which the public were to associate with the Labour Party. To achieve this they decided to give a new authority to communications and advertising professionals, who were now brought in to form the Shadow Communications Agency. The minutes of a 1986 campaign strategy meeting (24 February 1986) record the decision:

A paper from the Director of Campaigns and Communication was before the meeting. In it, he referred to the need to secure sound professional support for future Campaign Communications activity and the availability of a range of outside expertise to meet this need. It was proposed to structure this expertise in the form of a Shadow Communications Agency.

It was a fateful decision since it moved Labour into the direction of promoting images, rather than ways of understanding. The Party leadership had misunderstood the strength of the Conservative position. Beneath the glossy packaging which the New Right had used, there were two very powerful elements. The first was a relatively coherent ideology that could seem to make sense, whatever its disastrous potential effects in practice. The popular phrases deployed by Mrs Thatcher concerning 'the wealth-makers' and 'not taxing successful industry and commerce' and 'rewarding effort' had a strong resonance in the culture of the Conservatives' 'natural' supporters in the middle and lower-middle classes.

The second strength was the actual relationship which the Conservatives enjoyed with the 'wealth-owners', i.e. those who controlled the industrial and financial economy. If Labour abandoned the ideological territory of the economy, then the claim of the Conservatives to be the obvious Party to manage this area would be strengthened – especially since they were the stated preference of the 'business class'.

None the less, Labour pressed on with its new direction and the red flag became the red rose. One of the key factors influencing this move had been a BBC *Panorama* programme made by Michael Cockerell, called *The Marketing of Margaret*. It was broadcast shortly after the 1983 election and it contrasted the new communications machine of the Tories with what it portrayed as the shambles of the Labour campaign. John Underwood, the Labour Party director of communications after Peter Mandelson, reflected thus upon the programme's effect:

> The Cockerell programme did have a profound impact. There was a very strong feeling that Labour had to take on these communications developments. There is no question that in the 1987 election they used professional communication techniques for the first time. This was behind the rise and rise of Peter Mandelson. . . . The story of 1983 to 1987 was that it was the flight not just from ideology but from policy. Neil Kinnock and Peter Mandelson spoke constantly of transforming the *image* of the Labour Party.
>
> (interview, July 1992)

In this period Labour's new communication strategists believed that Kinnock and his wife were a youthful and glamorous couple who could be marketed in something approaching a presidential style. Hence, in the run up to the 1987 election there were triumphal rallies with stars such as Glenda Jackson introducing Kinnock as 'Britain's next Prime Minister'. A special Labour broadcast was commissioned to promote Kinnock, dubbed by some as 'Neil and Glenys – The Movie'. It was made by Hugh Hudson (director of *Chariots of Fire*) and is described by Cockerell as 'a vaseline-lensed biography of the Labour leader, with musical accompaniment' (1988: 323). The projection of the positive Kinnock image continued in fact right up to the 1992 election with what one editorial referred to as 'Mr Kinnock's relentlessly orchestrated round of babies, balloons and beaming bounds' (*Guardian*, 9 April 1992).

The strategy did not succeed in terms of establishing Kinnock's credibility with a wide public. But the promotion of him in this way had other important consequences. The intention was to give him a bouncy up-beat image. He had to be associated with brightness and success, so pictures of bleak industrial landscapes or economic destruction were thought to be inappropriate. Labour thus began to vacate the crucial territory of how the population understood their own history. They did it in favour of a philosophy appropriate only to influencing short-term consumer purchases. These issues were discussed with senior Labour Party figures at different times through the 1980s. In a letter to us, Brian Gould, the Labour spokesman for trade and industry, spelt out the approach and the difficulties of stressing 'bad news' on the economy: 'Our problem is that no one thanks the bringers of bad news and it is very hard to get the communications strategy right without appearing "whingers"' (14 January 1988).

It is interesting that Gould should use the word 'whingers'. In the 1980s this had become a catchword of the New Right and was used repeatedly by them to criticize the doubters in their own Party. It is symptomatic of how much ground the Labour Party had lost that the word should enter their own vocabulary as a potential description of themselves.

In the event, Labour's bouncy images were no match for the actual economic growth which the Conservative Chancellor Nigel Lawson had produced before and after the 1987 election. In June 1988, Peter Shore, the veteran Labour politician very frankly acknowledged that 'on economic and external policy, there is not the sense of confidence we [once] had' (Channel 4, *Week in Politics*, 24 June 1988).

There were other factors in 1987 which may have contributed to Labour's election defeat, such as the confusion over their defence policy and the obvious divisions which still existed in the Party over this. But the decision to focus on projecting positive images rather than winning ideological or policy battles was crucial – not least because it continued to form the Labour approach in the following years. The key decision-makers in the Party actually believed that the 1987 campaign had been a success, but that the Party had been held back by the 'negative' associations which it still had for some key groups of voters. The main negatives were seen as the unilateralist defence policy and the continued presence of the left-wing 'Militant Tendency'. As John Underwood commented: 'The period after 1987 was about removing the negatives – dumping unpopular policies rather than replacing them with anything else. . . . But the first rule of communications is that you can only tell the truth better' (interview, July 1992). His point was that the image techniques and getting the lighting and camera angles right could not make up for the absence of policy. By the end of the 1980s the Labour Party had actually reduced the areas which could clearly differentiate them from the Conservatives. As John Underwood observed: 'After removing all the negative policies by 1992, in marketing parlance, the party had lost its U.S.P. [Unique Selling Point].' He also pointed to the irony of John Smith's alternative 'budget' which was presented to the media just before the 1992 election. It was based on a clear political philosophy and was redistributive in the sense of moving wealth from the top of society to those most in need. As such, it was one part of the counter to New Right thinking which Labour could have developed through the 1980s. But by this time the political framework to understand it in this way was no longer present in popular political debate. Instead of understanding it in terms of its principle and intention, the budget was discussed in terms of its details, i.e. how many people exactly would be better off. In John Underwood's words:

> The Smith budget was redistributive – but there was no over-arching vision of the future into which the budget fitted. Arguments about it came down to its details rather than what it was for. Was John Smith right that eight out of ten would benefit or were the Tories right that people would all pay £1,200 extra tax?
>
> (interview, July 1992)

It was a long time since the leaders of the Labour Party had spoken out clearly about who owned the economy and of the parameters of wealth. In Britain, the great bulk of private wealth is in fact owned by the top 20 per cent of the population. But in seeking the elusive 'middle ground' the Labour Party had substantially moved away from rhetoric which raised issues such as class or private ownership.

THE 1992 ELECTION

The election of April 1992 was closely fought and more difficult for the Conservatives than in 1987. But once again, Labour lost the election largely because key groups of voters decided that they could not trust Labour on the economy. Larry Whitty, the Labour Party general secretary, concluded in his report on the defeat that 'Fears of high tax plus the general unease about our economic competence or general distrust of the party and its leadership took their toll' (report to Labour NEC, June 1992). Another report by David Hill, the party's director of communications, acknowledged the power of Conservative strategy in establishing elements of popular consciousness over a long period of time:

Our major long-term problem appears to be the fact that we carry too much baggage from the late 1970s and early 1980s to persuade people that they can fully trust us.

Even though many of those voting were very young during these times, *they have been subjected to constant reminders.*

(June 1992, emphasis added)

The key failure in Labour's approach was the absence of such 'constant reminders' of the crucial economic moments of the 1980s. That is not to say that there were no inputs from Labour throughout that period. There were comments and speeches from politicians such as John Smith, Brian Gould and Gordon Brown on issues such as the balance of payments and the low level of growth and investment. But in the millions of political words spoken in this period, the Labour effort was essentially at the periphery. There was no major drive to build an alternative popular understanding of what had gone wrong and what was to be done about it. This also highlights a key difference between the British and US elections of 1992. In the USA, the Democrats destroyed the Republicans by focusing relentlessly on the economic failures of Reagan and Bush. In the Labour Party *Manifesto* of 1992, there was no discussion of the Conservative economic record.

From 1987, the Labour Party sought to remove what were seen as the negative elements affecting voters and to stress the positive associations that the public made with the Party (for example the National Health Service). The assumption was that by keeping all of the positive elements dancing before the consumers' eyes, the product would take on an acceptable 'glow'. But political decisions and beliefs are more complex than consumer purchases. It is possible to change the colour of a soap-powder packet without the public seeing this as an expression of bad faith. But those changes in Labour policies designed to increase its market appeal (for example on defence) were actually seen by voters as evidence that the Labour leadership was untrustworthy. This was a clear result of opinion research conducted after the election in the marginal constituencies of areas such as Essex (Fabian Society 1992).

Stressing the 'positive' elements also neglects the underlying frameworks of understanding which people use to interpret new political information. For example, the underlying belief might be that a good health service or education system requires a sound economy. If so, there is no point in stressing simply health and education even if the market research shows that the Party does 'well' on these issues. The consequences of using an advertising philosophy for political selling had not been thought through. As one senior Labour Party worker from the Shadow Communications Agency remarked ruefully in an interview (July 1992): 'You went hard on the things that you think will win you votes. But you can never do enough on health to make up for the economy.'

Labour and 'economic competence'

Labour had focused much of its propaganda effort on the personal qualities of Neil Kinnock and the Conservative leader, Margaret Thatcher. The intention was to praise the first and to damn the second for having a personal style which was autocratic and domineering. An approach based on personalities was one result of the flight from ideology and policy. It was necessary to focus on the superficial qualities of the product, because the deeper social and political arguments had been largely ruled out. The Conservatives, therefore, confused Labour greatly when they dropped Margaret Thatcher as leader in 1990 and brought in the more 'moderate' John Major. The Conservatives still had serious problems, but they enjoyed one decisive advantage over Labour: this was the close relationship which they had with the business class – the owners of financial and industrial capital. It has always been Labour's problem to argue convincingly about what they would do in the face of the unremitting hostility of this group. How could Labour manage, control or change the capitalist economy? In each election that Labour had won since 1945, they had provided an answer to this. Under Attlee in 1945, it had been that they would take over key sections of the economy and run them in the public interest. In 1964, Wilson had some success in portraying the traditional political and economic establishment as being incompetent. It would be Labour that would introduce the 'white heat of technology'. Later, in 1974, Wilson had presented the political leadership of the Conservatives as socially divisive after two miners' strikes and the three-day week and state of emergency introduced by Edward Heath. According to Wilson, a Labour policy of social consensus would get the economy moving again and the country back to work.

But by the end of the 1980s, the Labour Party had no answer as clear as any of these. They had missed the opportunity of labelling the Conservatives with fearful images of social division (such as the street riots of 1981). On the crucial question of the economy, Labour's approach was to develop links with the business class and to try to show that Labour was competent in economic management. This point was made very clearly by Brian Gould in a Channel 4 broadcast in 1987 in which he set out his views on the future of the Labour Party:

> We have to show that we can produce wealth as well as arguing that it should be better used and more fairly distributed. What we have to do is to show that Labour knows how to run the economy – and do it more efficiently than the Tories.
>
> (Channel 4, 19:00, 25 September 1987)

In the period before the 1992 election, John Smith embarked on an extended programme of developing contacts in the City. From 1990, he visited merchant bankers, brokers, dealers and industrialists in the City of London in what was referred to in the Labour Party as the 'Prawn Cocktail Circuit'. Labour's *Manifesto* for 1992 conveyed the general sentiment of this with the headline 'A Government which Business can do Business with' (Labour Party, 1992: 11).[2]

But there is a fundamental problem for Labour if it becomes closely associated with the interests and preferences of the business class. What happens when that class makes it clear that it already has a political party which it prefers, and predicts economic chaos at the very mention that Labour might be elected? It was this which gave the Conservatives a decisive advantage and in pressing it home they had key allies in the media.

The media link

By the end of the 1980s, financial and City news had become central areas of media reporting, especially on television. This was one consequence of the dominance of the Conservatives and their promotion of the merits of share-ownership, entrepreneurs and business-dealing in general. Consequently, movements in the City were routinely reported and 'experts' from merchant banks and finance houses were consulted for their apparently neutral opinions on the latest trade or financial news. This gave them an important status as 'impartial' commentators.[3] 'Good news' for them and for television was a healthy stock market and rising shares. In electoral reporting, the preferences of the City were made absolutely clear by referring to such share movements. On ITN, when Labour took the lead in opinion polls the City sounded near to collapse:

> NEWSCASTER: Billions of pounds were wiped off the value of shares this morning, as the City, which traditionally prefers Conservative governments, took fright at the clear Labour lead in opinion polls.
> INDUSTRIAL CORRESPONDENT: It was headlines like these [refers to headline in *The Times*] showing Labour pulling into the lead which helped to turn City dealing room screens red. At the start of trading this morning billions of pounds were wiped off shares.
>
> (ITN, 12:30, 1 April 1992)

The BBC told a similar story, reporting that 'In the City worries about a Labour victory pushed share values down sharply' (BBC 1, 18:00, 1 April 1992). Such coverage has a long history. Before the 1987 election, the 'good news' for the City was that the Conservatives were taking the lead: 'The Tory lead in the polls may be wafer thin but it's good enough for the City where dealers and investors are in confident mood. Share prices are going up and up' (BBC 2, 22:25, 6 February 1987).

If the City and the business class are seen as crucial movers in economic health, then such coverage must help the Conservatives. This is especially so if there is no counter-ideology providing constant reminders of the damage which the Conservatives and the City have actually done to the economy. In this sense virtually all of the media could be seen as operating against the interests of Labour merely by reporting the movements and intentions of this class in the face of a Labour victory. For example, the *Guardian* (26 March 1992) reported on its front page about the movement of millions of pounds out of the country: 'Millions of pounds are leaving Britain with every opinion poll that puts the Opposition ahead, winging out via electronic transfer systems to all points of the compass.' The article pointed out that £870 billion, or half of the total personal wealth (excluding houses) was controlled by just 5 per cent of the population and that: 'By freighting a large proportion of this mobile capital abroad, the rich are reducing further the spending power in the economy.' A large transfer of capital into other currencies would also mean a run on the pound with an incoming Labour government pushed into putting up interest rates. The *Guardian* would not of course draw the same political conclusions from this as the right-wing press. But this analysis is not so different from the front-page 'warnings' in papers such as the *Daily Mail* (7 April 1992) 'WARNING: A Labour government will lead to higher mortgage payments. There is no doubt about it. Interest rates will rise within days of Kinnock entering Number Ten.' This was also the sense of the *Sun*'s message on its election-day front page: '*If Kinnock wins today will the last person to leave Britain please turn out the lights*' (9 April 1992). We can find other versions of such warnings on television news, in this case from a City expert speaking on ITN: 'If Labour were to win, I think people would be worried about public spending, public borrowing and what might happen to the exchange rate' (ITN, 12:30, 1 April 1992). It is no surprise that opinion poll research after the election showed serious worries among some voters about Labour's economic competence.[4]

One of the questions raised at the time of the 1992 election was whether the media were responsible for Labour's defeat. The answer is that they must be seen as contributing to it since the issue of economic competence was so crucial. Shortly before the election, opinion polls showed Labour at approximately 40 per cent of the popular vote and the Conservatives at around 37 per cent. The actual result gave the Conservatives 41.9 per cent and Labour 34.2 per cent. The 8 per cent of voters separating the two parties might well have been influenced by the media, once these people were confronted with the possibility that an 'incompetent' and 'untrustworthy' Labour Party would actually be elected. But there is another point which underlies this – the responsibility which Labour had for the formation of its own image. Throughout the 1980s it had vacated key areas of political argument and in the end had no answer to those who moved against them, who are a very small proportion of the electorate. The crucial issue for Labour is why it went into the election with only 40 per cent of the vote. In thirteen years of government the Conservatives had achieved a series of 'records' unparalleled this century on riots, crime, unemployment, the destruction of manufacturing and the trade balance, as well as major controversies over health, education and the poll tax. When the Conservatives had first come to power in 1979 Labour had achieved 37 per cent of the vote. Yet after thirteen extraordinary years the Labour vote was still only 34 per cent. It is clearly not enough for Labour to blame the tabloid press for its defeat. We cannot make judgements about the impact of media without analysing the input of Labour itself. Some of the crucial decisions which made the Party unelectable came from within it.

AFTER THE 1992 ELECTION

The Labour Party still confines itself to discussing the economy in terms of the European Exchange Rate Mechanism (ERM), managed exchange rates, shadowing currencies and the other technicalities of fiscal policy. But public understanding of such issues appears to be very limited. Our past research on television audiences has indicated this and so have our recent pilot studies of public knowledge of the economy. The bulk of the population can, however, understand that the economy must be rebuilt and that this may need radical government intervention. Indeed, they may well expect it, since there is a widespread belief that it is the 'job' of governments to make the economy work well. There is also some general understanding of the basic ideas on the need for efficient industries, for education, training and new technology as well as the development of transport, construction and communications. This is why the threatened death of the coal industry in late 1992 was so elemental and struck such a chord in public consciousness. It was symbolic of the decline of Britain and was understood in a way that the failure of the ERM is not. The collapse of the Conservative economic programme should have been good news electorally for Labour. But in practice, the public is now confused on the key economic issues because Labour did not develop a media strategy to highlight the failures of the economy in the 1980s. Instead of using the media to establish key elements of popular understanding about what was going wrong and what should be done, they relied instead on the shallow science of imagistics.

POSTSCRIPT: 'MODERNIZED' LABOUR AND POLITICAL POWER

Since the 1992 election, the Labour Party's modernizers under Tony Blair have inherited this communications-policy strategy and are now taking it to its logical conclusion. This is that the Labour Party is now unable to present a plausible political programme which would clearly distinguish it from the Conservatives and which could make sense of the dramatic social and material changes which concern its own potential supporters. In the absence of such a programme, Labour is increasingly in a position where only its sound-bites, its image and its general posture as 'the opposition' distinguish it from the Conservatives. This is in part a communications problem in the sense that Labour has not used its political advertising to explain the failure of monetarism or the impact of this on the social fabric and therefore what would need to be done to rebuild a socially oriented economy. But it is also a crucial policy question, for in eliminating the 'negatives' and seeking legitimacy with the City and business classes, the modernizers have limited the range of policy options which are available. For example, a persistent criticism of the British economy has been the lack of organic links between financial and industrial capital and specifically that the City pursues its own short-term interests to the detriment of industry. This view has recently been popularized by Will Hutton in his best-selling volume *The State We're In* (London: Cape, 1994). As he recently commented in the *Guardian*:

> British finance is still haunted by the gentlemanly preoccupation with deals and making money rather than making things; and the disdain for the 'provinces', 'manufacturing' and 'technology' runs very deep. Put it all together and Britain looks surprisingly as if it is regressing to the mid-19th century. A Conservative oligarchy exploits the semi-modern state to hand out favours and patronage, while the financial system scours the world for the highest return as its own industrial hinterland falters.
>
> (*Guardian*, 17 February 1995)

It is not easy to see how the Labour Party in its present trajectory could form concrete policy proposals on such a question. In the absence of clear alternative policies, Labour must rely on popular dislike of the Conservative government and on projecting a desirable 'image' to the electorate. This has led to criticisms from both the Right and Left of the political spectrum that the Labour Party has become a 'sound bite opposition'. As Ian Aitken has recently written:

> The shadow cabinet is now so anxious to avoid an identifiable policy on anything beyond the amendment of its own constitution that it finds it impossible to exercise the one function that justifies its presence at Westminster. If so, it gives some credence to Mr Major's assertion that this is a sound bite opposition.
>
> (*Observer*, 11 February 1995)

The *Sun* put the case more forcibly, arguing that there was now little difference between Labour and Conservatives on policy issues, and very acutely noted a potential danger for Labour:

> Who'll be the next Prime Minister. . . . Tony Major or John Blair? More and more, it's becoming hard to tell them apart. . . . There's only one danger in Blair's tactic; voters may well prefer the real thing to the imitation.
>
> (*Sun*, 16 February 1995)

This convergence is in part a consequence of the decision to remove socialist policies which were deemed to be unpopular. One ironic result of this has been that when there is popular discontent at the effects of a Conservative policy such as privatization, it is difficult for Labour to comment, without revealing the contradictions in its own position. By the beginning of 1995, privatization had become a major political issue following revelations on high pay awards for the directors of the once publicly owned industries such as British Gas. A Gallup poll in the *Daily Telegraph* of 3 February 1995 showed majorities of 70 per cent and above in favour of restoring industries such as railways and water to public ownership. Following further revelations on the high profits of British Gas, polls reported in the *Daily Mirror* showed that 'electors are now more concerned about greedy bosses than unemployment, rising crime, NHS cuts or the crisis in schools' (24 February 1995).

The Labour Party, however, following its own communications and policy imperatives was at this time involved in an intensive argument over whether it should reduce its commitment to public ownership. As Keith Waterhouse noted in the *Daily Mail*:

> What privatisation now means, in the public mind, is a license to print money to pay the bonanza salaries and other jackpot benefits of chief executives. Privatisation is now private in the sense of hands off, keep out. And Tony Blair chooses this moment in history to tour the country persuading the brothers and sisters to ditch Clause 4. Some sense of timing.
>
> (*Daily Mail*, 6 February 1995)

On 23 February Tony Blair was widely reported as attacking British Gas for boosting its profits by cutting 11,000 jobs and closing gas showrooms. Such tactics were denounced by him as 'the unacceptable face of privatisation' (BBC 1, 18:00, 23 February 1992). This is a good sound-bite but avoids the key issue of what is the 'acceptable' face of privatization for Labour. When these industries were privatized, Labour did not offer a vociferous, principled opposition or mount major campaigns in support of public ownership. In practice, around 20 per cent of the population actually purchased shares. The Labour Party could therefore have argued that 80 per cent of the population were being deprived of the ownership of key industries, the profits of which should go into public spending. Now that the industries are privatized and Labour is arguing for a strong private sector, it is disingenuous to complain that they are acting like others in the 'free market' by cutting jobs to boost profitability. The executives of the new companies have justified their own actions in exactly these terms. In classic liberal economics the individual firm makes its decisions on the basis of its market position and the social costs of this are irrelevant. It is not hard to see, for example, that a private electricity company may wish to obtain gas as a power source at the cheapest market price. If this then has devastating effects on another British industry (i.e. coal) then this is really not its concern. Similarly the chief executives of the once public industries are likely to want salaries which they regard as being at the level of the private sector. These are exactly the sort of issues which originally led to the belief that the logic of economic markets had to be controlled in terms of social priorities. If the Labour Party does come to office on a tide of public indignation at the practical effects of 'popular capitalism' then it will have to face the real problems involved in forcing social priorities on to a market economy. In this real world without public ownership of key industries, good sound-bites and imagery will not be enough.

NOTES

1   We put this point to John Underwood as a former Labour Party director of communications. He agreed and said that the only 'Labour phrasing' he could think of was terming the 'community charge' the 'poll tax' and referring to health-service changes as 'privatizing'. But as he said, the tangential nature of these phrases actually confirmed the general point.
2   Labour's *Manifesto* also contained positive policies in developing investment in manufacturing, in research and development and in skills and training. But such proposals remain empty phrases unless they have a resonance in a strong popular understanding about what has gone wrong and what corrective measures need to be undertaken.
3   Peter Golding noted of his own study of the 1992 election that 'a MORI poll last month showed that 90 per cent of top financial executives would be voting Conservative. Yet this particular group of analysts ... are called upon with increasing regularity as neutral analysts in election news' (*Guardian*, 6 April 1992 and Loughborough University Communications Research Centre).
4   A study of 'floating voters' by John Curtice of Strathclyde University for the BBC 1 programme, *On the Record*, showed a Conservative lead over Labour before the election of 18 points, on the issue of 'the Party best able to handle economy'. Just after the election, this lead was measured at 41 points.

REFERENCES

Cockerell, M. (1988) *Live from Number 10*, London: Faber & Faber.
Fabian Society (1992)*Qualitative Research Amongst Waverers in Labour's Southern Target Seats*, London: Fabian Society.
Labour Party (April 1992) *Election Manifesto*, London: Labour Party Publications.
Miller, W. et al. (1990) *How Voters Choose*, Oxford: Clarendon Press.
Philo, G. (1990) *Seeing and Believing*, London: Routledge.

Chapter 11

Television, politics and the rise of the New Right

Greg Philo

The Glasgow Media Group began its research in 1975. In retrospect this can be seen as a high point in the period of postwar social consensus. Harold Wilson, the Labour Prime Minister had initiated the social contract between the government, industry and the unions, which was intended to regulate wage claims and inflation. We showed in our research how television news endorsed the government's view on this and how the social contract fitted the social-democratic and consensual ethos of television. This ethos with its assumptions about social hierarchies, rights of access for the powerful and the routines of parliamentary democracy meant that broadcasters often viewed extra-parliamentary and grassroots agitation from the unions or the Left of the Labour Party with some suspicion. The purpose of this chapter is to outline subsequent developments in the media and in political communications and to illustrate them with material from our later research. The last twenty years have produced an extraordinary series of changes to our society and to its broadcasting institutions. The fracturing of consensus politics and the dominance of the New Right have been key factors in this. Journalists work within new institutional and legal constraints, while politicians are more than ever concerned to control and package the flow of information into the media. What are the consequences of these changes for an independent and critical journalism? This is by no means an exhaustive account of the period, but there are important tendencies which can be identified.

In 1979, the Conservative Party was elected under Margaret Thatcher. From the turbulent political period which followed, there are three key issues which we will analyse here. The first is the sustained attack on broadcasting which was mounted by the Conservatives in the 1980s. This antagonism, especially towards the BBC, followed from the key differences between the philosophies of the New Right and of traditional social democracy. The second is the extensive use which the Conservatives made of the media and public-relations techniques in promoting their new policies and political ideology. Third, we will look at the comparative weakness of central government in the early 1990s following the fall of Margaret Thatcher. This weakness of the centre had important consequences for broadcasting, since in some ways it strengthened the position of journalists. Yet the social structure within which they operated as well as the legal and commercial basis of broadcasting had all been decisively changed.

TELEVISION AND SOCIAL DEMOCRACY

In chapter 9 we argued that broadcasters did not take easily to the ideological perspective of the New Right. Television and especially the BBC were imbued with the politics of consensus. Since World War II, the BBC had seen itself as an authentic national voice, both representing and appealing to the values of the 'whole' population. In this sense it had a vested interest in a politics which might unite the nation. The ethos of such a politics was broadly liberal, humanist and social-democratic. The essence of this social-democratic approach was to minimize the harmful effects of a capitalist free market. These had been starkly illustrated by the economic recession and unemployment of the 1930s. The social costs of this period had led to intense political agitation and to the demand that the experience should not be repeated. The film *Love on the Dole* from the novel by Walter Greenwood provides an interesting example of the political changes in this period. All through the 1930s government censors had stopped the making of the film. But in 1941 it was finally produced and featured Deborah Kerr as the young woman who sells herself to escape from poverty and to get work for her family. As the *Sunday Pictorial* wrote when it appeared:

> Time after time, our censors have waxed apoplectic at the suggestion that ... *Love on the Dole* was a fit subject for a film.... If every man and woman in Britain could see this film, I don't think we would ever go back to the dreadful pre-war years when 2 million men and women were allowed to rot in idleness.

> (quoted in Richards 1986)

The film concludes with a quote from A.V. Alexander: 'Our working men and women have responded magnificently to any and every call made upon them. Their reward must be a new Britain. Never again must the unemployed become forgotten men of peace' (*Love on the Dole*, British National, 1941). This spirit was also reflected in parliament with Labour and some Conservative politicians supporting demands for the 'new Britain' in the postwar period. In February 1943, parliament debated the Beveridge Report which laid the foundations for the welfare state. The Conservative MP, Quintin Hogg (later Lord Hailsham), addressed his own party in the House of Commons as follows:

> Some of my hon. Friends seem to overlook one or two ultimate facts about social reform. The first is that if you do not give the people social reform, they are going to give you social revolution. The maintenance of our

institutions has been one of the principles of the Conservative party from time immemorial. The wise man who said that the maintenance of our institutions was the first Conservative principle made the improvement of the condition of the people the third. . . . Let anyone consider the possibility of a series of dangerous industrial strikes following the present hostilities and the effect it would have on our industrial recovery.

(Hansard, 17 February 1943: 1818)

After the war, in 1945, a Labour government was elected with a majority of 148. British politics then entered a social democratic and consensual period which lasted through a succession of Labour and Conservative administrations until the end of the 1970s. The essence of this political approach was to reduce class conflict by providing social services such as free education, health, social security and housing. It also included a sustained commitment to full employment with a high degree of state intervention in the economy and the public ownership of control of national industries. This would mean in theory that resources were reallocated from the top of the society towards its lower sections. This assumption was endorsed by Conservative governments and leaders such as Harold Macmillan. The Cabinet Papers from 1961 show the Chancellor of the Exchequer, Derek Heathcot Amory, calling for a moderation of profits as well as wages. As he notes: 'Labour costs are not the only problem, it is right that all should share in the benefits of increasing productivity' (Heathcot Amory 1961). Edward Heath, as Conservative Prime Minister in 1972, made his own statement of 'one nation' Toryism: 'In the kind of country we live in, there cannot be any "we" or "they". There is only "us", all of us' (quoted in Morely 1981: 373).

The election of Margaret Thatcher as Conservative Prime Minister in 1979 signified a major departure from such politics. The consensual state had assumed (at least in theory) a reallocation of resources from the top towards the lower sections of society. The approach of the New Right put this process into reverse. The intention was that state spending would be reduced on social services and that the government would no longer intervene in industry to promote full employment. Specifically, they would no longer subsidize failing industries. Indeed the 'monetary' conditions would be set (through, for example, high interest rates) whereby many firms would be hard-put to survive. Employees would, therefore, have to accept whatever wages were on offer or suffer the consequences of their firms going bankrupt. After the 1983 election in Britain, this political programme was developed to encompass the selling of profitable public industries into private hands. Another key area of New Right policy concerned the trade unions who were expected to oppose these political policies and to resist the lowering of wages. They were weakened by new laws and by the use of state funds to defeat them in specific conflicts (e.g. financing the use of oil-fired power stations to defeat the miners' strike of 1984/5). The new process of distributing resources would be completed by substantial tax cuts for the better-off, who would in practice also benefit by purchasing shares in the new private industries at very low rates and by using their economic position to benefit from the share and property markets. With such incentives, it was claimed that a new spirit of enterprise and growth would be released into the economy and there could eventually even be a 'trickle-down effect' which would benefit the less privileged.

The New Right approach clearly implied redistribution towards the better-off. But at the end of the 1970s, the strength of postwar consensual values was still such that this element of New Right philosophy was not at the forefront of Conservative political statements. Instead, the focus initially was on general tax cuts, the promise of economic efficiency, rationalization, stopping bureaucratic waste and combating the alleged dire effects of trade unions.

BROADCASTING AND THE NEW RIGHT

In practice, after 1979 the new Conservative government pursued a policy of high interest rates and a strong currency with the aim of reducing inflation. This created market conditions which were very difficult for the manufacturing industry. By 1983, manufacturing capacity had been seriously cut and unemployment had risen to over 3 million people (from 1.5 million in 1979). The issue of unemployment raised crucial differences between the philosophy of the New Right and earlier politics. For the consensual state, full employment was a major priority and a serious rise in the number of unemployed would be seen by all political parties as a failure of policy. But from the perspective of the New Right, unemployment was caused by factors such as the restrictive practices of trade unions, and crucially by workers not accepting the appropriate wage level. In the theory of the free market, those who were unemployed should move away from failing industries and seek work in the new businesses which (theoretically) market opportunities were creating. But the new Conservatives had difficulties in highlighting these views because of the extreme sensitivity of unemployment as a political issue. Consensual values were still strong and unemployment was widely seen as the responsibility of the state. Norman Tebbit, the Conservative Party chairman came near to stating the New Right position at the National Party Conference in 1981, when he implied that the unemployed should not complain or riot but 'get on their bikes' as his father had done and look for work: 'I know those problems. I grew up in the 30's with an unemployed father. He did not riot – he got on his bike and looked for work and he kept looking until he had found it (Tebbit 1981: 3).' And he listed the 'causes' of unemployment:

So put it together: recession; other nations fighting to take our markets; overmanning; pay rises out stripping productivity year after year; profits, the seed corn of future jobs, being robbed and looted to pay unjustified higher wages; a bad record of industrial disputes; and ... the Employment Protection Act, too, cannot always help in these matters. In the face of that is unemployment a surprise?

(ibid.: 6)

This speech was widely publicized and created a storm of controversy. So much so, that the 'on your bike' reference became part of political folklore. The coverage which television gave to unemployment was therefore a major potential irritation to the Conservatives. Because it was such a sensitive issue, the criticisms which were made of broadcasters were not as overt as in other conflicts. But they can be seen, for example, in the allegations made by the Media Monitoring Unit, on bias in broadcasting. This unit was established with the help of Lord Chalfont, who wrote the introduction to its first report:

There is a widespread belief in political circles – although this is not necessarily shared by the general public – that news and current affairs on television are neither objective nor impartial, and that they are, in fact, persistently biased in favour of the Left.

(Clark, 1986: ii)

Lord Chalfont was widely seen as a prominent right-wing figure and was later appointed by Margaret Thatcher to be deputy chairman of the controlling body for independent television, the Independent Television Commission. As Michael Cockerell writes:

To most broadcasters, Lord Chalfont had few redeeming virtues. A former Labour junior minister, he had moved steadily to the hard Right. On his own admission he saw the BBC as a nest of 'Communists, militants and left-wing agitators of all persuasions'.... He was a leading figure in a string of right-wing pressure groups set up to counter 'left-wing subversion' in the media and elsewhere.

(Cockerell 1989: 348)

The reports issued by the Media Monitoring Unit were very critical of television content. Each programme viewed was given a classification to denote possible 'bias'. It is interesting that two documentaries which dealt with unemployment (on the closure of steel works and on Cornish tin mines) are classified by the unit as 'programmes attacking the Right and promoting the Left' (Clark 1986: 13, 31). Programmes such as *World in Action* and *Panorama* are also criticized:

A two-part *World in Action* report entitled 'State of the Nation' compared the fortunes of three families from contrasting backgrounds from the early 1950's to the present day. The two programmes were unremittingly negative in their view of Britain today.... In typical fashion *Panorama* contrasted the fortunes of the 'haves' and 'have nots' in Harold

Macmillan's old Stockton constituency but concentrated on the plight of the 'have nots'.

(Clark 1988: xi)

We might recall the state papers of Harold Macmillan's Conservative government which suggested that his cabinet might have regarded an emphasis on the 'have nots' as quite appropriate. In this sense the conflict between the government and broadcasters in the 1980s came not because journalists had moved to the Left, but because the Conservatives had moved to the Right. This conflict was also apparent in other areas such as defence and foreign affairs, where the new Conservatives pursued strong interventionist policies and developed a close relationship with the USA. The British fought a war with Argentina in 1982 and supported the bombing of Libya by the USA in 1986. Both these events produced major public conflicts between the Conservative Party and the BBC.

PRESSURING THE BROADCASTERS

At the time of the Falklands War, the BBC was criticized by Conservative MPs and by the right-wing tabloid press for not being supportive enough of 'our' side (see chapter 5). Alan Protheroe, Assistant Director-General at the BBC from 1982 to 1987, gives his own account of the type of news which would have pleased the critics:

> Their ideal for the 9 o'clock news would have been a man in uniform backed by the Union Jack. The signature tune would have been replaced by the National Anthem and it would have been a kind of Ra, Ra, Ra news bulletin. It would really have been the dirty Argentines and the proud British – which of course is ... farcical – and I'm not exaggerating too much when I describe it that way.
>
> (speaking on World in Action, 29 February 1988)

There was a series of conflicts over specific programmes and what was seen as the detached style of the BBC. In May 1982, the managing-director of BBC Radio, Richard Francis, defended the Corporation while speaking to the International Press Institute in Madrid. His remarks were widely reported and they are interesting because they highlight exactly the difference between the two approaches: 'The widow of Portsmouth is no different from the widow of Buenos Aires. The BBC needs no lesson in patriotism' (quoted in Harris 1983: 83).

The Conservative critics could not accept such a comparison precisely because one widow was on 'our' side and the other wasn't. This division between 'their' victims and 'our' victims occurs again in the Conservative attack on BBC coverage of the US bombing of Libya in 1986. Norman Tebbit, as Conservative Party chairman, produced a report which criticized the structure and language of the BBC news. He asserted that coverage of the effects of the bombing was in Libya's interests. He accepted that casualties would be covered as an issue, but objected to them being given *prominence* in the news. Tebbit's report had this to say of the BBC coverage:

> [The BBC] also devoted far more of the opening paragraph than ITN did to words and phrases designed to arouse anti-American emotion: 'across the world there is great concern'.
> *'Deaths and injuries to men, women and children as they slept in their homes'*, *'Colonel Gaddafi's own family was hit'*, *'in intensive care with serious injuries'*.
> The point is not whether these statements should be made but whether they should be given such prominence in the first, 'audience conditioning' part of the report.
>
> (Conservative Central Office 1986: 7; emphasis in original)

The suggestion is that 'their' casualties should not go in the first 'audience-conditioning' part of the report. The Conservative critics had also wanted a more up-beat introduction. The report criticized the actual introduction which the BBC had used. This had been: 'We'll be assessing the world reaction to what the Americans have done, and the political repercussions for Mrs Thatcher' (BBC 1, 21:00, 15 April 1986). The report suggested that the following phrasing could have been used instead: 'We'll be looking at the events that prompted America's retaliation and its chances of success' (Conservative Central Office 1986: 8).

The Tebbit report also contrasted ITN and BBC coverage. ITN was praised for stating clearly that 'the Libyans are now trying to use the Americans' raid as a propaganda weapon for themselves' (ITN, 22:00, 15 April 1986). We are now back on the terrain of making distinctions between two types of victims – 'ours' who are simply innocent and 'theirs' who are propaganda. If television coverage rejects such a distinction and chooses to highlight the fate of innocent casualties, then it is applying a humanist criterion to news reporting. It is asserting the basic right of casualties to be innocent, whichever country they happen to be in. By contrast, the Tebbit report wanted to substitute a system of two types of reporting – one for 'us' and one for 'them'. If the right to be innocent is downgraded in this way, then it does make sense to have the upbeat introduction which the Conservatives desired and to reduce the prominence of statements about casualties. But it was a demand which cut across the BBC's perception of itself as being concerned with fairness, balance, and the expression of human and democratic values.

Coverage of the Falklands conflict and the Libyan bombing had provoked attacks from Tory MPs in parliament and from Norman Tebbit at the Party's Central Office. But there was another source of pressure very close to the broadcasters. The Prime Minister had the power to appoint the BBC's Board of Governors. From the early 1980s, the effects of this began to be felt.

Stephen Hearst was advisor to the Director-General from 1982 to 1986 and he describes the change which took place:

> Until the eighties it wouldn't have occurred to the professional staff of the BBC to suspect that the governors were anything other than independent. After the eighties one began to suspect that the governors were more likely to be appointed for Conservative sympathies than for other reasons.
>
> (speaking on *World in Action*, 29 February 1988)

In 1980, George Howard, a wealthy landowner, was made chairman of the Board of Governors, and William Rees-Mogg, ex-editor of *The Times* and a former Conservative parliamentary candidate was appointed as deputy chairman. There was increasing concern about pressure on the BBC through this period and in 1988 Granada Television's *World in Action* made a programme on the issue. It described how the Board of Governors was composed in the early 1980s:

> Critics say the Falklands War reinforced Mrs Thatcher's determination to curb the BBC and to appoint governors she thought would do it. In 1982 she appointed Daphne Park, the right-wing head of her old Oxford College – she replaced Baroness Serota, a Labour peer. Next came Sir John Boyd as trade-union representative. Boyd, perhaps the most right-wing of general secretaries, replaced the middle of the road Alf Allan. Then Malcolm MacAlpine was appointed. His family's building company has given the Conservative Party more than £300,000. Later Mrs Thatcher rejected Moira Shearer, a Liberal, as representative of the Arts and chose instead the Queen's cousin and traditionalist Lord Harewood. In 1983, Mrs Thatcher appointed a new chairman, Stuart Young, brother of David Young, then shortly to become one of her Cabinet Ministers.
>
> ('The Taming of the BBC', *World in Action*, 29 February 1988)

In this period there were a number of well-publicized attacks on the BBC by the government and by Conservative MPs. In 1985, the BBC produced a programme in its *Real Lives* series, which was a profile of two elected representatives from the Northern Ireland Assembly. One was a Loyalist and the other a Republican and leading member of Sinn Féin. The Conservative home secretary asked the BBC to ban the programme, a decision which was then confirmed by the Board of Governors. This led to strikes both in the BBC and ITN (in sympathy) and the programme was eventually shown. But coverage of Northern Ireland was a continual source of tension (see chapter 4). In 1988 the government attacked Thames Television for its programme *Death on the Rock* which dealt with the killing of three IRA members by the SAS in Gibraltar (Bolton 1990). There was another major controversy over a BBC series called *The Secret Society*. One of these programmes on the Zircon spy satellite suggested that the government was concealing this project from parliament. In January 1987, Special Branch police officers raided the offices of BBC Scotland and took away three van-loads of papers, videotapes and film.

These were only some of the most publicized conflicts arising from what broadcasters describe as constant pressure from the government and their own Board of Governors.[1] Alan Protheroe recalls this time as Assistant Director-General of the BBC: 'One did get rather tired of being involved in rather ritualistic crucifixions, every other Thursday when one appeared before the Board of Governors of the BBC' (speaking on *World in Action*, 29 February 1988). The effect of such pressure is to create an atmosphere of intense caution amongst programme makers. One producer who has spent more than twenty years in the BBC described this to us:

> [In the 1980s], the Conservatives used a kind of salami-cutting technique by attacking the BBC day after day and constantly put the management into a defensive posture.... We were self-censoring as a result of our superiors constantly saying 'can you just rest it for a while?'
>
> (interview, 27 April 1993)

This producer described to us how in 1987 shortly after the Conservative's third election victory, he had produced a programme on the long-term effects of unemployment. One contributor had mentioned the depression in Germany before World War II and its relation to the rise of Nazism. On seeing it, one of his superiors immediately insisted that it was removed, saying 'Don't be naive, Tebbit will be down on us like a ton of bricks' (interview, 27 April 1993). Intimidation can be very effective in curbing potential criticism. But the Conservatives also had their own agenda which they wished to promote and for this they developed new and innovative techniques of political communication.

SELLING THE 1980s

Governments are potentially in a very strong position to affect the supply of politically sensitive information. In some circumstances, they can impose legal controls over who may be interviewed on television or what information may be broadcast or printed (see chapters 4 and 5). But the government is also a major supplier of information in its own right. It is the key source for data on major issues such as the economy, unemployment, public spending and health. Each Whitehall department has its own press and public relations personnel and these form collectively the Government Information Service. Government leaders also supply information to the media through the lobby system. This is the system of unattributable briefings given to selected correspondents in the House of Commons. It has been criticized exactly because the source of the information cannot be disclosed (see chapter 5).

The Conservatives under Mrs Thatcher were intent on changing the political map of Britain and this required a major propaganda initiative. Of course, all governments attempt to present their own policies favourably and governments before 1979 had used the lobby system for unattributable briefings. But Mrs Thatcher and her press secretary Bernard Ingham achieved a centralization and control of government information services which had not been seen before. Writing in 1988, Robert Harris described this development:

> As her power and self-confidence have grown, so have his; as she has built a network of officials across Whitehall sympathetic to her ideas, so has he: 'Bernard's Babies' are now installed in information departments throughout the government.
>
> (Harris 1988: 15)

Once a week in a conference room in No. 10 Downing Street, Bernard Ingham would hold a meeting with the heads of information from each of the main government departments:

> The purpose of these weekly sessions ... is, according to one senior Whitehall figure, straightforward news management: 'ensuring bits of good news don't clash, masking bad news at one department by bringing forward good from another, stopping reporters playing one department off against another, deciding whether a television producer, on past experience can be trusted, and so on'.
>
> (ibid.)

In theory, government information services are supposed to supply 'neutral' facts rather than political propaganda. But many critics at the time argued that such lines had become blurred. At the annual conference of Professional Civil Servants in 1988, there were calls for a code of ethics to protect members who were expected to '"expound untruths on behalf of the government"' (quoted ibid.). One information officer at the Department of Employment gave examples of colleagues being required to write:

> 'articles of a party political nature on behalf of their ministers for insertion in the press'; government campaigns 'on the poll tax, changes to social security arrangements, privatisation'; the Action for Jobs Campaign – 'which said little about the Department of Employment's services but much about the Conservative party's views on unemployment and the unemployed'.
>
> (ibid.)

There are two specific complaints being made here. The first was about the quality of the information being distributed and the second was about the extensive use of public funds for what could be seen as political advertising campaigns. In January 1989 a Channel 4 documentary outlined a series of detailed cases on the distortion of political statistics. Its argument was interspersed with news clips of speeches by Conservative politicians:

JOURNALIST: Statistics do not just help you win the argument, they give you power. . . .

MRS THATCHER [on platform]: It's time we took the credit for some of the things we have achieved – the 8 million patients treated in hospitals each year. . . .

JOURNALIST: . . . Power to write the history of the past. . . .

NORMAN FOWLER [employment minister]: Since the election, unemployment has come down by 655,000, the biggest fall in unemployment for over 40 years. . . .

JOURNALIST: . . . and power to decide the policy of the future.

KENNETH CLARKE [health minister]: We will provide to the health authorities another £98 million of taxpayers money to carry out our obligations.

(Channel 4, *Dispatches*, 18 January 1989)

This programme looked initially at processes of news management. These include the down-playing of undesirable statistics by releasing them on the same day as other major events. In this example, bad news about the health service is drowned by the saturation coverage given to a royal wedding at Westminster Abbey:

The 23rd of July 1986 was the day of the royal wedding, a day of celebration. But it was also the day on which the government announced the publication of the delayed Health and Personal Social Services Statistics for 1986 – the contents of which gave the government little to celebrate about. For they revealed that between 1979 and 1984, 196 hospitals, 17,025 beds, 3,051 doctors and 20,000 ancillary staff, and 35 hospital schools were lost.

(ibid.)

But it was on the issue of the construction of politically sensitive data that the programme's analysis was most telling. It showed how government claims about new spending on health actually included money from the sale of assets. In other words if a hospital was knocked down and the land sold, this was counted as 'new money' being spent on health. The programme described such sales:

In the looking-glass world of health statistics, this site counts £29 million towards total government spending on the Health Service. It is not a hospital that is being built on this site either, but luxury canal-side flats. Just two years ago on this site was a hospital with 157 beds and 20 wards employing 400 staff treating 45,000 patients a year. It was pulled down to make way for the private developers.

(ibid.)

And as the commentator notes: 'With this use of figures, if the government sold the entire Health Service to private developers, it could claim to be spending more than ever before on the Health Service' (ibid.).

The use of figures on unemployment was also very contentious. In 1982, the government changed the basis on which these figures were calculated. They were originally measured as the number of people asking for work, but this was altered to the number receiving benefit. This was one of more than twenty changes made, which had the effect of reducing the unemployment figures by approximately 1 million people. The government was also criticized for establishing 'training schemes' which were designed to lower the unemployment figures rather than provide real job opportunities. In 1990 it was reported that: 'An internal civil service report suggested that between July 1986 and June 1989, of 608,000 people referred for jobs only 6,000 secured one' (*Guardian*, 8 June 1990).

The second major area of controversy was the claim that public funds were used to promote political propaganda. It was strongly suggested that the purpose of campaigns such as 'Action for Jobs' was mainly to promote the Conservatives' 'image' on unemployment rather than give information to the unemployed. In September 1989 a BBC *Panorama* programme looked back over this period and analysed the impact of the campaign. It showed how David Young (later Lord Young) was recruited to the Cabinet from industry by Margaret Thatcher. Henceforth, the Department of Trade and Industry was promoted in television advertisements as the 'Department of Enterprise', but the key role of David Young was in relation to unemployment. He devised the Action for Jobs campaign which was extensively promoted in the media from July 1986 until May 1987 (one month before the general election). *Panorama* commissioned a study of the campaign by the London Media Company, who found that it was targeted to reach high-income viewers and professional classes most of all, rather than the unemployed:

> The Campaign deliberately picked 'up-market' slots (on television) in and around ITN's *News at Ten*. They were chosen far more than, for instance, *Coronation Street* which has a big audience but not the same up-market profile . . . regionally, the ads were run most heavily in the south-east where unemployment is lowest.
>
> (BBC 1, *Panorama*, 4 September 1989)

There was another key area of government advertising which promoted the philosophy of the new Conservatives. This was the sales campaigns for the privatization of the nationally owned industries, which were on a scale not seen before. When British Telecom was sold, the deputy editor of *Marketing Week* wrote that the two advertising agencies involved had: 'worked their way through £7.6 million in little more than 3 months, the sort of money which even the UK's biggest advertisers would need a year to dispose of' (Koski 1984: 7). And, as he writes, beneath the soft advertising sell was the political philosophy of 'people's capitalism':

What makes the B.T. Campaign special is the role it played in promoting the government philosophy behind the flotation of the company, albeit indirectly. It is a philosophy which seeks to increase the number of private individuals owning shares to produce a system of people's capitalism, a share-owning democracy, ... the ads might have invited us all to 'share in British Telecom's future', but the invisible ink between the lines urging us to share in capitalism's future had become clear enough by the time application for shares needed to be made.

(Koski 1984: 7)

One of the largest and most heavily promoted sales was of the government's stake in British Petroleum. This came in October 1987 after the Conservatives' third electoral victory. By this time the government advertising machine was pushing at something of an open door in terms of obtaining free publicity from television. In the early stages of the promotion, the sale was made into a news item on the basis that the government had *announced the date* on which the price of the shares would be announced:

More details today of the government's biggest share offer so far – the sale of its one-third holding in BP. To entice investors, BP is offering shareholders a dividend for this year of 8p per share and the company has revealed exactly when the share price will be made public.

(BBC 1, 13:00, 25 September 1987)

This 'news' then becomes the rationale for promotional interviews with a government minister and the deputy chairman of BP. On the BBC evening news, the promotional seal is set by the industrial editor, who seems to be licking his lips at the share prospect of it all: *'It's an appetising buy* and there are still extra attractions for small investors including an almost immediate 8p dividend per share' (BBC 1, 21:00, 25 September 1987). Three weeks later the announcement of the share price occasioned another burst of media coverage. Both BBC and ITN ran major items on BP's oil fields in Alaska. These were shown the day before the announcement as a kind of trailer to it. ITN was quite un-self-conscious about producing news items which 'smooth the way' for the government's share sale. The 'hook' which it used to tell viewers that the story is coming up after the break ran as follows: 'A report next ... and the word from Alaska to smooth the way for BP shares' (ITN, 22:00, 14 October 1987). The ITN news then took on the flavour of a company prospectus:

NEWSCASTER: BP's most important source of oil lies in the land beneath Alaska, Prudhoe Bay, a name that could mean profits for shareholders.
JOURNALIST [in Alaska]: Exploration continues – the latest finds are further east. Sandstone rocks are oozing oil and suggest that reserves could be vast. Big new fields are coming on stream elsewhere.... Two and a half

miles beneath the surface it is estimated there is enough oil for another thirty years.

(ibid.)

This news actually mirrors the government's advertisements of the time. These had featured groups of BP workers who were identified by close-up shots of the BP logo. The news item featured the same technique by focusing on and then drawing away from the BP logo on an oil-worker's helmet. The BBC news that evening is more circumspect and speaks of 'Alaskan oil ... now helping the government to a big profit on its BP sale' (BBC 1, 18:00, 14 October 1987). The BBC correspondent is also less sanguine than his ITN counterparts on how many people will decide to buy shares. But both BBC and ITN are drawn as if by invisible threads to focus on the agenda set by the latest public-relations output on the share issue. On the following day, the price of shares is displayed at BP headquarters by a team of Marines who climb down the side of the building to reveal it in giant letters. The BBC journalist on the spot is not altogether happy about having to cover such an obvious stunt. He notes that it is 'pointless' since the price has already been known for three hours before the unveiling (BBC 1, 18:00, 15 October 1987). But the purpose of the exercise is to provide the news pictures which accompany and 'legitimize' the item. The pictures make it possible to feature yet more publicity material on the share offer:

> More than six million people have already registered to buy. Successful applicants must pay 120p on each share now and 105p by next August on each share they get. The final payment, another 105p, will be due in April 1989, and to encourage long-term investment, there will be a bonus of one free share for every ten held until October 1990.
>
> (ITN, 12:30, 15 October 1987)

The BBC's headline for its lunchtime news was 'Share Sale of the Century' (BBC 1, 13:00, 15 October 1987). A City expert, an oil analyst, is interviewed:

> NEWSCASTER: I asked him whether the BP share price was a good deal.
> OIL ANALYST: Yes, the offer is very attractive for the UK general public....
> NEWSCASTER: Are you going to buy any yourself?
> OIL ANALYST: Yes, of course.
>
> (BBC 1, 13:00, 15 October 1987)

The publicity campaign thus became a news item in its own right and occasioned interviews with and appearances by a succession of government ministers, City figures, BP executives and oil experts who murmur 'that's great' and 'liquid gold' (ITN, Alaskan report, 22:00, 14 October 1987). There are no critical voices from the opposition in the above news items and nothing which comments on the 80 per cent of the public who would no longer have a stake in the industry once the sale had gone through. The campaign marked a high point of Conservative dominance, with a political policy effectively advertised within routine news coverage. The BBC had sounded the occasional note of caution but there was much talk of the coming success. After the announcement of the share price, ITN concluded: 'This issue is not likely to fail – today's razzmatazz was just to make absolutely sure of success' (ITN, 12:30, 15 October 1987).

Some no doubt wished they had been better informed. Nemesis awaited this share issue four days later in the form of the great stock-market crash of 'Black Monday', on 19 October 1987. The price of BP shares on the open market was driven down to well below the £3.30 at which the government was offering its own stake for sale. The razzmatazz ended in something close to debacle.

ENTERPRISE TELEVISION AND THE ECONOMIC MIRACLE

The dominance of the Conservatives in this period also had a major impact on several other areas of programming which began to echo the new politics. The key element of the Conservative message from the mid-1980s was their claim to have revitalized the economy. William Keegan, writing in the *Observer* at the time, commented on the level of public relations resources which were being focused on the 'economic miracle':

> I cannot resist noting that about a quarter of the UK delegation to the OECD Ministerial Meeting were Press and Propaganda officers of one sort or another. Clearly, a lot of resources are now being devoted to the propagation of the British Economic Miracle.
>
> (22 May 1988)

The economy had indeed expanded, especially in the period before and after the 1987 election. Public spending had increased, but the crucial factor was a huge expansion in personal borrowing. The Conservatives had encouraged this by removing restrictions on credit and bank lending from 1980 onwards. Personal credit (including mortgages) increased from £90 billion at the end of 1980 to £282 billion by the end of 1987. Bank lending increased by one-third in the year before the 1987 general election (Lloyd 1993: 510). One effect of this was to produce a dramatic rise in house prices as the government changed the rules on the permitted levels of borrowing, such that buyers were able to obtain mortgages of 100 per cent on prospective purchases. The apparent growth of economic activity together with the increasing flow of money and consumption were important in creating the so-called 'feel good' effect, especially in the south-east of the country where the Conservatives were politically strongest. This area profited greatly from the growth of the financial/service sectors, and the extraordinary rise in house and property prices was initially concentrated there. But the economic growth was very largely in the service sector and masked deep structural problems in the wider economy.

The major problem facing Britain and other western economies in this period was the threat of competition from the powerful economies of the Far East. Their strength came from a combination of relatively low wages combined with high technology plus new management and 'lean-production' techniques. Britain had not had a particularly high-wage economy in the postwar period. Its persistent failure was on investment levels relative to its major industrial competitors. When the Glasgow Media Group published its first work in 1976, we noted that a Toyota worker in Japan was working with equipment worth the equivalent of £11,780 while a British Leyland car worker had only £1,000 worth. By 1989, Japan was investing $250 billion a year in machinery and equipment overall, compared with $54 billion in Britain (Hutton and Story 1989). Monetarism had little to offer to redress such a crucial area of imbalance. Indeed, the application of monetarist policies to the economy, with high interest rates between 1979 and 1981, had seriously damaged British manufacturing, reducing output by between 15 and 20 per cent. This was felt particularly in areas such as the West Midlands which had specialized in engineering and machine-tool production. This reduction was critical because when the economy expanded with the credit boom British industry could not adequately meet the demand. The very predictable result was an unparalleled balance-of-payments crisis at the end of the 1980s, as imports grew to far greater volumes than could be matched by British exports. The most perceptive commentators had pointed to this danger well before the 1987 election. Will Hutton was at that time working for BBC's *Newsnight* and produced a prophetic report on the decline of British manufacturing and the consequences for the country's ability to pay its way in the world:

> Britain is increasingly being knocked out of the trade fight. For every car we send to Germany, for example, they send over six back to us, our trade deficit with them last year was £5.4 billion. . . . name an industry and over the past ten years Britain's competitive position has weakened – machinery and data processing, our share of world markets has fallen from 15.6 per cent in 1975 to 7.5 per cent in 1984. . . . Electrical machinery is down from 5.5 per cent to 2.3 per cent. Internal combustion engines, 12.7 per cent to 6.4 per cent. Tyres, 8 per cent to just over 5 per cent, even pottery from a 19 per cent world share in 1975 to under 12 per cent in 1984. . . . In 1975 Britain's international accounts looked like this. Manufacturing surplus was around twice as high as the service sectors. . . . Ten years later the surplus in manufacturing had turned into a deficit, services were still in the black, though food and raw materials had to be paid for, but North Sea oil had come to the rescue. The surplus was £1.3 billion but according to predictions, especially commissioned for *Newsnight*, in ten years time the

manufacturing deficit will be even larger.... [There will be] a massive deficit of possibly £9 billion.

(BBC 2, *Newsnight*, 28 January 1987)

The report ended with this exchange between a US businessman and the *Newsnight* reporter:

BUSINESSMAN: If you are not a manufacturer, if you don't have a manufacturing base, you don't have an economy. People haven't created wealth and they won't have any money to buy the merchandise – and it will be all over.
REPORTER: All over?
BUSINESSMAN: Yes, what do they say on that little sign somewhere, last person to leave the country please turn out the lights.

(ibid.)

The report erred only on the side of caution. Two years later, in 1989, the balance-of-payments deficit reached £19.01 billion. But for many commentators in 1987 and 1988, the dominance of the Conservatives seemed assured. The warnings were unheeded and as the credit boom took hold, television began to celebrate the apparent 'economic miracle'.

Two months after the above *Newsnight* feature, ITN reported that a letter had been sent to *The Times* by five former Treasury advisors, who were severely critical of the government's economic policy. They were calling for a budget which would reduce unemployment. One of their number, Sir Fred Atkinson, was interviewed on the lunchtime news and was treated very critically by the newscaster, for whom the basic strength of the British economy was taken as axiomatic. The newscaster asks the following questions:

NEWSCASTER: Sir Fred, if I could come to you first – you're asking for a change of course – that's the usual cry is it? Do you want more public spending?
[Sir Fred Atkinson replies that he does want more public spending.]
NEWSCASTER: All of the advisors who signed that letter are pre-Thatcher men. You're being dismissed in Whitehall today as yesterday's men thinking in terms of yesterday's policies.
[Sir Fred Atkinson replies that there were good things about yesterday's policies].
NEWSCASTER: But you also had raging inflation – up to 27 per cent we had at one time.
[Sir Fred Atkinson replies that 'During most of that period we had about the same rate of inflation as we have now'.]

(ITN, 13:00, 16 March 1987)

The newscaster then turns to a City expert and asks what sort of budget the

Chancellor is likely to provide. The expert reports the government view that not much more can be done for jobs and that the economy is growing strongly. There are no criticisms made of this and the strength of the economy is reiterated by the newscaster who notes that 'we do have a strongly growing economy now – is the rise in inflation inevitable?' (ibid.). After their election victory in June 1987, the Conservatives were in a very powerful position. The Labour opposition had substantially abandoned political arguments about the economy (see chapter 10). The economic success story thus became part of the routine script of television. In August 19987, a BBC financial reporter noted that: 'With Britain's economy currently one of the success stories of the world, the authorities are concerned that growth doesn't get out of hand' (BBC 1, 13:00, 6 August 1987). His words parallel those of Nigel Lawson, the Conservative Chancellor, who is interviewed in the same bulletin: '[I have maintained] the sound financial conditions which have made this country the fastest-growing economy in all of the major countries in the world.'

The theme of the fastest-growing economy is developed in the following month with the release of new government figures for manufacturing output. These are reported by ITN in the language of contemporary political advertising. The economy is now 'leaner' and 'fitter':

The latest official figures for the economy showed industrial production growing faster this year than in Germany, France or Japan. [There has been] a radical shake-out in our traditional industries [but] a considerably leaner and apparently fitter manufacturing sector has hauled itself back to record output levels but there is clearly still some way to go. . . . These industrial output figures finally reflect the fact that the British economy is amongst the fastest-growing in the world.

(ITN, 22:00, 16 September 1987)

The figures showed that manufacturing output had in fact only just climbed back to where it had been when the Conservatives came to power in 1979. One month's or one year's figures for manufacturing output are not a reliable guide to long-term growth. But the script for the economic miracle still held strong for the next budget in March 1988. Economic news around this was underpinned by talk of 'boom', 'strength' and 'buoyancy':

The pound has gone up because of Britain's basic economic strength.

(BBC 1, 13:00, 8 March 1988)

Britain's economy is booming.

(trailer for BBC 1, *Money Programme*, against background of what the 'experts' were predicting for the Budget, 23:00, 10 March 1988)

It is that sort of buoyancy [in the economy] that has pushed unemployment to its lowest levels for six years.

(ITN, 12:30, 17 March 1988)

Two months later, the serious crisis in Britain's trade balance began to develop; but it is still not signalled as a major problem on the news:

NEWSCASTER: Britain's trade went further into the red last month. . . .
ECONOMICS CORRESPONDENT: No one thought this would be a good year for Britain's trade, but it is looking worse than the government expected.

(BBC 1, 21:00, 27 May 1988)

The BBC was still taking its mood from the City and the Chancellor. As long as they were not concerned, then there was apparently no reason for the BBC to panic:

Some City experts now expect the year's deficit to be nearer £6 billion, but took today's news in their stride, despite the fact that the figures were at the gloomier end of expectations. The City knows all to well that the figures go on being revised for many months afterwards *and by the time anyone knows what they really mean, they've more or less ceased to matter.* For the Chancellor, the money is still flowing in, which finances all those imports and *as long as no one else starts panicking, there is no reason why he should.*

(BBC 1, 21:00, 27 May 1988)

But the next month's figures cannot be shrugged off. The City panics and so does television:

HEADLINE: Britain's worst ever monthly trade figures hit shares and the pound.
SUMMARY: Britain's trade was in the red last month to the tune of £1,200 million, the worst figures on record. The gap between imports and exports was twice as bad as economists had predicted.

(BBC 1, 21:00, 2 June 1988)

And on ITN:

HEADLINE: The worst ever trade figures, dearer mortgages a likely result.
SUMMARY: The latest trade figures are the worst ever. Britain's trade was in the red by more than a billion and a half pounds last month as people spent more and more on foreign imports. And now it is thought inevitable that interest rates will rise yet again.

(ITN, 22:00, 27 June 1988)

Interest rates did indeed rise and the economy moved into the second major recession in ten years. The economic miracle proved to be something of a mirage. In the thirteen years from 1979 to 1992 manufacturing output rose by just 4.5 per cent in Britain, the lowest figure for any major industrial economy. In the same period, output in Japan rose by over 60 per cent (Central Statistical Office 1992 [February]).

But the apparent miracle was a key factor in the dominance of the

Conservatives from the middle of the 1980s. This dominance had crucial effects on the content as well as the structure of broadcasting. The routine deference to City 'experts' for opinions on economic news, for example, was a product of this time and, as we show elsewhere (see chapter 10), this was important in the 'framing' of key issues in the 1992 election. The predominance of City 'experts' on television began to irritate even the *Sun* who commented on it in the days after Nigel Lawson resigned as Chancellor of the Exchequer: 'One by one, the sharp City yuppies went on television after Nigel Lawson's resignation to warn of impending doom. . . . Why do the BBC and ITV allow these self-appointed experts to spout their rubbish' (editorial, *Sun*, 1 November 1989).

To view the economy through the eyes of the City is clearly a very partisan position. This was a point made in Channel 4's *Right of Reply* programme in a special feature made by John Dyer. He interviewed Peter Jay, the BBC's economics correspondent, who acknowledged this key issue:

> I personally happen to agree very strongly with what I think was perhaps the most interesting and concrete point in [John Dyer's report], namely the tendency that grew up during the 1980s on television and otherwise to present the economy through the spectacles of the City – to give the public the impression that the people who were doing the reporting thought that the City was some kind of Mount Olympus from which the economy could be viewed. . . . I believe that was profoundly mistaken.
>
> (Channel 4, *Right of Reply*, 6 April 1991)

The dominance of the New Right was reflected in other areas of programming as well. 'Enterprise' became a more routine concept and the BBC made a series of programmes under the title *Enterprise Culture*. They were clearly a response to the spirit of the age, although some of their content now looks so strange that it appears almost satirical. One of the programmes deals with a shoe-shine business which operates in City dealing rooms. The workers shine the shoes of those who are (literally and metaphorically) in the world above them. The owner of the business tells this story:

> There was I, polishing the shoes [in a dealing room], and there was a young man standing up on the phone and the whole dealing floor was looking in his direction. All of a sudden there was silence and all the phones came down and there was just this one man remained standing . . . and I thought what's going on here, so I asked this bloke, 'what's the matter with him?' Then the next minute everyone started applauding and jumping up and shouting and screaming – and I said, 'what's he done?' and he said, 'Oh, he's made himself a millionaire'.
>
> (BBC 1, 'Making a Million', *Enterprise Culture*, 30 May 1989)

There were other stories of enterprise which were featured in this period. The government promoted a scheme for schools to run small businesses and this became a news item:

> NEWSCASTER: All schools should be running their own small businesses, says the Trade and Industry Secretary, Lord Young. The government is launching the second phase of a project it calls mini-enterprise in schools and now they're looking for would-be entrepreneurs to take part.
>
> REPORTER: This is the sort of board meeting the government wants to see at every school in the country. At Capeman School in Whitby the business is salt, brought in as waste at a nearby potash mine, sold off by the bag at a tidy profit.
>
> (BBC 1, 18:00, 23 September 1987)

On children's television, *Toad of Toad Hall* no longer felt the need to steal motor cars and became instead a dealer in shares. He explains the system to his bemused companions:

> It's simple – all you do is buy shares in some little company and buy them cheap and then the company does fearfully well and then everyone wants its shares and you sell 'em for thousands more. . . . We'll all be rich as rich!!!
>
> (Cosgrove/Thames TV, 1986)

But all Toad's plans come to nought. The assets of the Arctic Pineapple Corporation are frozen, the Atlantic Tunnel scheme collapses and the Square Wheeled Bicycle has a rough ride. These events from Toad Hall, broadcast in 1986, were paralleled the following year when the real stock market collapsed. As in art, so follows life: 'The City panics and £50 billion disappears – and Wall Street is down over 500 points tonight in the crash of '87' (headlines, BBC 1, 21:00, 19 October 1987).

It was this stock-exchange collapse on 'Black Monday' that ruined the BP sale. This together with the balance-of-payments crisis of the following year signalled some of the deeper problems which underlay the economy and the apparent failure of the Conservative strategy. At the end of the 1980s, the Tories were also beset with difficulties over the poll tax, which they had introduced, and arguments within their own party over Europe. These conflicts led to the fall of Margaret Thatcher as their political leader and to her replacement with the apparently less controversial John Major. And yet the period in which the New Right had achieved its least challenged dominance illustrates crucially the impact a strong centralized state can have on a broadcasting system which is formally independent.

RESISTANCE

It would be wrong to see the 1980s as a period in which the flow of information into and from the media was simply controlled by the state. The dominance of the New Right was least partially contested by pressure groups such as CND or Greenpeace and by trade unions and the opposition political parties. There were major conflicts and struggles for public support and sympathy which were fought largely through the media. For example, the 'Battle for London' between 1981 and 1986, arose from the government's intense antipathy towards the Greater London Council and its left-wing leader, Ken Livingstone. The government's decision to abolish the council was hotly contested by the GLC itself and it was successful in winning substantial public support. This was in the face of intense hostility towards the GLC from virtually all the tabloid press. These papers ran an extended campaign focusing on GLC grants handed out to 'Queers Lib' and 'bizarre minority groups' from the 'lunatic fringe' (*Daily Mail*, 16 February 1983 and 22 April 1983; *Sun*, 20 September 1984; quoted in Curran 1987: 119). They were also intensely antipathetic towards 'red' Ken Livingstone, dubbed by the *Sun* as 'the most odious man in Britain' (12 October 1981).

The GLC was apparently fairly low in public esteem in the early 1980s. But, by January 1984, 50 per cent of Londoners were opposed to its abolition – a figure which rose to 66 per cent by April 1985. The GLC had successfully mobilized support for its cheap-fares policy and crucially had presented the decision to close it as being motivated by political prejudice rather than by a desire to improve local government. One of the crucial factors here was the split between the quality and tabloid press. Quality papers, notably the *Guardian* and the *Observer*, were sympathetic towards the GLC. While the circulation of such papers was not great, they had an important effect in that their support encouraged, indeed required, the broadcast media to take the GLC's case seriously. The tabloids made the GLC into 'news', but television and radio had in this case to invoke the formal requirements of 'balance', since the quality papers had legitimized the alternative case. The broadcast media are a crucial source of information for the bulk of the population, and this was therefore an important advance for the GLC. James Curran gives this example from his study of the conflict:

> Radio, television and every quality national daily all reported on 19th January 1984 that the GLC Tory leader, Alan Greengross, had supported Ken Livingstone in demanding a directly elected London Council. . . . The only GLC stories reported that day in the national popular press were a report of 'the latest daftness from Ken Livingstone's apparatchniks' at the Old Vic Theatre and an editorial denouncing the GLC's latest grant to resettle black female prisoners in the community as an example of 'its search for ever more imaginative and offensive ways of wasting the rate payer's money [*Daily Express*]'
>
> (Curran 1987: 128)

The GLC also engaged in the direct promotion of its policies by producing a free sheet newspaper and between 1981 and 1985 commissioning a number of advertising campaigns. In the most extensive of these, the GLC spent £5 million attacking the government's cancellation of the GLC elections, which had been scheduled for 1985.

The swing in public support towards the GLC did not prevent its eventual abolition. But, interestingly, it did have a marked effect on the approach of the tabloid press. As Curran notes:

> All three national newspapers in the Mirror Group were converted to the GLC's cause, beginning with the *Sunday Mirror*'s dramatic conversion in January 1984 – only a few months after it had been pressing the Government to speed up the GLC's abolition. The *New/London Standard*, long the leading prosecutor of the GLC, also came round to supporting a directly elected authority for London. And a large section of the press, including such pro-government papers as the *Mail on Sunday* and the *Daily Express*, broke ranks and opposed the cancelling of the GLC elections. While most of the popular press continued to be critical of the GLC, its criticism became less shrill and vehement.
>
> (Curran 1987: 130)

These changes are very important since they indicate the difficulties which a very partisan press can face when it is campaigning for policies which are not accepted by its readership. Newspapers exist within a highly competitive market. If the disjunction between their preferred policy and the views of their readership becomes so great that it could affect sales, then editors may have to think again. This is the continual problem facing a paper such as Rupert Murdoch's *Sun* which advocates Conservative politics to a readership which very substantially votes for the Labour Party. At times, the *Sun* has employed individual columnists to broaden its appeal. In 1991 it featured a regular column from none other than Ken Livingstone under the banner 'A View from Labour'.

There were a number of other conflicts in the 1980s in which the use of public-relations techniques and advertising by oppositional groups was very marked. The ambulance drivers in their pay dispute with the government in 1989 were able to carry a great deal of public support with them. This contrasted sharply with the public-sector disputes of 1979 in which they had also been involved. These had been dubbed the 'Winter of Discontent' and had featured very prominently in anti-union propaganda by the Conservative Party (see chapter 10). In 1989, the ambulance drivers selected their tactics very carefully, effectively working without pay and maintaining emergency services. Their public-relations offensive was a top priority. The unions involved in the dispute held daily meetings to discuss tactics and to agree a specific message for each day. Public statements were then co-ordinated and delivered, primarily through Roger Poole, the chief spokesperson. Regional officers then liaised with union headquarters on specific messages for local interviews. In the period since 1979, Roger Poole's union NUPE had appointed an experienced press officer and developed a very media-friendly and accessible press office. The success of the ambulance drivers was so marked that BBC's *Newsnight* ran a special feature on it. 'This is a public-relations triumph ... the battle for public support has been won, for now at least by the unions. A government which once seemed the master of PR has been beaten at its own game' (BBC 2, *Newsnight*, 18 December 1989).

This success cannot be attributed only to good public relations. By 1989 the government's economic strategy was being increasingly questioned. Its budget of the previous year had distributed an extraordinary level of tax cuts to the very well-off, intensifying the perceived disparity between rich and poor. The ambulance drivers were thus on very fertile ground in terms of presenting themselves as an underpaid and very 'worthy' group who really deserved to be supported. But overall, the organization of their campaign for public support was very important and it signified a growing use by trade unions of public-relations techniques.

Perhaps one of the most significant areas of resistance to Conservative policy was the struggle over the community charge or poll tax which stretched from 1986 until 1991, when the government was forced to formally abandon the measure and introduced the council tax to replace it. Popular resistance to the poll tax began in Scotland amongst groups of unemployed workers. These attracted media attention by criticizing and breaking up warrant sales (i.e. the forced sales of individuals' properties to pay the tax). It was an extraordinarily unpopular measure which proved to be a media and public-relations disaster for the Conservatives. Deacon and Golding (1991) argue that television and the press played a major role in informing the public about the tax and that media coverage was consistently hostile towards it. This was true even of newspapers which traditionally supported the Conservatives. Media coverage was influenced by the very extensive public-relations programme organized by local authorities and other groups opposed to the tax. Deacon and Golding suggest that another critical factor was the profound division within the Conservative Party over the policy. It was difficult for Conservative papers to follow a 'Party line', given that some of the most vocal critics were from the Party. But there is much more to this than saying simply that the Tory press were confused because political 'mentors' were divided. The editors of papers such as the *Sun* and the *Daily Mail* are at least as politically acute as Conservative politicians. They have a clear sense of how what is politically desirable (for them) interacts with what is politically possible. Some sections of the Conservative Party and most of the media appreciated very quickly that a regressive tax which shifted the burden of payment onto the less well-off would be hugely unpopular at the end of the 1980s. Here was the same fertile ground the ambulance drivers had found themselves on in their public-relations campaign.

This is an essential point because it signifies that the potential success of public relations must always be understood in relation to prevailing social and economic circumstances. The Conservative press obviously wish to promote Conservative views but they tread a fine line between how they invite their readers to understand the world and the actual material conditions and experience of those who buy their papers. It is the fine line which all political communicators tread. This does not mean that there is an immediate and necessary relationship between a change in 'reality' and the public perception of this change. But it does seem clear that some major changes in material circumstances such as the increases in unemployment in the 1980s or the radical drop in house prices pose very great difficulties for 'good' public relations and effective media management. The credibility gap can indeed yawn wide but where and when it exactly does so forms the site of a constant struggle between contending forces. It is a struggle in which the structural position of the state and its information managers is one of privilege and potential dominance. But it is a dominance which is contested by oppositional groups and through the interplay of the different organizational and commercial priorities of the media.

By the end of the 1980s, the collapse of the poll tax and the evident decline of the economy signalled serious problems for the government. When the political and economic programme of the Conservatives was seen to fail, broadcasting could recover some of its critical edge, but it was now in a changed society.

NEW STRUCTURES

A series of legal changes in the 1980s and 1990s directly affected broadcasting. These included the broadcasting ban, introduced in October 1988, which related to coverage of Northern Ireland and interviews with members of organizations such as Sinn Féin (see chapter 4). In 1989 a new Official Secrets Act was passed. It became an offence for a civil servant to make 'a damaging disclosure' – defined in effect as anything which 'endangers the interests of the United Kingdom abroad'. This Act was clearly aimed at civil servants such as Clive Ponting who, after the Falklands War, had revealed crucial information on the sinking of the Argentine battleship *Belgrano*. This had seriously embarrassed the Conservative government and though Ponting had been prosecuted he was found not guilty. The government had also been embarrassed by the revelations of Peter Wright in the Spycatcher affair. The new Act removed the defence that a civil servant could claim to be acting in the 'public interest'.

In 1990 a new Broadcasting Act was passed which had a major impact on the structures of the commercial organizations and more indirectly on the BBC. It was a crucial move in the direction of deregulation and a 'free market' in broadcasting. Commercial broadcasting had been regulated by the Independent Broadcasting Authority, a government-established body which had formally owned the transmission network. It had powers to enforce regulation on the quality of television and the proportion of time given to programmes such as current affairs as well as the time of day at which such output was to be transmitted. The new Act replaced the IBA with the Independent Television Commission (ITC) which was intended to be a 'light-touch' regulator operating as a licensing body not as a broadcaster. The proposals as originally conceived by the government would have given licences to the highest bidders, without any significant 'quality' threshold. But in the event there was extensive lobbying against this from organizations such as the Campaign for Television Quality (which included many prominent television personalities) and from within the IBA.[2]

In practice there was a strong consensus amongst professionals in both the private and public sector about the cultural, informative and educational role of television. This view was not shared by entrepreneurs such as Rupert Murdoch, with his interests in satellite television, who clearly stood to gain from deregulation.[3] One result of this debate was that the government agreed to establish a higher quality threshold including the obligation to provide 'a diverse programme service'. But the regulatory powers once held by the IBA had been very substantially weakened, crucially in the areas of current affairs and minority programming. The ITC could not now insist that a programme such as *World in Action* be shown in peak time. The effects of this were felt early in 1994 when this programme was taken off the air for a period by Granada television. The reason given for its removal was that it would enable the company to compete more effectively with the soap operas being broadcast by the BBC. As Sylvia Harvey has written, the pressure is towards a ratings-driven system to the detriment of minority and controversial programmes:

> In 1988/89 what critics of the proposed new licensing procedure feared was that high bidding, combined with a significant diminution in regulatory powers, would result in generally lower standards, in less money being spent on programmes, in less diversity of programming, and in the emergence of an almost entirely ratings driven system, pushing controversial and minority-interest programmes to the edges of the schedule and the lower reaches of the budget. It is perhaps the last of these concerns that proved to be the most prescient and the most accurate in terms of subsequent developments.
>
> (Harvey 1992: 16)

The 1990 Broadcasting Act also included provisions for Channel 4 television. Its position has been different from that of the main ITV channel since it had a remit to offer a more diverse and innovative television service appealing to tastes and interests not generally catered for by ITV (Mulholland 1992). But as Sylvia Harvey notes, Channel 4 is still under potential pressure from advertisers: 'It remains to be seen to what extent Channel Four comes under internal or external pressure to maximise its audience, and to prioritise the kinds of programmes attracting the kinds of viewers that advertisers most want to reach' (Harvey 1994: 20).

In the final stages of the broadcasting bill, an amendment was made which affected all TV channels. In July 1990, Home Office ministers announced that there would be a code of impartiality, which would impose the requirement of 'balance' on *individual* programmes (rather than requiring that the output as a *whole* should be balanced). Investigative journalists such as John Pilger saw this as a direct attempt to muzzle critical current-affairs programmes. As he wrote at the time:

> The point about this amendment is that it has nothing to do with truth and fairness ... control is the real aim. The amended bill will tame and, where possible, prevent the type of current affairs and documentary programmes that have exposed the secret pressures and corruption of establishment vested interests, the lives and duplicity of government ministers or officials.
>
> (Pilger 1992: 78)

A further stipulation of the Broadcasting Act was that both the BBC and ITV (Channel 3) would be required to commission 25 per cent of their original programmes from independent companies. This had a major effect on the cost structure of the BBC and resulted in staff cuts. In fact the BBC was already introducing radical changes to become more 'responsive' to market forces. The most important of these was the new system of 'product choice' by which producers of programmes could buy in production facilities (crews, technicians, camera people, etc.) from independent companies. The BBC's own in-house facilities were thus made to be in competition with those outside. In theory producers could choose what was needed to maintain quality, but there were persistent complaints that the underlying drive was always to go for the cheapest. Mary Goldring in her own study of the BBC described the effect of this system:

> Here is the sharp end of the change called producer choice – a change that has created two BBCs, them and us – producers and producer choices. ... It's a cattle market – BBC crews bidding against outside crews for producers' contracts. ... Producer choice is an elegant management concept but in terms of its effect on people it's about as sensitive and compassionate as the old dock labour scheme when people stood cap in hand at the gate for work.
>
> (Channel 4, *The Goldring Audit*, 6 April 1994)

Historically, the BBC had developed a very strong ethos of public service. It has also generated an intensive loyalty amongst its own employees who have often worked for lower incomes than their equivalents in independent television. The application of 'elegant management strategies' such as producer choice has meant in effect a rule by accountants and market criteria.

The new ethos is dominated by competition and fears of losing jobs. As Mary Goldring argues, morale in the new BBC is at a very low point:

> Internally it is a mass of gut-twanging apprehension at the misery the BBC is doing itself now and the misery the government is about to do it because the Charter is expiring in a couple of years. Eight previous occasions when the Charter has been renewed, extended, it's been a rubber-stamp job – but not this time. This time the future of the BBC *is* on the rack and from top to bottom the effect on the morale is palpable.
>
> (ibid.)

This is not a climate which is conducive to a critical or innovative approach to television – especially amongst its senior management:

> Everything the BBC says or has said for the last two years has been both eyes on Whitehall and the renewal of the Charter – the whipped spaniel posture, the determination not to give offence, the noisy sounds of reorganization, have been choreographed with an eye to the political effect.
>
> (ibid.)

Yet paradoxically there has been some space in the 1990s for a critical journalism, since central government in this period has been characterized by internal divisions and confusion over policy. The government of John Major has not had the ability to impose its will on journalists in the manner practiced by Mrs Thatcher at the height of Conservative dominance. Michael Cockerell in *Live from Number 10* writes of journalists interviewing Mrs Thatcher at the start of 1989. He quotes the descriptions of television critics: 'the tugging of the forelock would have been the most appropriate gesture' and a journalist 'probing as remorselessly as a day-old lettuce' (Cockerell 1989: 349). Two years earlier the BBC had actually apologized to Norman Tebbit as Chairman of the Conservative Party because it had failed to mention a good set of trade figures in an early evening news bulletin (*Observer*, 19 April 1987).

We can compare this with the climate in which John Major's government has operated, in what at times has looked almost like an 'open season' for attacks on it by journalists. For example, in May 1993 a television critic wrote of ITN 'gleefully' listing all the government's climbdowns on policy (*Glasgow Evening Times*, 11 May 1993). It was in the context of the government announcing a retreat in school tests in the face of pressure from teachers. Here is the bulletin to which the critic referred:

> This is the latest of a series of government climbdowns. The Prime Minister who once called leaving the ERM 'the soft option' and the chancellor together pulled us out last September. In January, Malcolm Rifkind saved four of the regiments the government had earlier said had to be axed. In March, Michael Heseltine reprieved 12 of the 31 pits whose

closure he had earlier said was unavoidable. Last week, Kenneth Clarke ordered changes to the so-called unit-fines system – fines linked to people's incomes, which had produced, he said, absurdities. And now, John Patten, by changing school tests, has admitted that the original idea was too complicated and that teachers *are* being overworked.

(ITN, 22:00, 11 May 1993)

In the following year, a *Daily Telegraph* poll was reported as showing John Major's popularity to be the lowest of any prime minister since the 1930s. (8 April 1994) The Scott inquiry into the Matrix Churchill affair was another disaster for the government and occasioned quite savage criticism in the media. Evidence to the inquiry effectively implied that there had been a government 'cover-up' of its role in permitting the supply of arms to Iraq prior to the Gulf War. Even the *Sun*, a long-term supporter of the Conservatives commented that the inquiry was about: 'The Establishment keeping quiet while innocent men faced jail. Ministers signing gagging orders to keep vital documents covered up' (1 March 1994). It is an indication of how far the government's esteem had fallen. A BBC radio journalist actually commented of the Attorney-General that: 'He must be worried that he is being lined up to take the rap for other members of the government' (BBC, Radio 4, 13:00, 1 March 1994).

These examples illustrate the paradox of contemporary broadcasting. It is in a contradictory position since it is operating within structures and legal constraints which are potentially very restrictive, but is doing so at a time when central government is divided and open to criticism. The management may be extremely nervous, but journalists can sometimes avoid the overt constraints and simply assume that the government will not complain because it is too weak or preoccupied with other problems. As long as the political centre is confused and divided then the prospects for a critical journalism may increase. But a corollary of this is that if the centre recovers then these prospects will again diminish, especially in the light of the new broadcasting structures and legal constraints which are now in place.

DE-REGULATION AND QUALITY OF NEWS AND CURRENT AFFAIRS

One effect of the intensification of commercial pressures within broadcasting is to increase the tendency for news to be reactive, event-driven and superficial. Television news has often been criticized for the 'fire-brigade' approach in which news teams fly in and out of crisis situations. The priority of such reporting is to obtain 'good pictures', with perhaps a couple of interviews with prominent figures as quickly as possible before the next assignment (see Philo 1993). Journalists have time only to film their own preconceptions – e.g. Africa is about crisis and famine, the Middle East and the *intifada* are about violence between Israeli soldiers and mobs of stone-throwers.

A number of producers have commented to us on how the new commercial structures are further reducing the potential of television to produce well-planned and in-depth news and current-affairs programmes. For example, when a television company has a long-running commitment to a current-affairs series then it is possible to propose and develop a number of programmes on a particular topic over an extended period. Series such as Granada's *World in Action* and the BBC's *Panorama* also attracted and retained people with a great deal of expertise and experience. But the new pressures mean that the trend for television production as a whole is now towards working on a short time scale, often with independent companies on low budgets who are commissioned to produce programmes and hopefully can 'buy in' whatever facilities or expertise they need. Sometimes this works, if the independent producer is very skilled or committed to a programme in a specific area (which can be seen in the quality of some Channel 4 output). But the trend towards cheap television with very rapid production cycles is likely to detract from the possibility of quality or the ability of television actually to explain the events of the world.

Greg Lanning worked for many years in Thames Television as well as the BBC and other companies, and is now working as an independent producer. He described to us some of the changes occasioned by the new systems of television production:

> If you were working in Thames or the BBC, there might [for example] be four or five people who had filmed in the Middle East. Because three of four teams of people were working together in the same space you have continual access to all their expertise, their contacts and understanding.
>
> When an idea is put up, it can be seriously examined in relation to the cumulative experience of the team. But when you are working as an independent, you are alone and there is no continuous input of ideas from anyone else. If you are working as an independent, you can ring people but there is no reason they would tell you anything. In fact the opposite, as they are searching for programme ideas themselves. There is a built-in bias in the system against sharing information and knowledge – because your livelihood depends on keeping it to yourself.
>
> (interview, 10 July 1994)

Some of the largest and most successful independent producers describe their own work as a treadmill in which there is constant pressure to generate new, 'saleable' programme ideas. What is at risk here is the continuity and quality of production which had been established in what were effectively centres of excellence within television. As Greg Lanning commented:

> There is [now] a tendency to put on ideas that are not properly researched

and ideas which are not fully formed. . . . If people are on a salary they can work on strands of ideas over a long period while still making other programmes. Not every week has to be paid for by a programme which is actually going out.

(ibid.)

The continuity given by salaried employment to extended current-affairs series meant that ideas and expertise could be developed over a long period and crucially that bad ideas could be rejected. But in the new system, no one has an interest in cancelling an idea that is bad once it has been accepted as a commission. Greg Lanning described to us how he was once sent to an Asian country to make a programme with an independent company. When the team arrived, the story that it intended to film simply did not stand up. But no one could alter the fact that a programme had to be made. The researchers would not say that there was no programme there as it would destroy their jobs – the producer couldn't say so for the same reason. The commissioning editor would not want to be told the bad news as it would then leave a gap in the schedule and the whole commissioning process would have to start again. So something else had to be put together on the spot as best it could be.

Overall, the quality of understanding offered by news and current affairs is likely to deteriorate under the pressures of an intense commercial climate. Consider the difficulties of explaining a complex conflict such as that between the Israelis and the Palestinians. A crucial issue in understanding this is the division and exploitation of natural resources within the occupied territories. Greg Lanning pointed out to us that before the *intifada* had started, Thames Television had already focused on the Israeli policy of sinking deep-drill wells that were effectively lowering the water table and causing Palestinian shallow wells to dry up. As he put it, 'to explain the *intifada*, you need to understand the significance of depriving Palestinian villages of their water supply'. But for much of the media the *intifada* was one more 'surprise' in a world of unexplained extraordinary events. The new technology of satellite links and 'instant' reporting can actually intensify the tendency of news to be event-driven. The new approach, pioneered by companies such as CNN, comes with a new ideology. Truth consists of 'being there' as it happens – as if being in the middle of the riot could explain why the stones are being thrown. As Greg Lanning commented: 'CNN is built on the idea that if you see it live you are seeing the truth – but this can miss out all the underlying processes' (ibid.). Reliance on the new technology is also likely to limit the range of explanations offered by interviewees and on-the-spot informants. The technology privileges those who can afford to have immediate access to it, which in practice will often be 'official' and government sources. They will always be available for sound-bites on satellite links. But there is no village spokesman in this position. To develop television which is critical and which explains required in-depth study and commitment. These are not the priorities of the commercial market which in its most unregulated form will be concerned only with grabbing the attention of audiences and delivering them to advertisers at the lowest possible cost.

A CRITICAL JOURNALISM

There are two other key factors which affect the possibility of a free and critical journalism. The first is that British society as a whole is becoming less democratic as the independence of the civil service is eroded and the number of quasi-governmental organizations (quangos) run by political appointees increases.[4] The state is becoming more centralized and this at a time of persistent high unemployment. Controls are increasing in a context where people are frightened for their own jobs. The independence of institutions which were once associated with the free expression of speech and opinion is thus eroded. A journalist recently wrote of the changed climate within universities, where power has now moved from academics towards administrators and fund-raisers:

> You can sense greater caution among academics these days. For the first time, none of those I spoke to wanted to be quoted for this article. 'You see we've all got mortgages,' said one old contact, not liking himself very much as he said it.
>
> (*Guardian*, 15 February 1994)

When the water industry was privatized, there were complaints from within it that free discussion was being curtailed in case it should damage the prospects for the sale:

> It has been an honourable and long standing tradition that engineers and scientists in the industry have freely discussed their problems. (e.g. of water quality, supply, treatment and of environmental pollution) through conferences, seminars, work shops and technical papers in their various professional journals. However, during the past two years all such papers have been vetted by a central committee and withdrawn or modified if it was felt that the open discussion of problems might in any way jeopardise the selling of shares.
>
> (letter to the *Observer*, 10 December 1989)

The priorities of markets and money thus affect more than balance sheets – they shape our social life, our interpersonal relations, our speech, what people are willing to say and thus what can be reported.

The second major factor which limits a critical and innovative journalism is that the agendas for political debate in key areas such as the economy are largely set by senior politicians and within the context of our existing political structures. Journalists work with routine assumptions about status and who has the 'legitimate' right to speak. In practice this gives defined rights of access to government leaders and leaders of the opposition (irrespective of how similar these are in their views). As we have seen, such coverage may also feature unelected 'experts' from the City of London or other financial interests. Broadcasting does not stray far beyond such parameters to criticize or set any independent agendas, even if much of the population does not feel well informed or properly represented by such structures.[5] Consider the manner in which political leaders have dealt with the crucial question of Britain's economic decline. One of the key issues in explaining this decline has been the historical division in this country between financial and industrial capital. For over a hundred years Britain was the financial and commercial centre of the world economy. The City provided banking, insurance and shipping services, while sterling was the basis of the international monetary system. This financial economy also benefited extensively from investment abroad, within the empire and outside it.[6] The crucial point is that there was no organic link between the financial economy and British-based industry, which was in a sense simply one customer amongst many. There has been no state-co-ordinated programme in Britain to bring together financial and industrial interests to target key areas for investment and growth (as for example in Japan). Britain's ascendancy in the world economy originally derived from the revenues taken from its empire and its early lead in industrialization. This ascendancy was challenged from the nineteenth century by the growth of powerful industrial rivals, but the British economy was never re-structured to respond to this. Instead, the short-term concerns of financial capital and the lack of any co-ordinated long-term strategy for investment produced a terminal decline in key areas of the industrial economy. As Will Hutton writes:

> The run-down of the British Industrial 'mittelstand' – our small and medium-sized businesses – and the proliferation of property, retailing and financial services originates in the terms, support and choices of British finance. It is in every sense distant from industry – spatially, legally and financially. Decisions are taken in London; loans and time horizons are chronically short-term; profits, as fee driven as possible, are taken early. Behind the banks, venture capitalists and large investing institutions stands an army of merchant bankers, auditors, lawyers and surveyors – all with the same need for returns now and shaping by their values, lifestyles and interests the contours in which our economic life has gone.
>
> (*Guardian*, 25 January 1993)

The implication is that the economy would require radical restructuring, for Britain to exist as an efficient capitalist society, let alone to build a social-democratic or radical alternative. But no political leader of a major party will acknowledge the depth of the decline or the extent of these problems for fear of being accused by each other of 'talking Britain down'.[7] The Labour Party leadership in the 1980s actually avoided discussing the economy and sought closer links with the City in a bid for legitimacy (see chapter 10). In this sense Britain is still in a post-imperial dream from which the population is not yet to be wakened, at least by its political leaders and the media. There are moments when nightmare scenarios come fitfully to the surface of public consciousness – as when the government revealed in October 1992 that the coal-mining industry was effectively disappearing. For a short time there was popular agitation against the latest round of pit closures and coverage of this in the press and on television. But in the absence of political leadership, the issue disappeared and political discussion could thus retreat into the familiar territory of personalities, divisions, upsets and scandal. Yet foreign industrialists can apparently see the deeper problems with some clarity. In February 1994, the Rover group, which was all that remained of British-owned volume car production, was sold to the German company, BMW. The president of the Toyota motor company, Nobuhiko Kawamato, commented that: 'The money game is fine but industry is the only way for a country to survive, and I wonder how the British expect to make a living in the future' (*Guardian*, 22 February 1994). To raise such issues in a consistent fashion would require an innovative and critical journalism and a truly independent broadcasting. But at present the parameters and agendas of media comment are still largely set by politicians and political structures which themselves stand so much in need of critical scrutiny.

NOTES

1   The hostility of Mrs Thatcher to the BBC was such that there were many, both within and outside the Corporation, who feared for the survival of public broadcasting. In the mid-1980s she was apparently in favour of forcing the BBC to take advertising and of abolishing the licence fee. This produced serious opposition from some Conservatives (such as William Whitelaw) and traditionalists who saw the BBC as a potential repository of high culture, standards, good taste and national values. This in part represented a split between nationally defined interests and the forces of international broadcasting, with the 'threat' of cheap, imported 'low cultural' products and the corrupting influences of 'foreign' pornography, etc. This was a powerful force in defence of the BBC and the proposals on advertising were effectively shelved following the Peacock report in 1986. We can see similar divisions within the Conservative Party over the proposals for independent broadcasting in the 1990 Broadcasting Act where the concern for 'good taste' and 'quality' became a major issue in opposition to demands for straightforward market criteria.

2   In the event, the ITC, albeit with more limited powers, has still mounted a struggle for quality. On 26 May 1994 it published a series of major criticisms on the performance of the new ITV network, stating that it had been cautious and unadventurous, with too heavy a reliance on predictable game shows and light-entertainment formats (*Guardian*, 27 May 1994).

3   In its final form, the Broadcasting Act took special account of the interests of

Rupert Murdoch, creating the category of 'non-domestic satellite'. Rules on cross-media ownership were not applied to his organization and he has been able to build a near monopoly in satellite television while still controlling a third of the country's newspaper circulation (Higham 1994: 17).

4   *The Economist*, for example has written of 'the pernicious growth of government patronage that has accompanied the spread of quangos. *Public Bodies 93*, a publication from the Cabinet Office, says that ministers are responsible for 42,600 appointments. In any year ministers make or renew about 10,000 of them. In written answers to parliamentary questions, the government has revealed that it advertised only 24 of these appointments in 1992' (6 August 1994).

5   By 1993 it was reported that 80 per cent of the population regarded television as its main source of news as against 20 per cent for newspapers (Goodman 1993: 4).

6   Such assets totalled £4 billion by 1914 (Gamble 1981: 56). On the eve of World War I, Britain's net overseas assets totalled 180 per cent of GDP. By 1993 it was calculated that Britain had become an international debtor with net liabilities of around £20 billion or 4 per cent of GDP (Martin, 1994: 15).

7   The Conservative Party election broadcast of 7 June 1994 had in its concluding comments the phrase 'Don't let Labour run Britain down'.

REFERENCES

Bolton, R. (1990) *Death on the Rock and Other Stories*, London: W.H. Allen.

Central Statistical Office (1992) *Economic Trends*, London: HMSO.

Clark, S. (1986) *Media Monitoring Report*, London: Media Monitoring Unit.

—— (1988) *Media Monitoring Update*, London: Media Monitoring Unit.

Cockerell, M. (1989) *Live from Number 10*, London: Faber & Faber.

Conservative Central Office (1986) *Media Monitoring Report*, London: Conservative Party Publications.

Curran, J. (1987) 'The boomerang effect: the press and the battle for London 1981–6', in J. Curran , A. Smith and P. Wingate, *Impacts and Influences*, London: Methuen.

Deacon, D. and Golding, P. (1991) 'When ideology fails: the flagship of Thatcherism and the British local and national media', *European Journal of Communication*, vol. 16, no. 3 (September).

Fishkin, J. (1991) *Democracy and Deliberation*, New Haven: Yale University Press.

Gamble, A. (1981) *Britain in Decline*, London: Macmillan.

Goodman, G. (1993) 'Too much to read?', *British Journalism Review*, vol. 4, no. 1.

Harvey, S. (1992) 'Broadcasting regulation and the public sphere: the 1991 UK television licence allocations', unpublished paper presented at *Screen* conference, Glasgow 1992.

—— (1994) 'Channel Four Television: from Annan to Grade', in S. Hood (ed.), *Behind the Screen*, London: Lawrence & Wishart.

Harris, R. (1983) *Gotcha! The Media, the Government and the Falklands Crisis*, London: Faber & Faber.

—— (1988) 'The Authorised Version', *Observer*, 5 June.

Heathcot Amory, D. (1961) State Papers quoted in the *Guardian*, 1 January 1991.

Higham, N. (1994) *Marketing Week*, 11 March.

Hutton, W. and Story, J. (1989) 'The slide to Skid Row', *New Statesman & Society*, 13 October: 13.

Koski, J. (1984) 'The hidden message in the Telecom sell-off promotion', *Guardian*, 10 December.

Lloyd, T.O. (1993) *Empire, Welfare State, Europe*, Oxford: Oxford University Press.

Martin, B. (1994) 'Britain grows used to being a beggar' *Guardian*, 6 June.

Morely, D. (1981) 'Industrial conflict and the mass media', in S. Cohen and J. Young, *The Manufacture of News*, London: Constable.

Mulholland, C. (1992) 'Delivering the goods', *Spectrum*, Winter 1992.

Philo, G. (1993) 'From Buerk to Band Aid: the media and the 1984 Ethiopian famine', in J. Eldridge (ed.), *Getting the Message*, London: Routledge.

Pilger, J. (1992) *Distant Voices*, London: Vintage.

Richards, J. (1986) 'The secret diaries of the film censors', Channel 4, 30 March.

Tebbit, N. (1981) Conference Speech, Conservative Research Department, 32 Smith Square, Westminster, London.

Index